AF597454
poems
70,000
Lenna Jawdat

2026

This book is a work of poetry and personal reflection. The views, interpretations, and expressions contained herein are solely those of the author and are presented as an exploration of grief, memory, inheritance, and history. They do not purport to represent the views of any institution, organization, government, or collective body.

Any historical references, archival materials, photographs, newspaper clippings, or other documentary sources included in or referenced by this work are used for contextual, educational, or artistic purposes. Such materials are drawn from widely available public sources and are cited where applicable. Their inclusion does not imply endorsement by, or affiliation with, the original creators or publishers. This work does not claim to be a comprehensive historical account. Rather, it is an artistic engagement with documented events and their enduring emotional and cultural impact, as experienced and interpreted by the author.

Illustration on page 130 by Fadia Jawdat and Ahmad Kadi.

Published by Central Avenue Poetry, an imprint of Central Avenue Marketing Ltd.
centralavenuepublishing.com

70,000: POEMS

Trade Paper: 978-1-77168-454-5
Ebook: 978-1-77168-455-2

Printed in United States of America

1. POETRY / Middle Eastern 2. POETRY / Subjects & Themes - Political & Protest

1 3 5 7 9 10 8 6 4 2

For my ancestors & my descendants.
May we live to see a Free Palestine.

[Exercise 1.0. Imagine:

the entire written record of your people's existence, gone]

In 1948, the state of Israel was created, and its military quickly took over as much land as they were able, expelling 700,000 Palestinians from their homes. Once the homes were emptied, they could be plundered. Amongst the stolen items, 70,000 books were taken from Palestinian homes and private libraries.

"At the time, the books' plunder affair was a small sideshow of the main events of the war. But seen through a wider historical perspective, the books' looting together with the destruction of the Palestinian urban centers, constitute the destruction of an entire culture. This is a major outcome of the 1948 war. Thousands of the books were recycled into paper while others were absorbed into the library's general collection, making it impossible to trace them today. Six thousand of these books were eventually categorized as foreign and placed in the Eastern Studies Department of The National Library, although technically still owned by the Custodian of Absentee Property. The fate of these books is much like that of the Palestinian people: unlawfully taken from their homes, expelled and made foreign in their own land. Baring [sic] the label 'AP,' for Abandoned Property the books are the focal point of The Great Book Robbery project."[1]

1 Mondoweiss, "The Great Book Robbery," January 25, 2012.

70,000 books stolen. (Lab Report)

Aim: To document a loss.

They say the human mind cannot comprehend numbers when they get too large to count. What is seventy thousand? I set out to write each number, document them one by one as a mark on a page, to get a sense of the magnitude. To wrap my mind

a
r
r → o
a u
d n
n d
a

Materials:
Paper, pens, patience.

Method:

1. The blank pages are empty and waiting. Hunch over them.
2. Neatly write out each number on a new line.
3. If they come freely, you will pause. Wonder
whether to continue.
Anyone can count.
4. You will write the numbers as small as you are able.
Cram them, crimp them, gather them in pleats.
5. You will fold them into tiny fortune tellers.
6. You will use the fortune tellers as portals to a world where
books have never been destroyed.

25M

1	35	69	103	137	171	205	240	274
2	36	70	104	138	172	206	241	275
3	37	71	105	139	173	207	242	276
4	38	72	106	140	174	208	243	277
5	39	73	107	141	175	209	244	278
6	40	74	108	142	176	210	245	279
7	41	75	109	143	177	211	246	280
8	42	76	110	144	178	212	247	281
9	43	77	111	145	179	213	248	282
10	44	78	112	146	180	214	249	283
11	45	79	113	147	181	215	250	284
12	46	80	114	148	182	216	251	285
13	47	81	115	149	183	217	252	286
14	48	82	116	150	184	218	253	287
15	49	83	117	151	185	219	254	288
16	50	84	118	152	186	220	255	289
17	51	85	119	153	187	221	256	290
18	52	86	120	154	188	222	257	291
19	53	87	121	155	189	223	258	292
20	54	88	122	156	190	224	259	293
21	55	89	123	157	191	225	260	294
22	56	90	124	158	192	226	261	295
23	57	91	125	159	193	227	262	296
24	58	92	126	160	194	228	263	297
25	59	93	127	161	195	229	264	298
26	60	94	128	162	196	230	265	299
27	61	95	129	163	197	231	266	300
28	62	96	130	164	198	232	267	301
29	63	97	131	165	199	233	268	302
30	64	98	132	166	200	234	269	303
31	65	99	133	167	201	235	270	304
32	66	100	134	168	202	236	271	305
33	67	101	135	169	203	237	272	306
34	68	102	136	170	204	238	273	307

Observations:

1. If your hand cramps, right where thumb bone meets wrist, switch to a marker. The smooth felt of Sharpie will glide across the surface and you will settle into an easy trance.
2. You will need breaks more and more fre que nt ly.
   Be gentle with yourself.
3. If each number represents one book
   and each book is 60,000 words
   then 4.2 billion words were taken.
4. If we speak 10,950,000 words per year, that's nearly 384 years of speech.

   I'm 35 and cannot imagine 11 lifetimes

   of words being taken from me.

   Can't imagine the entire verbal record of my existence

   (gone).

Imagine living your whole life in silence.

What would you do with the empty space, the catch in your throat?

308
309
310
311
312
313
314
315
316
317
318
319
320
321
322
323
324
325
326
327
328
329
330
331
332
333
334
335
336
337
338
339
340
341

342
343
344
345
346
347
348
349
350
351
352
353
354
355
356
357
358
359
360
361
362
363
364
365
366
367
368
369
370
371
372
373
374
375
376

377
378
379
380
381
382
383
384
385
386
387
388
389
390
391
392
393
394
395
396
397
398
399
400
401
402
403
404
405
406
407
408
409
410
411

412
413
414
415
416
417
418
419
420
421
422
423
424
425
426
427
428
429
430
431
432
433
434
435
436
437
438
439
440
441
442
443
444
445
446

447
448
449
450
451
452
453
454
455
456
457
458
459
460
461
462
463
464
465
466
467
468
469
470
471
472
473
474
475
476
477
478
479
480
481
482
483
484
485
486
487
488
489
490
491
492
493
494
495
496

497
498
499
500
501
502
503
504
505
506
507
508
509
510
511
512
513
514
515
516
517
518
519
520
521
522
523
524
525
526
527
528
529
530
531
532
533
534
535
536
537
538
539
540

541
542
543
544
545
546
547
548
549
550
551
552
553
554
555
556
557
558
559
560
561
562
563
564
565
566
567
568
569
570
571
572
573
574
575
576
577
578
579
580
581

582
583
584
585
586
587
588
589
590
591
592
593
594
595
596
597
598
599
600
601
602
603
604
605
606
607
608
609
610
611
612
613
614
615
616
617
618
619
620
621
622
623
624
625
686
627
628
629
630
631
632
633
634
635
636
637
638
639
646
647

648
649
650
651
652
653
654
655
656
657
658
659
660
661
662
663
664
665
666
667
668
669
670
671
672
673
674
675
676
677
678
679
680
681
682
683
684
685
686
687
688
689
690
691
692
693
694
695
696
697
698
699
700
701
702
703
704
705
706
707

708
709
710
711
712
713
714
715
716
717
718
719
720
721
722
723
724
725
726
727
728
729
730
731
732
733
734
735
736
737
738
739
740
741
742
74
74
74
74
74
74
74
75
75
75
75
75
755
756
757
75
759
760
761
762
763

I take back my words. Swallow them whole.
In this reality I am on mute. I've never
told you that I love you. I've never apologized.
Sure I'm still the girl who feigned sleep
when a kid I didn't know put my hand
down his pants. Still the one who struggles
to ask for help with homework or the mortgage.
Still the girl who smiles meekly while classmates
trade quips about Arab terrorists.
Classic freeze, feign, fawn.
But in this version I've never screamed
with glee as I galloped through a field
or called a friend to giggle and gush.
I am wallpaper. In this version, I have
not spent a lifetime searching for
just the right words in the perfect order
to express myself better than a house cat,
to soothe your heartache, pave over the potholes
in your memory. I've never spun sounds into silk
to dress your wounds. I am invisible. My sentence
an absence, four more years. I sit in the shadows.
I stay stunned.

Silent.

5. You will not fret about wasted paper.
You will pay no mind
to the scarcity of trees.

Pine, fir, spruce, hemlock, and larch,
balsam poplar pulp
soft, coniferous, ever-green.

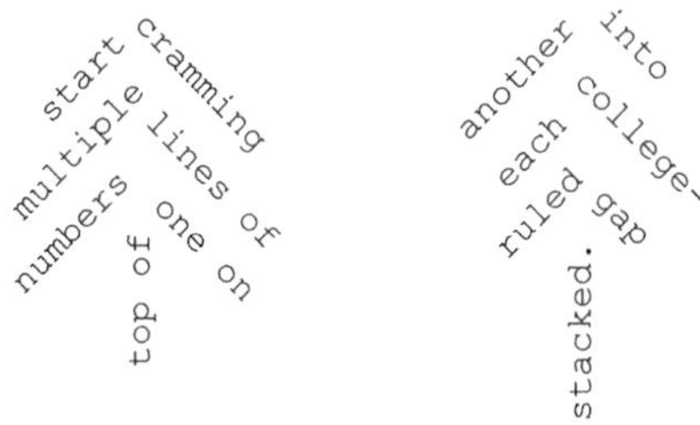

Scarcity.
As in, being in short supply; shortage.
As in “a time of scarcity.”

764 765 766 767 768 769 770 771 772 773 774 775 776 777 778 779 780 781 782 783 784 785 786 787 788 789 790 791 792 793 794 795 796 797 798 799 800 801 802 803 804 805 806 807 808 809 810 811 812 813 814 815 816 817

818 819 820 821 822 823 824 825 826 827 828 829 830 831 832 833 834 835 836 837 838 839 840 841 842 843 844 845 846 847 848 849 850 851 852 853 854 855 856 857 858 859 860 861 862 863 864 865 866 867 868 869 870 871 872 873 874 875 876 877 878 879 880 881 882 883 884

885 886 887 888 889 890 [illegible] 901 902 903 [illegible]

[illegible] 971 972 973 974 975 [illegible] 980 981 982 983 984 985 986 987 988 989 990 991 992 993 994 995 996 997 998 999 1000 1001 1002 1003 1004 1005 1006 1007 1008 1009 1010 1011 1012 1013 1014

1015 1016 1017 1018 1019 1020 1021 1022 1023 1024 1025 1026 1027 1028 1029 1030 1031 1032 1033 1034 1035 1036 1037 1038 1039 1040 1041 1042 1043 1044 1045 1046 1047 1048 1049 1050 1051 1052 1053 1054 1055 1056 1057 1058 1059 1060 1061 1062 1063 1064 1065 1066 1067 1068 1069 1070 1071 1072 1073 1074 1075 1076 1077 1078 1079 1080 1081 1082 1083 1084

1085 1086 1087 1088 1089 1090 1091 1092 1093 1094 1095 1096 1097 1098 1099 1100 1101 1102 1103 1104 1105 1106 1107 1108 1109 1110 1111 1112 1113 1114 1115 1116 1117 1118 1119 1120 1121 1122 1123 1124 1125 1126 1127 1128 1129 1130 1131 1132 1133 1134 1135 1136 1137 1138 1139 1140 1141 1142 1143 1144 1145 1146 1147 1148 1149 1150 1151 1152 1153 1154 1155 1156 1157 1158 1159

1160 1161 1162 1163 1164 1165 1166 1167 1168 1169 1170 1171 1172 1173 1174 1175 1176 1177 1178 1179 1180 1181 1182 1183 1184 1185 1186 1187 1188 1189 1190 1191 1192 1193 1194 1195 1196 1197 1198 1199 1200 1201 1202 1203 1204 1205 1206 1207 1208 1209 1210 1211 1212 1213 1214 1215 1216 1217 1218 1219 1220 1221 1222 1223 1224 1225 1226 1227 1228 1229 1230 1231 1232 1233 1234

1235 1236 1237 1238 1239 1240 1241 1242 1243 1244 1245 1246 1247 1248 1249 1250 1251 1252 1253 1254 1255 1256 1257 1258 1259 1260 1261 1262 1263 1264 1265 1266 1267 1268 1269 1270 1271 1272 1273 1274 1275 1276 1277 1278 1279 1280 1281 1282 1283 1284 1285 1286 1287 1288 1289 1290 1291 1292 1293 1294 1295 1296 1297 1298 1299 1300 1301 1302 1303 1304 1305 1306 1307 1308 1309

1310 1311 1312 1313 1314 1315 1316 1317 1318 1319 1320 1321 1322 1323 1324 1325 1326 1327 1328 1329 1330 1331 1332 1333 1334 1335 1336 1337 1338 1339 1340 1341 1342 1343 1344 1345 1346 1347 1348 1349 1350 1351 1352 1353 1354 1355 1356 1357 1358 1359 1360 1361 1362 1363 1364 1365 1366 1367 1368 1369 1370 1371 1372 1373 1374 1375 1376 1377 1378 1379 1380 1381 1382 1383 1384 1385 1386 1387 1388 1389 1390

1391 1392 1393 1394 1395 1396 1397 1398 1399 1400 1401 1402 1403 1404 1405 1406 1407 1408 1409 1410 1411 1412 1413 1414 1415 1416 1417 1418 1419 1420 1421 1422 1423 1424 1425 1426 1427 1428 1429 1430 1431 1432 1433 1434 1435 1436 1437 1438 1439 1440 1441 1442 1443 1444 1445 1446 1447 1448 1449 1450 1451 1452 1453 1454 1455 1456 1457 1458 1459 1460 1461 1462 1463 1464 1465 1466 1467 1468 1469 1470 1471

1472 1473 1474 1475 1476 1477 1478 1479 1480 1481 1482 1483 1484 1485 1486 1487 1488 1489 1490 1491 1492 1493 1494 1495 1496 1497 1498 1499 1500 1501 1502 1503 1504 1505 1506 1507 1508 1509 1510 1511 1512 1513 1514 1515 1516 1517 1518 1519 1520 1521 1522 1523 1524 1525 1526 1527 1528 1529 1530 1531 1532 1533 1534 1535 1536 1537 1538 1539 1540 1541 1542 1543 1544 1545 1546 1547 1548

1549 1550 1551 1552 1553 1554 1555 1556 1557 1558 1559 1560 1561 1562 1563 1564 1565 1566 1567 1568 1569 1570 1571 1572 1573 1574 1575 1576 1577 1578 1579 1580 1581 1582 1583 1584 1585 1586 1587 1588 1589 1590 1591 1592 1593 1594 1595 1596 1597 1598 1599 1600 1601 1602 1603 1604 1605 1606 1607 1608 1609 1610 1611 1612

Implications:

1. If each book, on average, is 330 pages,
this 770 scribbled on the page
represents 254,100 pages.
2. If a tree produces
10,000 to 20,000 sheets of paper,
770 = 13 to 26 trees.
3. If 770 on the page represents 508 reams of paper,
one would need more than 90 times as many reams for 70,000.
508 x 90.91 = 46,182.28 reams.
4. Let's say a ream of paper costs $5.
46,182 reams x 5 = $230,910.
5. At the bottom of page 4 I've gotten to 2,066.
It's been 2 and a half hours. 4 generations of
lifetimes gone in a flash.

You will turn the page sideways and crosshatch
numbers over numbers, like early settlers writing
letters on valuable onionskin paper.

You will turn the page over. The ink bleeds

`through   ɥƃnoɹɥʇ`

`...2332.     .ƧƐƐƧ...`

1613 1614 1615 1616 1617 1618 1619 1620 1621 1622 1623 1624 1625 1626 1627 1628 1629 1630 1631 1632 1633 1634 1635 1636 1637 1638 1639 1640 1641 1642 1643 1644 1645 1646 1647 1648 1649 1650 1651 1652 1653 1654 1655 1656 1657 1658 1659 1660 1661 1662 1663 1664 1665 1666 1667 1668 1669 1670

1671 1672 1673 1674 1675 1676 1677 1678 1679 1680 1681 1682 1683 1684 1685 1686 1687 1688 1689 1690 1691 1692 1693 1694 1695 1696 1697 1698 1699 1700 1701 1702 1703 1704 1705 1706 1707 1708 1709 1710 1711 1712 1713 1714 1715 1716 1717 1718 1719 1720 1721 1722 1723 1724 1725

1726 1727 1728 1729 1730 1731 1732 1733 1734 1735 1736 1737 1738 1739 1740 1741 1742 1743 1744 1745 1746 1747 1748 1749 1750 1751 1752 1753 1754 1755 1756 1757 1758 1759 1760 1761 1762 1763 1764 1765 1766 1767 1768 1769 1770 1771 1772 1773 1774 1775 1776 1777 1778 1779

1780 1781 1782 1783 1784 1785 1786 1787 1788 1789 1790 1791 1792 1793 1794 1795 1796 1797 1798 1799 1800 1801 1802 1803 1804 1805 1806 1807 1808 1809 1810 1811 1812 1813 1814 1815 1816 1817 1818 1819 1820 1821 1822 1823 1824 1825 1826 1827 1828 1829 1830 1831 1832 1833 1834 1835 1836 1837

1838 1839 1840 1841 1842 1843 1844 1845 1846 1847 1848 1849 1850 1851 1852 1853 1854 1855 1856 1857 1858 1859 1860 1861 1862 1863 1864 1865 1866 1867 1868 1869 1870 1871 1872 1873 1874 1875 1876 1877 1878 1879 1880 1881 1882 1883 1884 1885 1886 1887 1888 1889 1890 1891 1892 1893

1894 1895 1896 1897 1898 1899 1900 1901 1902 1903 1904 1905 1906 1907 1908 1909 1910 1911 1912 1913 1914 1915 1916 1917 1918 1919 1920 1921 1922 1923 1924 1925 1926 1927 1928 1929 1930 1931 1932 1933 1934 1935 1936 1937 1938 1939 1940 1941 1942 1943 1944 1945 1946 1947 1948 1949

1950 1951 1952 1953 1954 1955 1956 1957 1958 1959 1960 1961 1962 1963 1964 1965 1966 1967 1968 1969 1970 1971 1972 1973 1974 1975 1976 1977 1978 1979 1980 1981 1982 1983 1984 1985 1986

1987 1988 1989 1990 1991 1992 1993 1994 1995 1996 1997 1998 1999 2000 2001 2002 2003 2004 2005 2006 2007 2008 2009 2010 2011 2012 2013 2014 2015 2016 2017 2018 2019 2020 2021 2022 2023 2024 2025 2026 2027 2028 2029 2030 2031

2032 2033 2034 2035 2036 2037 2038 2039 2040 2041 2042 2043 2044 2045 2046 2047 2048 2049 2050 2051 2052 2053 2054 2055 2056 2057 2058 2059 2060 2061 2062 2063 2064 2065 2066

2067 2068 2069 2070 2071 2072 2073 2074 2075 2076 2077 2078 2079 2080 2081 2082 2083

2084 2085 2086 2087 2088 2089 2090 2091 2092 2093 2094 2095 2096 2097 2098 2099 2100 2101

2102 2103 2104 2105 2106 2107 2108 2109 2110 2111 2112 2113 2114 2115 2116 2117 2118 2119 2120 2121 2122 2123 2124

2125 2126 2127 2128 2129 2130 2131 2132 2133 2134 2135 2136 2137 2138 2139 2140 2141 2142 2143 2144 2145 2146 2147

2148 2149 2150 2151 2152 2153 2154 2155 2156 2157 2158 2159 2160 2161 2162 2163 2164 2165 2166 2167 2168 2169

2170 2171 2172 2173 2174 2175 2176 2177 2178 2179 2180 2181 2182 2183 2184 2185 2186 2187 2188 2189 2190 2191 2192

2193 2194 2195 2196 2197 2198 2199 2200 2201 2202 2203 2204 2205 2206 2207 2208 2209 2210 2211 2212 2213 2214 2215 2216 2217

2218 2219 2220 2221 2222 2223 2224 2225 2226 2227 2228 2229 2230 2231 2232 2233

2234 2235 2236 2237 2238 2239 2240 2241 2242 2243 2244 2245 2246 2247 2248 2249 2250 2251 2252

2253 2254 2255 2256 2257 2258 2259 2260 2261 2262 2263 2264 2265 2266 2267

2268 2269 2270 2271 2272 2273 2274 2275 2276 2277 2278 2279 2280 2281 2282 2283 2284

2285 2286 2287 2288 2289 2290 2291 2292 2293 2294 2295 2296 2297 2298 2299 2300 2301 2302

2303 2304 2305 2306 2307 2308 2309 2310 2311 2312 2313 2314 2315 2316 2317 2318 2319 2320 2321 2322 2323 2324 2325 2326 2327 2328 2329 2330 2331 2332 2333 2334

I zip past **1882**, the year when the first waves of financially-backed Zionist mass emigration to Palestine begins; **1896**, when the Jewish Colonization Association begins operating in Palestine; **1897**, the first World Zionist Congress conference held and the World Zionist Organization established.

1917 - The Balfour Declaration

67 words, none of them "Palestinian" or "Arab,"
only "non-Jewish," a subtle disappearance.

His Majesty's government (British,
who, one may note, are merely colonists of the land,
collectors of cards in a hand)
view with favour the establishment in Palestine
of a national home for the Jewish people
and will use their best endeavours to facilitate the achievement of this object—[2]

. . . without accounting for 94% of the population of the place in question

. . .

Meanwhile, this British proclamation is barely audible
as it floats down to Earth in Palestine with a muffled thud.
Government censorship that bans news of the declaration
and newsprint scarcity due to naval blockades
silences media, word of mouth slow to follow on land.

Scarcity. Scare-city.

2 Wikisource, "Balfour Declaration."

1919 - "in Palestine we do not propose even to go through the form of consulting the wishes of the present inhabitants of the country[...]. The four Great Powers are committed to Zionism. And Zionism, be it right or wrong, good or bad, is rooted in age-long traditions, in present needs, in future hopes, of far profounder import than the desire and prejudices of the 700,000 Arabs who now inhabit that ancient land."

— Arthur Balfour

2335 2336 2337 2338 2339 2340 2341 2342 2343 2344 2345 2346 2347 2348 2349 2350 2351 2352 2353 2354 2355 2356 2357 2358 2359 2360 2361 2362 2363 2364 2365 2366 2367 2368

2369 2370 2371 2372 2373 2374 2375 2376 2377 2378 2379 2380 2381 2382 2383 2384 2385 2386 2387 2388 2389 2390 2391 2392 2393 2394 2395 2396 2397 2398 2399 2400 2401 2402

2403 2404 2405 2406 2407 2408 2409 2410 2411 2412 2413 2414 2415 2416 2417 2418 2419 2420 2421 2422 2423 2424 2425 2426 2427 2428 2429 2430 2431 2432 2433 2434 2435 2436

2437 2438 2439 2440 2441 2442 2443 2444 2445 2446 2447 2448 2449 2450 2451 2452 2453 2454 2455 2456 2457 2458 2459 2460 2461 2462 2463 2464 2465 2466 2467 2468 2469 2470

2471 2472 2473 2474 2475 2476 2477 2478 2479 2480 2481 2482 2483 2484 2485 2486 2487 2488 2489 2490 2491 2492 2493 2494 2495 2496 2497 2498 2499 2500 2501 2502 2503 2504

2505 2506 2507 2508 2509 2510 2511 2512 2513 2514 2515 2516 2517 2518 2519 2520 2521 2522 2523 2524 2525 2526 2527 2528 2529 2530 2531 2532 2533 2534 2535 2536 2537 2538

2539 2540 2541 2542 2543 2544 2545 2546 2547 2548 2549 2550 2551 2552 2553 2554 2555 2556 2557 2558 2559 2560 2561 2562 2563 2564 2565 2566 2567 2568 2569 2570 2571 2572 2573 2574 2575 2576 2577 2578

2579 2580 2581 2582 2583 2584 2585 2586 2587 2588 2589 2590 2591 2592 2593 2594 2595 2596 2597 2598 2599 2600 2601 2602 2603 2604 2605 2606 2607 2608 2609 2610 2611 2612 2613 2614 2615 2616 2617 2618 2619

2620 2621 2622 2623 2624 2625 2626 2627 2628 2629 2630 2631 2632 2633 2634 2635 2636 2637 2638 2639 2640 2641 2642 2643 2644 2645 2646 2647 2648 2649 2650 2651 2652 2653

"in Palestine

the present inhabitants of
the country . . . are
committed to

long
traditions, present needs, future hopes

of the 700,000 Arabs who now
inhabit that ancient land."

— revision

2654 2655 2656 2657 2658 2659 2660 2661 2662 2663 2664 2665 2666 2667 2668 2669 2670 2671 2672 2673 2674 2675 2676 2677 2678 2679 2680 2681 2682 2683 2684 2685 2686 2687 2688 2689 2690 2691 2692 2693 2694

2695 2696 2697 2698 2699 2700 2701 2702 2703 2704 2705 2706 2707 2708 2709 2710 2711 2712 2713 2714 2715 2716 2717 2718 2719 2720 2721 2722 2723 2724 2725 2726 2727 2728 2729 2730 2731 2732 2733 2734 2735 2736 2737 2738 2739

2740 2741 2742 2743 2744 2745 2746 2747 2748 2749 2750 2751 2752 2753 2754 2755 2756 2757 2758 2759 2760 2761 2762 2763 2764 2765 2766 2767 2768 2769 2770 2771 2772 2773 2774

2775 2776 2777 2778 2779 2780 2781 2782 2783 2784 2785 2786 2787 2788 2789 2790 2791 2792 2793 2794 2795 2796 2797 2798 2799 2800 2801 2802 2803 2804 2805 2806 2807 2808 2809

2810 2811 2812 2813 2814 2815 2816 2817 2818 2819 2820 2821 2822 2823 2824 2825 2826 2827 2828 2829 2830 2831 2832 2833 2834 2835 2836 2837 2838 2839 2840 2841 2842 2843 2844

2845 2846 2847 2848 2849 2850 2851 2852 2853 2854 2855 2856 2857 2858 2859 2860 2861 2862 2863 2864 2865 2866 2867 2868 2869 2870 2871 2872 2873 2874 2875 2876 2877 2878 2879

2880 2881 2882 2883 2884 2885 2886 2887 2888 2889 2890 2891 2892 2893 2894 2895 2896 2897 2898 2899 2900 2901 2902 2903 2904 2905 2906 2907 2908 2909 2910 2911 2912 2913 2914

I'm frantic, scribbling,

fear I'll never finish.

The tears spill, blur my vision.

My bicep burns,

shoulder clamped down,

shark jaw gripping chest—

I'm holding my breath.

Heartbeat speeds up

like a hamster on the treadmill of my ribs.

My legs want to run,

bounce, jiggle.

Partial collapse,

partial flight.

2915	2950	2983	3017	3051	3085	3119	3153
2916	2951	2984	3018	3052	3086	3120	3154
2917	2952	2985	3019	3053	3087	3121	3155
2918	2953	2986	3020	3054	3088	3122	3156
2919	2954	2987	3021	3055	3089	3123	3157
2920	2955	2988	3022	3056	3090	3124	3158
2921	2956	2989	3023	3057	3091	3125	3159
2922	2957	2990	3024	3058	3092	3126	3160
2923	2958	2991	3025	3059	3093	3127	3161
2924	2959	2992	3026	3060	3094	3128	3162
2925	2960	2993	3027	3061	3095	3129	3163
2926	2961	2994	3028	3062	3096	3130	3164
2927	2962	2995	3029	3063	3097	3131	3165
2928	2963	2996	3030	3064	3098	3132	3166
2929	2964	2997	3031	3065	3099	3133	3167
2930	2965	2998	3032	3066	3100	3134	3168
2931	2966	2999	3033	3067	3101	3135	3169
2932	2967	3000	3034	3068	3102	3136	3170
2933	2968	3001	3035	3069	3103	3137	3171
2934	2969	3002	3036	3070	3104	3138	3172
2935	2970	3003	3037	3071	3105	3139	3173
2936	2971	3004	3038	3072	3106	3140	3174
2937	2972	3005	3039	3073	3107	3141	3175
2938	2973	3006	3040	3074	3108	3142	3176
2939	2973	3007	3041	3075	3109	3143	3177
2940	2974	3008	3042	3076	3110	3144	3178
2941	2975	3009	3043	3077	3111	3145	3179
2942	2976	3010	3044	3078	3112	3146	3180
2943	2977	3011	3045	3079	3113	3147	3181
2944	2978	3012	3046	3080	3114	3148	3182
2945	2979	3013	3047	3081	3115	3149	3183
2946	2980	3014	3048	3082	3116	3150	3184
2947	2981	3015	3049	3083	3117	3157	3185
2948	2982	3016	3050	3084	3118	3152	3186
2949							

1929 - The Jewish Agency is formed to encourage Jewish immigration to Palestine.

1930 - 29% of Arab families in villages lose their land due to Jewish immigration.

Somewhere in the 3000s

I start to lose count

3562 3563 3564 3565 3566 3567 3568 3569 3570 3571 3572 3573 3574 3575 3576 3577 3578 3579 3580 3581 3582 3583 3584 3585 3586 3587 3588 3589 3590 3591 3592 3593 3594 3595 3596 3597 3598 3599 3600 3601 3602 3603 3604 3605 3606 3607 3608 3609

3610 3611 3612 3613 3614 3615 3616 3617 3618 3619 3620 3621 3622 3623 3624 3625 3626 3627 3628 3629 3630 3631 3632 3633 3634 3635 3636 3637 3638 3639 3640 3641 3642 3643 3644 3645 3646 3647 3648 3649

3650 3651 3652 3653 3654 3655 3656 3657 3658 3659 3660 3661 3662 3663 3664 3665 3666 3667 3668 3669 3670 3671 3672 3673 3674 3675 3676 3677 3678 3679 3680 3681 3682 3683 3684 3685 3686 3687 3688 3689 3690 3691

3692 3693 3694 3695 3696 3697 3698 3699 3700 3701 3702 3703 3704 3705 3706 3707 3708 3709 3710 3711 3712 3713 3714 3715 3716 3717 3718 3719 3720 3721 3722 3723 3724 3725 3726 3727 3728 3729 3730 3731 3732

3733 3734 3735 3736 3737 3738 3739 3740 3741 3742 3743 3744 3745 3746 3747 3748 3749 3750 3751 3752 3753 3754 3755 3756 3757 3758 3759 3760 3761 3762 3763 3764 3765 3766 3767 3768 3769 3770 3771 3772 3773 3774 3775

3776 3777 3778 3779 3780 3781 3782 3783 3784 3785 3786 3787 3788 3789 3790 3791 3792 3793 3794 3795 3796 3797 3798 3799 3800 3801 3802 3803 3804 3805 3806 3807 3808 3809 3810 3811 3812 3813 3814 3815 3816 3817

3818 3819 3820 3821 3822 3823 3824 3825 3826 3827 3828 3829 3830 3831 3832 3833 3834 3835 3836 3837 3838 3839 3840 3841 3842 3843 3844 3845 3846 3847 3848 3849 3850 3851 3852 3853 3854 3855 3856 3857 3858 3859 3860 3861 3862

3863 3864 3865 3866 3867 3868 3869 3870 3871 3872 3873 3874 3875 3876 3877 3878 3879 3880 3881 3882 3883 3884 3885 3886 3887 3888 3889 3890 3891 3892 3893 3894 3895 3896 3897 3898 3899 3900 3901 3902 3903 3904 3905 3906

After 3,859 I write 5,860 and get sidetracked in the 5,000s—a detour—
wishful thinking, maybe. I work my way up to 6,257
before somehow I end up back in the 5,000s.
5,259, 5,260, 5,261 . . .
4 hours of writing, 5 hours . . .

As I speed up, my mind gets ahead of my hand.
My numbers begin to stumble over each other.
I have to circle back to correct them, collect them.
I start bringing the pages with me.
Doodle numbers absentmindedly during other tasks.

As I speed up, my mind gets ahead of my hand.
My numbers begin to stumble over each other.
I have to circle back to correct them, collect them.
I start bringing the pages with me.
Doodle numbers absentmindedly during other tasks.

As I speed up, my mind gets ahead of my hand.
My numbers begin to stumble over each other.
I have to circle back to correct them, collect them.
I start bringing the pages with me.
Doodle numbers absentmindedly during other tasks.

As I speed up, my mind gets ahead of my hand.
My numbers begin to stumble over each other.
I have to circle back to correct them, collect them.
I start bringing the pages with me.
Doodle numbers absentmindedly during other tasks.

As I speed up, my mind gets ahead of my hand.
My numbers begin to stumble over each other.
I have to circle back to correct them, collect them.
I start bringing the pages with me.
Doodle numbers absentmindedly during other tasks.

As I speed up, my mind gets ahead of my hand.
My numbers begin to stumble over each other.
I have to circle back to correct them, collect them.
I start bringing the pages with me.
Doodle numbers absentmindedly during other tasks.

As I speed up, my mind gets ahead of my hand.
My numbers begin to stumble over each other.
I have to circle back to correct them, collect them.
I start bringing the pages with me.
Doodle numbers absentmindedly during other tasks.

As I speed up, my mind gets ahead of my hand.
My numbers begin to stumble over each other.
I have to circle back to correct them, collect them.
I start bringing the pages with me.
Doodle numbers absentmindedly during other tasks.

I begin to relate to my Bedouin ancestors
who trudged through long stretches of desert.
The mirage of relief,

oasis of dopamine
waits at the end
of the voyage.

When I go to bed I'm technically in the 4,000s
with an inflated sense of accomplishment, unearned.

Joints in need of oil.

Rock jaw
leaden legs.
Shoulders coiled tight.

MY PARTNER EXPRESSES
CONCERN:

This can't be
good for you.

Questions for further research

How many hours of labor does it take to write 70,000 books?
To edit, print, and bind?
How many hands were involved in papermaking?
How much would the ink alone weigh?
How many years of labor lost?
Whose stories are gone?

3907
3908
3909
3910
3911
3912
3913
3914
3915
3916
3917
3918
3919
3920
3921
3922
3923
3924
3925
3926
3927
3928
3929
3930
3931
3932
3933
3934
3935
3936
3937
3938
3939
3940
3941
3942
3943
3944
3945
3946
3947
3948
3949
3950
3951
3952
3953
3954
3955

3956
3957
3958
3959
3960
3961
3962
3963
3964
3965
3966
3967
3968
3969
3970
3971
3972
3973
3974
3975
3976
3977
3978
3979
3980
3981
3982
3983
3984
3985
3986
3987
3988
3989
3990
3991
3992
3993
3994
3995
3996
3997
3998
3999
4000
4001
4002
4003

4004
4005
4006
4007
4008
4009
4010
4011
4012
4013
4014
4015
4016
4017
4018
4019
4020
4021
4022
4023
4024
4025
4026
4027
4028
4029
4030
4031
4032
4033
4034
4035
4036
4037
4038
4039
4040
4041
4042
4043
4044
4045
4046
4047
4048
4049
4050
4051

4051
4052
4053
4054
4055
4056
4057
4058
4059
4060
4061
4062
4063
4064
4065
4066
4067
4068
4069
4070
4071
4072
4073
4074
4075
4076
4077
4078
4079
4080
4081
4082
4083
4084
4085
4086
4087
4088
4089
4090
4091
4092
4093
4094
4095
4096
4097

4098
4099
4100
4101
4102
4103
4104
4105
4106
4107
4108
4109
4110
4111
4112
4113
4114
4115
4116
4117
4118
4119
4120
4121
4122
4123
4124
4125
4126
4127
4128
4129
4130
4131
4132
4133
4134
4135
4136
4137
4138
4139
4140
4141
4142
4143
4144
4145

4146
4147
4148
4149
4150
4151
4152
4153
4154
4155
4156
4157
4158
4159
4160
4161
4162
4163
4164
4165
4166
4167
4168
4169
4170
4171
4172
4173
4174
4175
4176
4177
4178
4179
4180
4181
4182
4183
4184
4185
4186
4187
4188
4189
4190
4191

4192
4193
4194
4195
4196
4197
4198
4199
4200
4201
4202
4203
4204
4205
4206
4207
4208
4209
4210
4211
4212
4213
4214
4215
4216
4217
4218
4219
4220
4221
4222
4223
4224
4225
4226
4227
4228
4229
4230
4231
4232
4233
4234
4235
4236
4237
4238
4239

4240
4241
4242
4243
4244
4245
4246
4247
4248
4249
4250
4251
4252
4253
4254
4255
4256
4257
4258
4259
4260
4261
4262
4263
4264
4265
4266
4267
4268
4269
4270
4271
4272
4273
4274
4275
4276
4277
4278
4279
4280
4281
4282
4283
4284

4285
4286
4287
4288
4289
4290
4291
4292
4293
4294
4295
4296
4297
4298
4299
4300
4301
4302
4303
4304
4305
4306
4307
4308
4309
4310
4311
4312
4313
4314
4315
4316
4317
4318
4319
4320
4321
4322
4323
4324
4325
4326
4327
4328
4329
4330
4331
4332
4333

4334
4335
4336
4337
4338
4339
4340
4341
4342
4343
4344
4345
4346
4347
4348
4349
4350
4351
4352
4353
4354
4355
4356
4357
4358
4359
4360
4361
4362
4363
4364
4365
4366
4367
4368
4369
4370
4371
4372
4373
4374
4375
4376
4377
4378
4379
4380
4381
4382
4383

4384
4385
4386
4387
4388
4389
4390
4391
4392
4393
4394
4395
4396
4397
4398
4399
4400
4401
4402
4403
4404
4405
4406
4407
4408
4409
4410
4411
4412
4413
4414
4415
4416
4417
4418
4419
4420
4421
4422
4423
4424
4425
4426
4427
4428
4429
4430
4431
4432
4433
4434
4435
4436

4437
4438
4439
4440
4441
4442
4443
4444
4445
4446
4447
4448
4449
4450
4451
4452
4453
4454
4455
4456
4457
4458
4459
4460
4461
4462
4463
4464
4465
4466
4467
4468
4469
4470
4471
4472
4473
4474
4475
4476
4477
4478
4479
4480
4481
4482
4483
4484
4485
4486
4487
4488
4489
4490

4491
4492
4493
4494
4495
4496
4497
4498
4499
4500
4501
4502
4503
4504
4505
4506
4507
4508
4509
4510
4511
4512
4513
4514
4515
4516
4517
4518
4519
4520
4521
4522
4523
4524
4525
4526
4527
4528
4529
4530
4531
4532
4533
4534
4535
4536
4537
4538
4539
4540
4541
4542

4543
4544
4545
4546
4547
4548
4549
4550
4551
4552
4553
4554
4555
4556
4557
4558
4559
4560
4561
4562
4563
4564
4565
4566
4567
4568
4569
4570
4571
4572
4573
4574
4575
4576
4577
4578
4579
4580
4581
4582
4583
4584
4585
4586
4587
4588
4589
4590
4591
4592
4593
4594

4595
4596
4597
4598
4599
4600
4601
4602
4603
4604
4605
4606
4607
4608
4609
4610
4611
4612
4613
4614
4615
4616
4617
4618
4619
4620
4621
4622
4623
4624
4625
4626
4627
4628
4629
4630
4631
4632
4633
4634
4635
4636
4637
4638
4639
4640
4641
4642

4643
4644
4645
4646
4647
4648
4649
4650
4651
4652
4653
4654
4655
4656
4657
4658
4659
4660
4661
4662
4663
4664
4665
4666
4667
4668
4669
4670
4671
4672
4673
4674
4675
4676
4677
4678
4679
4680
4681
4682
4683
4684
4685
4686
4687
4688
4689

Palestine, or Falastin in Arabic, was named for the seafaring Philistine people who inhabited the land conquered by Romans in the second century C.E. You might remember the story of Goliath and the triumphant underdog, David. The giant Goliath was a Philistine. Goliath with his strength and weapons, defeated by a mere shepherd. I've always related strongly to this underdog story; felt more like David than Goliath. Israel with their big guns and fancy drones, Palestinians throwing rocks.

4690	4738	4793	4846	4900	4950	5001	5055
4691	4739	4794	4847	4901	4951	5002	5056
4692	4740	4795	4848	4902	4952	5003	5057
4693	4741	4796	4849	4903	4953	5004	5058
4694	4742	4797	4850	4904	4954	5005	5059
4695	4743	4798	4851	4905	4955	5006	5060
4696	4744	4799	4852	4906	4956	5007	5061
4697	4745	4800	4853	4907	4957	5008	5062
4698	4746	4801	4854	4908	4958	5009	5063
4699	4747	4802	4855	4909	4959	5010	5064
4700	4748	4803	4856	4910	4960	5011	5065
4701	4749	4804	4857	4911	4961	5012	5066
4702	4750	4805	4858	4912	4962	5013	5067
4703	4751	4806	4859	4913	4963	5014	5068
4704	4752	4807	4860	4914	4964	5015	5069
4705	4753	4808	4861	4915	4965	5016	5070
4706	4754	4809	4862	4916	4966	5017	5071
4707	4755	4810	4863	4917	4967	5018	5072
4708	4756	4811	4864	4918	4968	5019	5073
4709	4757	4812	4865	4919	4969	5020	5074
4710	4758	4813	4866	4920	4970	5021	5075
4711	4759	4814	4867	4921	4971	5022	5076
4712	4760	4815	4868	4922	4972	5023	5077
4713	4761	4816	4869	4923	4973	5024	5078
4714	4762	4817	4870	4924	4974	5025	5079
4715	4763	4818	4871	4925	4975	5026	5080
4716	4764	4819	4872	4926	4976	5027	5081
4717	4765	4820	4873	4927	4977	5028	5082
4718	4766	4821	4874	4928	4978	5029	5083
4719	4767	4822	4875	4929	4979	5030	5084
4720	4768	4823	4876	4930	4980	5031	5085
4721	4769	4824	4877	4931	4981	5032	5086
4722	4770	4825	4878	4932	4982	5033	5087
4723	4771	4826	4879	4933	4983	5034	5088
4724	4772	4827	4880	4934	4984	5035	5089
4725	4773	4828	4881	4935	4985	5036	5090
4726	4774	4829	4882	4936	4986	5037	5091
4727	4775	4830	4883	4937	4987	5038	5092
4728	4776	4831	4884	4938	4988	5039	5093
4729	4777	4832	4885	4939	4989	5040	5094
4730	4778	4833	4886	4940	4990	5041	5095
4731	4779	4834	4887	4941	4991	5042	5096
4732	4780	4835	4888	4942	4992	5043	5097
4733	4781	4836	4889	4943	4993	5044	5098
4734	4782	4837	4890	4944	4994	5045	
4735	4783	4838	4891	4945	4995	5046	
4736	4784	4839	4892	4946	4996	5047	
4737	4785	4840	4893	4947	4997	5048	
	4786	4841	4894	4948	4998	5049	
	4787	4842	4895	4949	4999	5050	
	4788	4843	4896		5000	5051	
	4789	4844	4897			5052	
	4790	4845	4898			5053	
	4791		4899			5054	
	4792						

5099 5100 5101 5102 5103 5104 5105 5106 5107 5108 5109 5110 5111 5112 5113 5114 5115 5116 5117 5118 5119 5120 5121 5122 5123 5124 5125 5126 5127 5128 5129 5130 5131 5132 5133 5134 5135 5136 5137 5138 5139 5140 5141

5142 5143 5144 5145 5146 5147 5148 5149 5150 5151 5152 5153 5154 5155 5156 5157 5158 5159 5160 5161 5162 5163 5164 5165 5166 5167 5168 5169 5170 5171 5172 5173 5174 5175 5176 5177 5178 5179 5180 5181 5182 5183 5184 5185 5186

5187 5188 5189 5190 5191 5192 5193 5194 5195 5196 5197 5198 5199 5200 5201 5202 5203 5204 5205 5206 5207 5208 5209 5210 5211 5212 5213 5214 5215 5216 5217 5218 5219 5220 5221 5222 5223 5224 5225 5226 5227 5228 5229 5230 5231 5232 5233 5234

5235 5236 5237 5238 5239 5240 5241 5242 5243 5244 5245 5246 5247 5248 5249 5250 5251 5252 5253 5254 5255 5256 5257 5258 5259 5260 5261 5262 5263 5264 5265 5266 5267 5268 5269 5270 5271 5272 5273 5274 5275 5276 5277 5278 5279 5280 5281 5282 5283 5284

5285 5286 5287 5288 5289 5290 5291 5292 5293 5294 5295 5296 5297 5298 5299 5300 5301 5302 5303 5304 5305 5306 5307 5308 5309 5310 5311 5312 5313 5314 5315 5316 5317 5318 5319 5320 5321 5322 5323 5324 5325 5326 5327 5328 5329 5330 5331 5332

5333 5334 5335 5336 5337 5338 5339 5340 5341 5342 5343 5344 5345 5346 5347 5348 5349 5350 5351 5352 5353 5354 5355 5356 5357 5358 5359 5360 5361 5362 5363 5364 5365 5366 5367 5368 5369 5370 5371 5372 5373 5374 5375 5376 5377 5378 5379 5380 5381 5382 5383

5384 5385 5386 5387 5388 5389 5390 5391 5392 5393 5394 5395 5396 5397 5398 5399 5400 5401 5402 5403 5404 5405 5406 5407 5408 5409 5410 5411 5412 5413 5414 5415 5416 5417 5418 5419 5420 5421 5422 5423 5424 5425 5426 5427 5428 5429 5430 5431 5432 5433 5434 5435 5436

I'm a hand-woven rug

being tugged apart...

5437
5438
5439
5440
5441
5442
5443
5444
5445
5446
5447
5448
5449
5450
5451
5452
5453
5454
5455
5456
5457
5458
5489
5490
5491
5492
5493
5494
549C
5496
5497
5498
5499
5500
5501
5502
5503
5504
5505

5506
5507
5508
5509
5510
5511
5512
5513
5514
5515
5516
5517
5518
5519
5520
5521
5522
5523
5524
5525
5526
5527
5528
5529
5530
5531
5532
5533
5534
5535
5536
5537
5538
5539

5540
5541
5542
5543
5544
5545
5546
5547
5548
5549
5550
5551
5552
5553
5554
5555
5556
5557
5558
5559
5560
5561
5562
5563
5564
5565
5566
5567
5568
5569
5570
5571
5572
5573
5574

5575
5576
5577
5578
5579
5580
5581
5582
5583
5584
5585
5586
5587
5588
5589
5590
5591
5592
5593
5594
5595
5596
5597
5598
5599
5600
5601
5602
5603
5604
5605
5606
5607
5608
5609
5610
5611
5612
5613

5614
5615
5616
5617
5618
5619
5620
5621
5622
5623
5624
5625
5626
5627
5628
5629
5630
5631
5632
5633
5634
5635
5636
5637
5638
5639
5640
5641
5642
5643
5644
5645
5646
5647
5648
5649

5650
5651
5652
5653
5654
5655
5656
5657
5658
5659
5660
5661
5662
5663
5664
5665
5666
5667
5668
5669
5670
5671
5672
5673
5674
5675
5676
5677
5678
5679
5680
5681
5682
5683
5684
5685
5686
5687
5688

5689
5690
5691
5692
5693
5694
5695
5696
5697
5698
5699
5700
5701
5702
5703
5704
5705
5706
5707
5708
5709
5710
5711
5712
5713
5714
5715
5716
5717
5718
5719
5720
5721
5722
5723
5724
5725
5726
5727
5728
5729
573

5731
5732
5733
5734
5735

Turn to the map. Something concrete.

But the paper crumbles in my hands.

1946

Land disappears

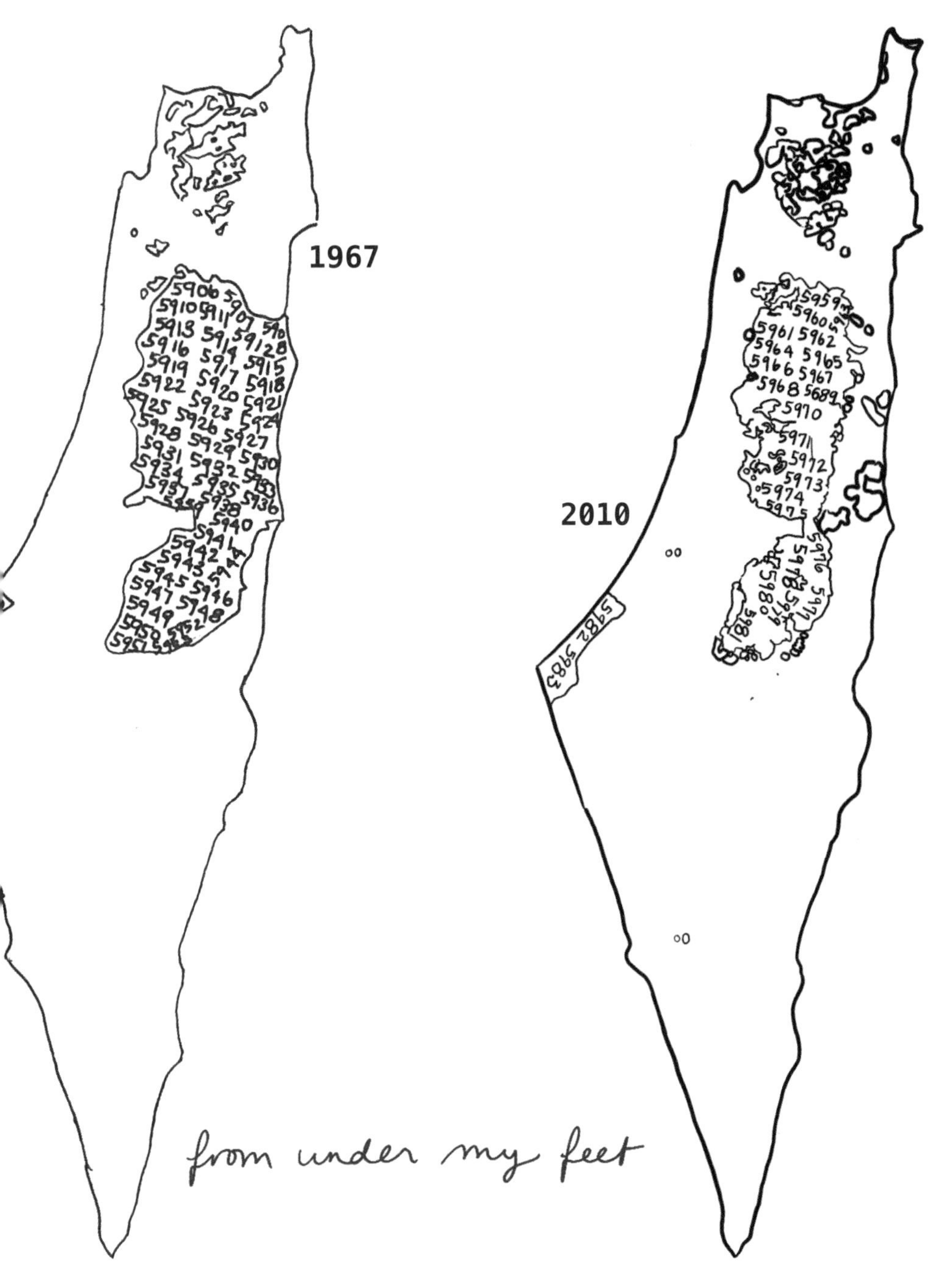
1967
2010
from under my feet

6,000 books held captive
in the archives at the National Library of Israel.
Inaccessible to Palestinians.

If **we** can't get the books back

I **will** document them somehow,

Each number a tombstone,

something to **return** to.

Run my fingers down each

line, each spine.

At the end of day 3,
I check my notes,
convinced I'd achieved
my goal, and realize
I was only one-tenth
of the way there.

When the numbers get this big, I can't compute.

If you actually stacked 70,000 books, they'd be 7,350 feet tall, which is equivalent to over 4 world trade center buildings.

And by 4 world trade center buildings, I am talking about the new World Trade Center, which, at 1,776 feet tall, is the Western Hemisphere's tallest building.

One World Trade Center building was completed in 2013 on the site of ground zero, where the former world trade center twin towers were struck down on September 11, 2001.

70,000 books stacked would be equivalent in height to over 5 of the original world trade center buildings.

5984 5985 5986 5987 5988 5989 5990 5991 5992 5993 5994 5995

5996 5997 5998 5999 6000.

6001 6002 6003 6004 6005 6006 6007 6008 6009 6010 6011

6012 6013 6014 6015 6016 6017 6018 6019 6020 6021 6022

6023 6024 6025 6026 6027 6028 6029 6030 6031 6032 6033

6034 6035 6036 6037 6038 6039 6040 6041 6042 6043 6044

6045 6046 6047 6048 6049 6050 6051 6052 6053

6054 6055 6056 6057 6058 6059 6060 6061 6062 6063

6064 6065 6066 6067 6068 6069 6070 6071 6072 6073 6074

6075 6076 6077 6078 6079 6080 6081 6082 6083 6084

6085 6086 6087 6088 6089 6090 6091 6092 6093 6094

6095 6096 6097 6098 6099 6100 6101 6102 6103 6104 6105

6106 6107 6108 6109 6110 6111 6112 6113 6114 6115 6116

6117 6118 6119 6120 6121 6122 6123 6124 6125 6126 6127

6128 6129 6130 6131 6132 6133 6134 6135 6136 6137 6138

6139 6140 6141 6142 6143 6144 6145 6146 6147 6148 6149

6150 6151 6152 6153 6154 6155 6156 6157 6158 6159

6160 6161 6162 6163 6164 6165 6166 6167 6168 6169

6170 6171 6172 6173 6174 6175 6176 6177 6178 6179

6180 6181 6182 6183 6184 6185 6186 6187 6188 6189

6190 6191 6192 6193 6194 6195 6196 6197 6198 6199 6200

6201 6202 6203 6204 6205 6206 6207 6208 6209 6210 6211

6212 6213 6214 6215 6216 6217 6218 6219 6220 6221 6222

6223 6224 6225 6226 6227 6228 6229 6230 6231 6232 6233

6234 6235 6236 6237 6238 6239 6240 6241 6242 6243

6244 6245 6246 6247 6248 6249 6250 6251 6252 6253 6254

6255 6256 6257 6258 6259 6260 6261 6262 6263 6264 6265

6266 6267 6268 6269 6270 6271 6272 6273 6274 6275

6276 6277 6278 6279 6280 6281 6283 6284 6285 6286

6287 6288 6289 6290 6291 6292 6293 6294 6295 6296 6297

6298 6299 6300 6301 6302 6303 6304 6305 6306 6037 6038

6039 6040 6041 6042 6043 6044 6045 6046 6047 6048 6049

6050 6051 6052 6053 6054 6055 6056 6057 6058 6059 6060

6061 6062 6063 6064 6065 6066 6067 6068 6069 6070 6071

6072 6073 6074 6075 6076 6077 6078 6079 6080 6081

6082 6083 6084 6085 6086 6087 6088 6089 6090 6091

6092 6093 6094 6095 6096 6097 6098 6099 6100 6101 6102

6103 6104 6105 6106 6107 6108 6109 6110 6111 6112 6113

6114 6115 6116 6117 6118 6119 6120 6121 6122 6123 6124

6125 6126 6127 6128 6129 6130 6131 6132 6133 6134 6135

6136 6137 6138 6139 6140 6141 6142 6143 6144 6145 6146

6147 6148 6149 6150 6151 6152 6153 6154 6155 6156 6157 6158

6159 6160 6161 6162 6163 6164 6165 6166 6167 6168 6169

6170 6171 6172 6173 6174 6175 6176 6177 6178 6179 6180

6181 6182 6183 6184 6185 6186 6187 6188 6189 6190

6191 6192 6193 6194 6195 6196 6197 6198 6199 6200 6201

6202 6203 6204 6205 6206 6207 6208 6209 6210

6211 6212 6213 6214 6215 6216 6217 6218 6219 6220

6221 6222 6223 6224 6225 6226 6227 6228 6229 6230 6231

6232 6233 6234 6235 6236 6237 6238 6239 6240

6241 6242 6243 6244 6245 6246 6247 6248 6249 6250

6251 6252 6253 6254 6255 6256 6257 6258 6259 6260

6261 6262 6263 6264 6265 6266 6267 6268 6269 6270

6271 6272 6273 6274 6275 6276 6277 6278

6279 6280 6281 6282 6283 6284 6285 6286 6287 6288 6289 6290 6291 6292 6293 6294 6295 6296 6297 6298

6299 6300 6301 6302 6303 6304 6305 6306

6307 6308 6309 6310 6311 6312 6313 6314 6315 6316 6317 6318 6319 6320 6321 6322 6323 6324 6325

6326 6327 6328 6329 6330 6331 6332 6333 6334 6335

6336 6337 6338 6339 6340 6341 6342 6343 6344 6345 6346 6347 6348 6349 6350 6351 6352 6353

6354 6355 6356 6357 6358 6359 6360 6361 6362

6363 6364 6365 6366 6367 6368 6369 6370 6371 6372 6373 6374 6375 6376 6377 6378 6379 6380 6381

6382 6383 6384 6385 6386 6387 6388 6389

6390 6391 6392 6393 6394 6395 6396 6397 6398 6399 6400 6401 6402 6403 6404 6405 6406 6407 6408

6409 6410 6411 6412 6413 6414 6415 6416 6417

6418 6419 6420 6421 6422 6423 6424 6425 6426 6427 6428 6429 6430 6431 6432 6433 6434 6435 6436

6437 6438 6439 6440 6441 6442 6443 6444

6445 6446 6447 6448 6449 6450 6451 6452 6453 6454 6455 6456 6457 6458 6459 6460 6461 6462

6463 6464 6465 6466 6467 6468 6469 6470 6471

6471 6472 6473 6474 6475 6476 6477 6478 6479 6480 6481 6482 6483 6484 6485 6486 6487 6488 6489 6490

6491 6492 6493 6494 6495 6496 6497 6498 6499 6500 6501 6502 6503 6504 6505 6506 6507 6508 6509 6510 6511 6512 6513 6514 6515 6516 6517 6518 6519 6520 6521 6522 6523 6524 6525 6526 6527 6528 6529 6530 6531 6532 6533 6534 6535 6536 6537 6538 6539 6540 6541 6542

6543 6544 6545 6546 6547 6548 6549 6550 6551 6552 6553 6554 6555 6556 6557 6558 6559 6560 6561 6562 6563 6564 6565 6566 6567 6568 6569 6570 6571 6572 6573 6574 6575 6576 6577 6578 6579 6580 6581 6582 6583 6584 6585 6586 6587 6588 6589 6590 6591 6592 6593 6594 6595 6596.

When I'm in my 20s, several of my friends go on "birthright," free trips to Israel for Jewish young adults 18-26.

My fiancé went on birthright.

It's where he met his ex-wife, so it's easy to dismiss as a poor decision.

My best friend went on birthright.

This is a fact I have not yet reconciled.

I've never been.

I search the internet about visiting Israel, and despite my U.S. passport, my Jewish fiancé, my plane ticket, I cannot find consensus on whether:

a. I would be allowed into the country upon landing in the airport.
b. I would be allowed into the country, but only through Jordan's Israeli-run West Bank boundary, or through Egypt's Sinai desert, which borders Gaza.
c. I would be allowed into the country through the airport, but only after being detained and questioned for several hours.
d. I would be deported upon arrival.

In my 20s, a close friend and I went on a spontaneous road trip with her partner and a friend of theirs I'd never met. On the long drive, we rolled down the windows and sang along to the radio. Katy Perry's "Firework," "S&M" by Rihanna, joyful, carefree dance hits from David Guetta, Pitbull, Ke$ha, until we lost radio signal. The air was humid, conspiratorial, and thick with possibility. When we arrived in our shared hotel room, somehow the topic of Israel and Palestine came up. One of my fellow travelers was apparently a member of AIPAC, an American Zionist organization which I wasn't familiar with at the time. I couldn't tell you what they said about Palestine because the topic was so charged that I immediately floated out of my body and hovered behind myself. Someone stepped in and defended Palestinians, which just escalated this person's conviction. Someone else asked me what I thought, and I said something vague and placating, hoping the topic would be dropped.

6743 6744 6745 6746 6747 6748 6749 6750 6751 6752 6753 6754 6755 6756 6757 6758 6759 6760 6761 6762 6763

6764 6765 6766 6767 6768 6769 6770 6771 6772 6773 6774 6775 6776 6777 6778 6779 6780 6781 6782 6783 6784

6785 6786 6787 6788 6789 6790 6791 6792 6793 6794 6795 6796 6797 6798 6799 6800 6801 6802 6803 6804 6805 6806

6807 6808 6809 6810 6811 6812 6813 6814 6815 6816 6817 6818 6819 6820 6821 6822 6823 6824 6825 6826 6827

6828 6829 6830 6831 6832 6833 6834 6835 6836 6837 6838 6839 6840 6841 6842 6843 6844 6845 6846 6847 6848 6849

6850 6851 6852 6853 6854 6855 6856 6857 6858 6859 6860 6861 6862 6863 6864 6865 6866 6867 6868 6869 6870 6871

6872 6873 6874 6875 6876 6877 6878 6879 6880 6881 6882 6883 6884 6885 6886 6887 6888 6889 6890 6891 6892 6893

6894 6895 6896 6897 6898 6899 6900 6901 6902 6903 6904 6905 6906 6907 6908 6909 6910 6911 6912 6913 6914 6915 6916

6917 6918 6919 6920 6921 6922 6923 6924 6925 6926 6927 6928 6929 6930 6931 6932 6933 6934 6935 6936 6937 6938 6939

6940 6941 6942 6943 6944 6945 6946 6947 6948 6949 6950 6951 6952 6953 6954 6955 6956 6957 6958 6959 6960 6961 6962 6963

6964 6965 6966 6967 6968 6969 6970 6971 6972 6973 6974 6975 6976 6977 6978 6979 6980 6981 6982 6983 6984

6985 6986 6987 6988 6989 6990 6991 6992 6993 6994 6995 6996 6997 6998 6999 7000 7001 7002 7003 7004 7005 7006

7007 7008 7009 7010 7011 7012 7013 7014 7015 7016 7017 7018 7019 7020 7021 7022 7023 7024 7025 7026 7027

After this friend breaks up with her partner, she gets married to someone else. She and her husband, both Jewish, will go on a babymoon trip to Israel. They will receive thousands of dollars toward their travel because they are Jewish and young and recently married. They will hang a photo from their trip in their living room: a cluster of sand-colored buildings, arched windows and minarets in the background, fishing boats on the blue water in the foreground. And when someone asks where the photo was taken they will say Yafo. It takes a minute for me to register the Jewish name for occupied Jaffa. The Palestinian houses filled with new occupants. And I will feel nausea kick me in the stomach and tears sting my eyes. And I won't know how to bring up, in casual conversation, that this place they were paid to visit is my grandmother's hometown, a place I have never been. A place I may never be able, or allowed, to see.

7028 029 030 7031 032 033 034 035 036 037 038 039 040

7041 7042 7043 7044 7045 7046 7047 7048 7049 7050 7051 7052 7053 7054 7055 7056

7057 7058 7059 7060 7061 7062 7063 7064 7065 7066 7067 7068 7069

7070 7071 7072 7073 7074 7075 7076 7077 7078 7079 7080 7081

7082 7083 7084 7085 7086 7087 7088 7089 7090 7091 7092 7093 7094 7095 7096

7097 7098 7099 7100 7101 7102 7103 7104 7105 7106 7107 7108 7109

7110 7111 7112 7113 7114 7115 7116 7117 7118 7119 7120 7121 7122 7123

7124 7125 7126 7127 7128 7129 7130 7131 7132 7133 7134 7135 7136 7137 7138 7139

7437 7438 7439 7440 7441 7442 7443 7444 7445 7446 7447 7448

7449 7450 7451 7452 7453 7454 7455 7456 7457 7458 7459 7460

7461 7462 7463 7464 7465 7466 7467 7468 7469 7470 7471 7472 7473

7474 7475 7476 7477 7478 7479 7480 7481 7482 7483

7484 7485 7486 7487 7488 7489 7490 7491 7492 7493 7494 7495 7496 7497 7498

7499 7500 7501 7502 7503 7504 7505 7506 7507 7508 7509

140 141 142 143 144 145 146 147 148 149

7150 7151 7152 7153 7154 7155 7156 7157 7158 7159 7160

7161 7162 7163 7164 7165 7166 7167 7168 7169 7170

7171 7172 7173 7174 7175 7176 7177 7178 7179 7180 7181 7182 7183 7184

7185 7186 7187 7188 7189 7190 7191 7192 7193 7194

7195 7196 7197 7198 7199 7200 7201 7202 7203 7204 7205 7206

7207 7208 7209 72

7210 7211 7212 7213 7214 7215 7216 7217 7218 7219 7220 7221

7222 7223 7224 7225 7226 7227 7228 7229 7230 7231 7232 7233 7234 7235

7510 7511 7512 7513 7514 7515 7516 7517 7518 7519

7520 7521 7522 7523 7524 7525 7526 7527 7528 7529

7530 7531 7532 7533 7534 7535 7536 7537 7538 7539 7540 7541

7542 7543 7544 7545 7546 7547 7548 7549 7550

7551 7552 7553 7554 7555 7556 7557 7558 7559

7560 7561 7562 7563 7564 7565 7566 7567 7568

7236 7237 7238 7239 7240 7241 7242 7243 244 7245 7246 7247 248 249 250 251 252 253 254

7255 7256 7257 7258 7259 7260 7261 7262 7263

7264 7265 7266 7267 7268 7269 7270 7271

7272 7273 7274 7275 7276 7277 7278 7279

7280 7281 7282 7283 7284 7285 7286 7287 7288 7289 7290 7291

7292 7293 7294 7295 7296 7297 7298 7299 7300 7301 7302

7303 7304 7305 7306 7307 7308 7309 7310 7311 7312

7569 7570 7571 7572 7573 7574 7575 7576 7577

7578 7579 7580 7581 7582 7583 7584 7585 7586 7587 7588

7589 7590 7591 7592 7593 7594 7595 7596

7597 7598 7599 7600 7601 7602 7603 7604 7605 7606

7607 7608 7609 7610 7611 7612 7613 7614 7615 7616

7617 7618 7619 7620 7621 7622 7623 7624

7625 7626 7627 7628 7629 7630 7631 7632

7313 7314 7315 7316 7317 7318 7319

7320 7321 7322 7323 7324 7325 7326

7327 7328 7329 7330 7331 7332 7333 7334 7335

7336 7337 7338 7339 7340 7341 7342

7343 7344 7345 7346 7347 7348 7349 7350 7351

7352 7353 7354 7355 7356 7357 7358 7359

7360 7361 7362 7363 7364 7365 7366 7367

368 369 370 371 372 373 374 75 376

7377 7378 7379 7380 7381 7382 7383 7384 7385 7386 7387

7388 7389 7390 7391 7392 7393 7394 7395 7396

7397 7398 7399 7400 7401 7402 7403 7404 7405 7406 7407

7408 7409 7410 7411 7412 7413 7414 7415 7416 7417 7418

7419 7420 7421 7422 7423 7424 7425 7426 7427

7428 7429 7430 7431 7432 7433 7434 7435 7436

7633 7634 7635
7636 7637 7638
7639 7640 7641
7642 7643 7644
7645 7646 7647
7648 7649 7650
7651 7652 7653
7654 7655 7656
7657 7658 7659
7660 7661 7662
7663 7664 7665
7666 7667 7668
7669 7670 7671
7672 7673 7674
7675 7676 7677

7678 7679 7680
7681 7682 7683
7684 7685 7686
7687 7688 7689
7690 7691 7692
7693 7694 7695
7696 7697 7698
7699 7700 7701
7702 7703 7704
7705 7706 7707
7708 7709 7710
7711 7712 7713
7714 7715 7716
7717 7718 7719

Each year, on Passover, they say, “Next year in Jerusalem!”

While it’s not necessarily a political statement, sometimes it stings like one.

I can’t help thinking of my own return.

Palestinians in diaspora are known to keep the keys to their homes that no longer exist. An entry pass to an eradicated place. A solid artifact, reminder of reality, when everything else is explained away, demolished.

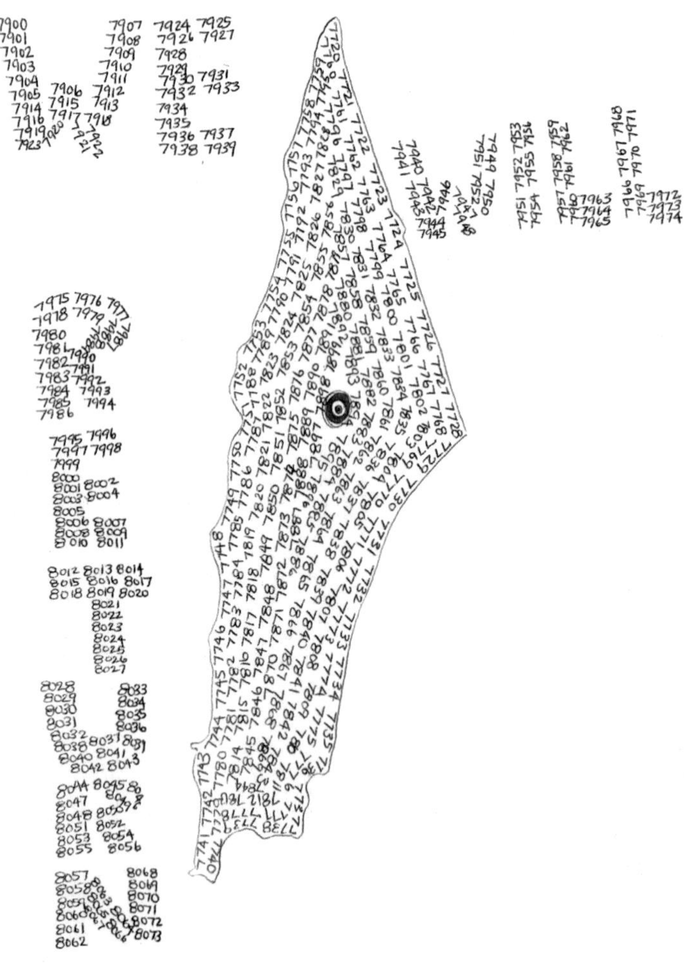

8261 8262 8263 8264 8265 8266 8267 8268 8269 8270 8271 8272 8273 8274 8275 8276 8277 8278 8279 8280 8281 8282 8283 8284 8285 8286 8287 8288 8289 8290 8291 8292 8293 8294 8295 8296 8297 8298 8299 8300 8301 8302 8303 8304 8305 8306 8307 8308 8309 8310 8311 8312 8313 8314 8315 8316

8317 8318 8319 8320 8321 8322 8323 8324 8325 8326 8327 8328 8329 8330 8331 8332 8333 8334 8335 8336 8337 8338 8339 8340 8341 8342 8343 8344 8345 8346 8347 8348 8349 8350 8351 8352 8353 8354 8355 8356 8357 8358 8359 8360 8361 8362 8363 8364

8365 8370 8366 8371 8367 8372 8368 8373 8369 8374

8375 8376 8377 8378 8379 8380 8381 8382 8383 8384 8385 8386 8387 8388 8389 8390 8391 8392 8393 8394 8395 8396 8397 8398 8399

8400 8405 8401 8406 8402 8407 8403 8408 8404 8409

8074 8075 8076 8077 8078 8079 8080 8081 8082 8083 8084 8085 8086 8087 8088 8089 8090 8091 8092 8093 8094 8095 8096 8097 8098 8099 8100 8101 8102 8103 8104 8105 8106 8107 8108

8109 8110 8111 8112 8113 8114 8115 8116 8117 8118 8119 8120 8121 8122 8123 8124 8125 8126 8127 8128 8129 8130 8131 8132

8413 8414 8415 8416 8417 8418 8419 8420 8421 8422 8423 8424 8425 8426 8427 8428 8429 8430 8431 8432 8433 8434 8410 8435 8411 8436 8412 8437

8448 8449 8450 8451 8452 8453 8454 8455 8456 8457 8458 8459 8460 8461 8462 8463 8464 8465 8466 8467 8468 8469 8470 8471 8472 8473 8474 8475 8476 8477 8478 8479 8480 8481 8482 8483 8484 8485 8486 8487 8488 8489 8490 8491 8492 8493 8494 8495 8496 8497 8498 8499 8500 8501 8502 8503

8213 8214 8215 8216 8217 8218 8219 8220 8221 8222 8223 8224 8225 8226 8227 8228 8229 8230 8231 8232 8233 8234 8212 8211 8210 8209 8208 8207 8206 8205

8438 8439 8440 8441 8442 8443 8444 8445 8446 8447

8504 8505 8506 8507 8508 8509 8510 8511 8512 8513 8514 8515 8516 8517 8518 8519 8520 8521 8522 8523 8524 8525 8526 8527 8528 8529 8530 8531 8532 8533 8534 8535 8536 8537 8538 8539 8540 8541 8542 8543 8544 8545 8546 8547 8548 8549 8550 8551 8552

8553 8554 8555 8556 8557 8558 8559 8560 8561 8562 8563 8564 8565 8566 8567 8568 8569 8570 8571 8572 8573 8574 8575 8576 8577 8578 8579 8580 8581 8582 8583 8584 8585 8586 8587 8588 8589 8590 8591 8592 8593 8594

8133 8134 8135 8136 8137 8138 8139 8140 8141 8142 8143 8144 8145 8146 8147 8148 8149 8150 8151 8152 8153 8154 8155 8156 8157 8158 8159 8160 8161 8162 8163 8164 8165 8166 8167 8168 8169 8170 8171 8172 8173 8174 8175 8176 8177 8178 8179 8180 8181 8182

8595 8596 8597 8598 8599 8600 8601 8602 8603 8604 8605 8606 8607 8608 8609 8610 8611 8612 8613 8614 8615 8616 8617 8618 8619 8620 8621 8622 8623 8624 8625 8626 8627 8628 8629

8630 8631 8632 8633 8634 8635 8636 8637 8638 8639 8640 8641 8642 8643 8644 8645 8646 8647 8648 8649 8650 8651 8652 8653 8654 8655 8656 8657 8658 8659 8660 8661 8662 8663 8664 8665 8666 8667 8668 8669 8670 8671 8672 8673 8674 8675 8676 8677 8678 8679 8680 8681 8682 8683 8684 8685 8686 8687

8688 8689 8690 8691 8692 8693 8694 8695 8696 8697 8698 8699 8700 8701 8702 8703 8704 8705 8706 8707 8708 8709 8710 8711 8712 8713 8714 8715 8716 8717 8718 8719 8720 8721 8722 8723 8724 8725 8726 8727 8728

8729 8730 8731 8732 8733 8734 8735 8736 8737 8738 8739 8740 8741 8742 8743 8744 8745 8746 8747 8748 8749 8750 8751 8752 8753 8754 8755 8756 8757 8758 8759 8760 8761 8762 8763 8764 8765 8766 8767 8768 8769 8770 8771 8772 8773 8774 8775 8776 8777 8778 8779 8780 8781 8782 8783 8784 8785 8786 8787 8788 8789

8183 8184 8185 8186 8187 8188 8189 8190 8191 8192 8193 8194 8195 8196 8197 8198 8199 8200 8201 8202 8203 8204

8235 8236 8237 8238 8239 8240 8241 8242 8243 8244 8245 8246 8247 8248 8249 8250 8251 8252 8253 8254 8255 8256

8790 8791 8792 8793 8794 8795 8796 8797 8798 8799 8800 8801 8802 8803 8804 8805 8806 8807 8808 8809 8810 8811 8812 8813 8814 8815 8816 8817 8818 8819 8820 8821 8822 8823 8824 8825 8826 8827 8828 8829 8830 8831 8832 8833 8834 8835 8836 8837 8838 8839 8840 8841 8842 8843 8844 8845 8846 8847 8848 8849 8850 8851 8852 8853

8854 8855 8856 8857 8858 8859 8860 8861 8862 8863 8864 8865 8866 8867 8868 8869 8870 8871 8872 8873 8874 8875 8876 8877 8878 8879 8880 8881 8882 8883 8884 8885 8886 8887 8888 8889 8890 8891 8892 8893 8894 8895 8896 8897 8898 8899 8900 8901 8902 8903 8904 8905 8906 8907 8908 8909

8910 8911 8912 8913 8914 8915 8916 8917 8918 8919 8920 8921 8922 8923 8924 8925 8926 8927 8928 8929 8930 8931 8932 8933 8934 8935 8936 8937 8938 8939 8940 8941 8942 8943 8944 8945 8946 8947 8948 8949 8950 8951 8952 8953 8954 8955 8956 8957 8958 8959 8960 8961 8962

8963 8964 8965 8966 8967 8968 8969 8970 8971 8972 8973

9021 9022 9023 9024 9025 9026 9027 9028 9029 9030 9031 9032 9033

9134 9135 9136 9137 9138 9139 9140 9141 9142 9143 9144 9145 9146

9168 9169 9170 9171 9172 9173 9174 9175 9176 9177 9178 9179 9180

9205 9206 9207 9208 9209 9210 9211 9212 9213 9214 9215 9216 9217

9243 9244 9245 9246 9247 9248 9249 9250 9251 9252 9253 9254 9255 9256

9282 9283 9284 9285 9286 9287 9288 9289 9290 9291 9292 9293 9294 9295 9296

9320 9321 9322 9323 9324 9325 9326 9327 9328 9329 9330 9331 9332

9355 9356 9357 9358 9359 9360 9361 9362 9363 9364 9365 9366 9367 9368

9391 9392 9393 9394 9395 9396 9397 9398 9399 9400 9401 9402 9403 9404

9428 9429 9430 9431 9432 9433 9434 9435 9436 9437 9438 9439 9440 9441

9464 9465 9466 9467 9468 9469 9470 9471 9472 9473 9474 9475 9476

9498 9499 9500 9501 9502 9503 9504 9505 9506 9507 9508 9509 9510

9034 9038 9042 9046 9050 9054 9058 9062
9035 9039 9043 9047 9051 9055 9059 9063
9036 9040 9044 9048 9052 9056 9060 9064
9037 9041 9045 9049 9053 9057 9061 9065

8974 8975 8976 8977 8978 8979 8980 8981 8982 8983 8984 8985 8986 8987 8988 8989 8990 8991 8992 8993 8994 8995 8996 8997 8998 8999

9104 9105 9106 9107 9108 9109 9110 9111

9066 9067 9068 9069 9070 9071 9072
9073 9074 9075 9076 9077 9078 9079
9080 9081 9082 9083 9084 9085 9086
9087 9088 9089 9090 9091 9092 9093 9094
9095 9096 9097 9098 9099 9100 9101 9102 9103

9000 9001 9002 9003 9004 9005 9006 9007 9008 9009 9010 9011 9012 9013 9014 9015 9016 9017 9018 9019 9020

9112 9113 9114 9115 9116 9117 9118 9119 9120 9121 9122 9123 9124 9125 9126 9127 9128 9129 9130 9131 9132 9133

9147 9148 9149 9150 9151 9152 9153 9154 9155 9156 9157 9158 9159 9160 9161 9162 9163 9164 9165 9166 9167

9181 9182 9183 9184 9185 9186 9187 9188 9189 9190 9191 9192 9193 9194 9195 9196 9197 9198 9199 9200 9201 9202 9203 9204

9218 9219 9220 9221 9222 9223 9224 9225 9226 9227 9228 9229 9230 9231 9232 9233 9234 9235 9236 9237 9238 9239 9240 9241 9242

9257 9258 9259 9260 9261 9262 9263 9264 9265 9266 9267 9268 9269 9270 9271 9272 9273 9274 9275 9276 9277 9278 9279 9280 9281

9297 9298 9299 9300 9301 9302 9303 9304 9305 9306 9307 9308 9309 9310 9311 9312 9313 9314 9315 9316 9317 9318 9319

9333 9334 9335 9336 9337 9338 9339 9340 9341 9342 9343 9344 9345 9346 9347 9348 9349 9350 9351 9352 9353 9354

9369 9370 9371 9372 9373 9374 9375 9376 9377 9378 9379 9380 9381 9382 9383 9384 9385 9386 9387 9388 9389 9390

9405 9406 9407 9408 9409 9410 9411 9412 9413 9414 9415 9416 9417 9418 9419 9420 9421 9422 9423 9424 9425 9426 9427

9442 9443 9444 9445 9446 9447 9448 9449 9450 9451 9452 9453 9454 9455 9456 9457 9458 9459 9460 9461 9462 9463

9477 9478 9479 9480 9481 9482 9483 9484 9485 9486 9487 9488 9489 9490 9491 9492 9493 9494 9495 9496 9497

9511 9512 9513 9514 9515 9516 9517 9518 9519 9520 9521 9522 9523 9524 9525 9526 9527 9528 9529 9530 9531

1932 - My teta is born in Jaffa, Palestine, a port city on the Mediterranean Sea that became a symbol of the Arab resistance against British colonizers.

Her parents are both Palestinian, and her great-uncle is the prominent 'Issa al-'Issa, publisher of the Palestinian newspaper *Falastin*, which criticizes the Zionist movement.

Jaffa is known for its special variety of oranges developed by Palestinian farmers in the mid-19th century. Jaffa oranges were a symbol of Palestinian identity, ingenuity, land, and pride.

Teta's father, Saba Malak, was the son of an orange grower and merchant, and started a printing business for the delicate packaging oranges were wrapped in before being exported.

1948 - In May, the state of Israel is established on Palestinian soil.

700,000 people flee their homes.

Teta, along with her parents and siblings, pack a couple of bags and take a vacation, hoping they can wait out the violence and uncertainty.

They never returned.

1952 - My mother is born in Beirut.

1956 - Israeli forces execute more than 450 male civilians in the refugee camps of Rafah and Khan Yunis.[3]

---

3 Sayigh, Yezid, *Armed Struggle and the Search for State: The Palestinian National Movement, 1949–1993*, Oxford University Press, 1997, p. 65.

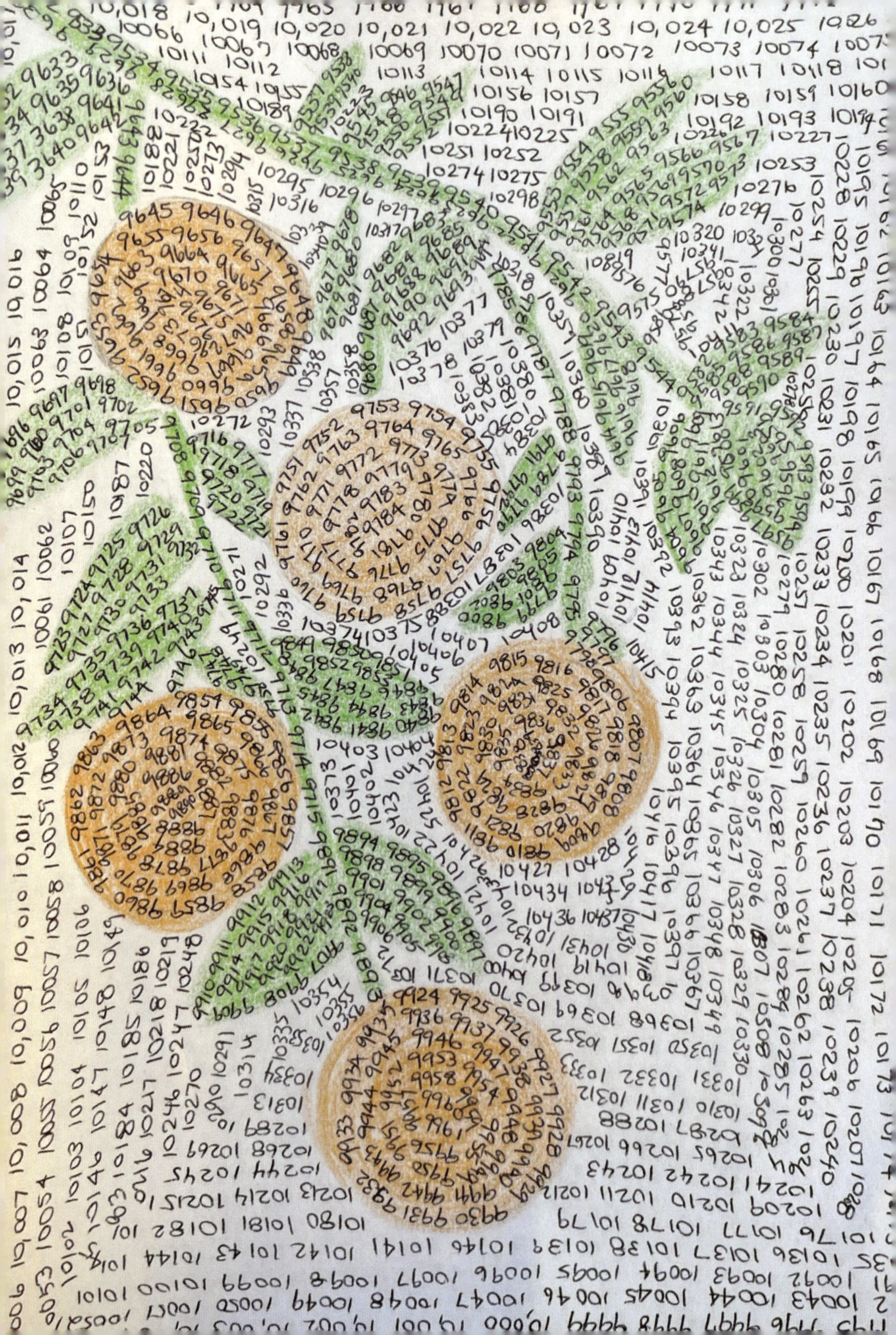

10066 10,019 10,020 10,021 10,022 10,023 10,024 10,025 10026

10111 10067 10068 10069 10070 10071 10072 10073 10074 10075

10112 10113 10114 10115 10116 10117 10118

Self Portrait as Jaffa Orange

I come from a long line of world-renowned
fruit, treasures thinly wrapped in stamped
paper: ellipsoids with low shoulders
and a faint areolar ring, ripped
from limbs, upright and thornless,

enchanted plants with sweet
fruit, fragrant, nearly seedless
and skin thick enough
to travel the world
in their Technicolor crinkle.
— That's us,
living in diaspora:
sweet on the inside, ripe with nostalgia
for the trees from which we were plucked.

My roots are so far from my fruit, I long
to belong to the homeland we've lost,
salty soil by the seaside.
On days when I feel most tender and pulpy, I long
for ancestral dirt, long to inhale her scent
hot with sun and wet with rain.

When my grandparents fled
their homes and groves were razed
and set ablaze. Corpses of our dead
littered the ground,
the earth choked with their blood—
oranges unable to grow.

They bulldozed fields and roads,
cut off water flow so the native
farmers could only grow
tensions.

Some remaining relatives were held up
at checkpoints and closed border crossings,
rotting as they waited.

Others survived the journey unbruised
to start a new legacy abroad, ripe with nostalgia.

Appropriating oranges,
plucking someone from their native tree,
to oppress them with advertisements, images
of what they once possessed, called home.
Gaslighting by citrus.

My grandmother arrested
in her development at 16
when she left
and spent the rest
of her life in mourning,
propagating resentment.

Like the trees we tried to replant overseas
—the seeds overtook her fruit's bitter body.

10438 10439 10440 10441 10442 10443 10444 10445 10446 10447 10448 10449 10450 10451
10498 10499 10500 10501 10502 10503 10504 10505 10506 10507 10508 10509 10570
10555 10556 10557 10558 10559 10560 10561 10562 10563 10564 10565
10609 10610 10611 10612 10613 10614 10615 10616 10617 10618 10619
10659 10660 10662 10662 10665 10664 10665 10666 10667 10668 10669
10708 10709 10710 10711 10712 10713 10714 10715 10716 10717 10718
10753 10754 10755 10756 10757 10758 10759 10760 10761
10794 10795 10796 10797 10798 10799 10800 10801

10814 10815 10816 10817 10818 10819 10820 10821 10822

As I write, I journey . . .

[To mountains]   [and valleys]   [cliffs and coasts]

To the sound of the muezzin, a siren,

calling the masses to prayer.

To the olive trees,

ancient gnarly beasts,

knotted and rough,

enormous warriors,

with tiny silver wings and green fruit.

To the lipstick smudge fields of poppies,

waist-high and swaying like a Coachella crowd.

To the orange groves, wheelbarrows piled with mounds of fruit.

85
86
87
88
89
90
91
92
93
94
95
96
97
98
99
00
01
02
03
04
05
06
07
08
09
10
11
12
13
14
15
16
17
18
19
20
21
22
23
24
25
126
127
28
29
130
131
132
33
34

11135
11136
11137
11138
11139
11140
11141
11142
11143
11144
11145
11146
11147
11148
11149
11150
11151
11152
11153
11154
11155
11156
11157
11158
11159
11160
11161
11162
11163
11164
11165
11166
11167
11168
11169
11170
11171
11172
11173
11174
11175
11176
11177
11178
11179
11180

11181
11182
11183
11184
11185
11186
11187
11188
11189
11190
11191
11192
11193
11194
11195
11196
11197
11198
11199
11200
11201
11202
11203
11204
11205
11206
11207
11208
11209
11210
11211
11212
11213
11214
11215
11216
11217
11218
11219
11220
11221
11222
11223

11224
11225
11226
11227
11228
11229
11230
11231
11232
11233
11234
11235
11236
11237
11238
11239
11240
11241
11242
11243
11244
11245
11246
11247
11248
11249
11250
11251
11252
11253
11254
11255
11256
11257
11258
11259
11260
11261

11262
11263
11264
11265
11266
11267
11268
11269
11270
11271
11272
11273
11274
11275
11276
11277
11278

11279
11280
11281
11282
11283
11284
11285
11286
11287
11288
11289
11290
11291
11292
11293
11294

11295
11296
11297
11298
11299
11300
11301
11302
11303
11304
11305
11306
11307
11308
11309
11310
11311

11312
11313
11314
11315
11316
11317
11318
11319
11320
11321
11322
11323
11324
11325
11326
11327
11328

11329
11330
11331
11332
11333
11334
11335
11336
11337
11338
11339
11340
11341
11342
11343
11344

11345
11346
11347
11348
11349
11350
11351
11352
11353
11354
11355
11356
11357
11358
11359
11360
11361
11362
11363
11364
11365
11366
11367
11368
11369
11370
11371
11372
11373
11374
11375
11376
11377
11378
11379
11380

11381
11382
11383
11384
11385
11386
11387
11388
11389
11390
11391
11392
11393
11394
11395
11396
11397
11398
11399
11400
11401
11402
11403
11404
11405
11406
11407
11408
11409
11410
11411
11412
11413
11414
11415
11416
11417
11418
11419
11420
11421
11422
11423
11424

I'm in a work meeting when a colleague mentions her recent trip to Israel. She calls it "birthright" even though she is over the age of 26. She's beaming when she says it was such a powerful and spiritual experience connecting with her Jewish roots. She's never thought of herself as Jewish, and as far as I know, has no historical or cultural connection to the land. It's a recent realization that she considers herself entitled to this land since birth.

She was born in the 1990s, so I guess she's only ever known the world post-Oslo Accord.

She believes it is her right, as someone with Jewish ancestors, to take a vacation in my motherland.

My mind blurs, eyes cross, vision fades out.

There are three other white colleagues in the meeting. Two of them are my friends. They are young and liberal. I hope one of them will say something, but I don't know what. No one says anything, so I brace myself and wait for the chitchat to end.

I fade away.

On social media, this colleague posts a video of herself touching the Western Wall. Blonde hair wisping in the wind. She slips her wishes into fractured rock. Fills the empty space with her wanting. Colonizes cracks. She says she is tearful and humble, reflecting and praying. She writes "peace and healing for all."[4]

Who does she mean by "all"?

What does it mean to wish someone healing while standing on occupied land?

4 *Spiritual bypassing. (verb) Using spirituality or belief in a higher power to sidestep or sugarcoat painful emotional issues, psychological wounds, unresolved traumas.

[wish] x x x x xx x x

xxx x x xx

X x x x x x x

xx x xx

X xx x [wish] x

[wish] x x

X x xx x x

xx [wish] [wish] x x x x

xx x x xxx x x xx

X x x x x x x

xx x xx

X xx x [wish] x

[wish] x x

X x xx x x

xx [wish] xx x

[wish] x [wish] x x

X x xx x x

xx [wish] [wish] x

x x x xx x x xxx x

x xx

X x x x x x x

xx X [wish] xx x x xx [wish] x

xx [wish] x xx x x xxx x

xx xx [wish] x x xx x x xx xx x [wish] x [wish] xx [wish] x

If I could touch that wall I would

[Western Wall, c. 1880]

2186 2187 188 2189 2190 2191 2192 2193 2194 2195 2196 2197 2198 2199

12200 12201 12202 12203 12204 12205 12206 12207 12208 12209 12210 12211 12212 12213

12214 12215 12216 12217 12218 12219 12220 12221 12222 12223 12224 12225 12226 12227 12228

12229 12230 12231 12232 12233 12234 12235 12236 12237 12238 12239 12240 12241 12242 12243

12244 12245 12246 12247 12248 12249 12250 12251 12252 12253 12254 12255 12256 12257 12258 12259

12260 12261 12262 12263 12264 12265 12266 12267 12268 12269 12270 12271 12272 12273 12274

12275 12276 12277 12278 12279 12280 12281 12282 12283 12284 12285 12286 12287 12288 12289

12290 12291 12292 12293 12294 12295 12296 12297 12298 12299 12300 12301 12302 12303 12304

12305 12306 12307 12308 12309 12310 12311 12312 12313 12314 12315 12316 12317 12318

12319 12320 12321 12322 12323 12324 12325 12326 12327 12328 12329 12330 12331 12332 12333

12334 12335 12336 12337 12338 12339 12340 12341 12342 12343 12344 12345 12346 12347 12348

12349 12350 12351 12352 12353 12354 12355 12356 12357 12358 12359 12360 12361 12362 12363 12364

12365 12366 12367 12368 12369 12370 12371 12372 12373 12374 12375 12376 12377 12378 12379 12380 12381

1962

12382 12383 12384 12385 12386 12387 12388 12389 12390 12391 12392 12393 12394 12395

12396 12397 12398 12399 12400 12401 12402 12403 12404 12405 12406 12407 12408 12409 12410

12411 12412 12413 12414 12415 12416 12417 12418 12419 12420 12421 12422 12423 12424

12425 12426 12427 12428 12429 12430 12431 12432 12433 12434 12435 12436 12437 12438

12439 12440 12441 12442 12443 12444 12445 12446 12447 12448 12449 12450 12451 12452 12453

12454 12455 12456 12457 12458 12459 12460 12461 12462 12463 12464 12465 12466 12467 12468

12469 12470 12471 12472 12473 12474 12475 12476 12477 12478 12479 12480 12481 12482 12483

12484 12485 12486 12487 12488 12489 12490 12491 12492 12493 12494 12495 12496 12497

12498 12499 12500 12501 12502 12503 12504 12505 12506 12507 12508 12509 12510 12511 12512

12513 12514 12515 12516 12517 12518 12519 12520 1252 12522 12523 12524 12525 12526

12527 12528 12529 12530 12531 12532 12533 12534 12535 12536 12537 12538 12539 12540 12541

12542 12543 12544 12545 12546 12547 12548 12549 12550 12551 12552 12553 12554

Early 1960s, my mother visits Palestine with her family and writes:

> "Jerusalem: The Dome of the Rock. What a magnificent Mosque. I think it was the first time I had actually gone inside a mosque and seen an example of Islamic architecture. I was in awe and in love [. . .] the "Rock" upon which at least 3 prophets (they told me) had some kind of interaction. Anyway, it was the first time I felt I was in a holy place, really felt it. At least it was a place worthy of respect. I remember to myself looking at the layers of Persian carpets on the ground and thinking to myself I couldn't possibly step here.
>
> "In Jerusalem we went up to the roof of some building with my mother's cousins from where we could see the 'Israeli side'! It was the first time I actually saw Israel and Israelis (however small and at a distance) realizing they were people like us, and their homes were like ours.
>
> "Beit Jalah [West Bank]: We visited an old aunt of my father's. She had a little farm and bred rabbits. She had goats too. She looked poor but peaceful.
>
> "Most of the relatives we visited had very little in their homes. It was lucky they had a roof over their heads and jobs. But it was obvious to me that they were impoverished by moving, relocating and leaving any wealth they might have had behind."

55 56 57 558 559 560 561 562 563 564 565 566 567 568 569 570 2571 2572 2573 2574 12575 12576 577 2578 2579 2580 2581 2582 583 584 2585 2586 2587 2588 2589 12590 12591 12592 12593 12594 12595 12596 12597 12598 2599 12600 12601 12602 12603 12604 12605 12606 12607 12608 12609 12610 12611

12612 12613 12614 12615 12616 12617 12618 12619 12620 12621 12622 12623 12624 12625 12626 12627 12628 12629 12630

12631 12632 12633 12634 12635 12636 12637 12638 12639 12640 12641 12642 12643 12644 12645 12646 12647 12648

12667 12668 12669 12670 12671 12672 12673 12674 12675 12676 12677 12678 12679 12680 12681 12682 12683 12684

12703 12704 12705 12706 12707 12708 12709 12710 12711 12712 12713 12714 12715 12716 12717 12718 12719 12720 12721

12740 12741 12742 12743 12744 12745 12746 12747 12748 12749 12750 12751 12752 12753 12754 12755 12756 12757

12777 12778 12779 12780 12781 12782 12783 12784 12785 12786 12787 12788 12789 12790 12791 12792 12793 12794

12814 12815 12816 12817 12818 12819 12820 12821 12822 12823 12824 12825 12826 12827 12828 12829 12830 12831 12832

12852 12853 12854 12855 12856 12857 12858 12859 12860 12861 12862 12863 12864 12865 12866 12867 12868 12869 12870 12871

12892 12893 12894 12895 12896 12897 12898 12899 12900 12901 12902 12903 12904 12905 12906 12907 12908 12909

12930 12931 12932 12933 12934 12935 12936 12937 12938 12939 12940 12941 12942 12943 12944 12945

12964 12965 12966 12967 12968 12969 12970 12971 12972 12973 12974 12975 12976 12977 12978 12979 12980 12981

13001 13002 13003 13004 13005 13006 13007 13008 13009 13010 13011 13012 13013 13014 13015 13016 13017 13018 13019 13020 13021 13022 13023

12631 12632 12633 12634 12635 12636 12637 12638 12639 12640 12641 12642 12643 12644 12645 12646 12647 12648

12649 12650 12651 12652 12653 12654 12655 12656 12657 12658 12659 12660 12661 12662 12663 12664 12665 12666

12685 12686 12687 12688 12689 12690 12691 12692 12693 12694 12695 12696 12697 12698 12699 12700 12701 12702

12722 12723 12724 12725 12726 12727 12728 12729 12730 12731 12732 12733 12734 12735 12736 12737 12738 12739

12758 12759 12760 12761 12762 12763 12764 12765 12766 12767 12768 12769 12770 12771 12772 12773 12774 12775 12776

12795 12796 12797 12798 12799 12800 12801 12802 12803 12804 12805 12806 12807 12808 12809 12810 12811 12812 12813

12833 12834 12835 12836 12837 12838 12839 12840 12841 12842 12843 12844 12845 12846 12847 12848 12849 12850 12851

12872 12873 12874 12875 12876 12877 12878 12879 12880 12881 12882 12883 12884 12885 12886 12887 12888 12889 12890 12891

12910 12911 12912 12913 12914 12915 12916 12917 12918 12919 12920 12921 12922 12923 12924 12925 12926 12927 12928 12929

12946 12947 12948 12949 12950 12951 12952 12953 12954 12955 12956 12957 12958 12959 12960 12961 12962 12963

12982 12983 12984 12985 12986 12987 12988 12989 12990 12991 12992 12993 12994 12995 12996 12997 12998 12999

This same colleague posts a photo of herself floating in the Dead Sea with a caption about the healing power of minerals.

**This is an Israeli tourism ad for the Dead Sea*

Solve for $\boldsymbol{x}$

If $\boldsymbol{x}^3$ = [flavor] = [crave] = [saline] = [blood pressure] = [أبيض] = ($\boldsymbol{x}$) flats = ($\boldsymbol{x}$) lick = ($\boldsymbol{x}$) box = ($\boldsymbol{x}$) shaker

If $\int$ ($\boldsymbol{x}$) = [summer] [osmosis] [longing] [sweat] [cerulean] [crystal] [soothe] [soak] [chaos] [blood] [electric] [pickle] [carve] [clean] [pillar] [rock] [spill] [crave] [crust] [تأكل] [crushed] [protection] [tears] toes[ ] [pool] [birth] [bomb] [بحر] [belonging] [womb] [wound] [current] [encrusted] [sparkle] [enchant] [الشمس] [erosion] [gene pool] [vacation] [conductor] [twinge] [طيب] [thaw] [مالح] [amphetamine] [melt] [cave] [pearl]

Craving Salt: A language approximation

Arabic	English
ملح	salt
ملح البحر.	sea salt.
الملح المعالَج باليود	Iodized salt
تناول الملح	Eat salt
مِلْحِ الطَّعَامِ	salt
مع حبة المَلح.	with a grain of salt.
سولت ليك	Salt Lake
مَاءُ مَالِحٌ	salty water
المياه المالحة	Salt water
من الملح	of salt
الملح	the salt

milh
milh albahra.
almalh almealaj bialywd
tanawal almilh
milh alttaeam
mae habat almalahi.
sult lik
ma' malih
almiah almaliha
min almilh
almilh

But when you think of your mom visiting the Dead Sea, you also remember how she had to cross an Israeli checkpoint. In your mind she's 10 years old, sitting in the back of the car. On the road trip she listened to records on a portable record player perched in her lap. You imagine her at that checkpoint in the back seat. Self-soothing with singles. She's enchanted by the magic of the music, of getting caught up in the car, when she's used to long stretches of silence. The way listening to music can transport you while the landscape changes outside the window. How the soundtrack makes it more real, even as you escape further into yourself. Your reverie is interrupted by a soldier, yelling through the front window. You're caught off guard. He's talking to you. You're suddenly aware of the tension in the car. As if everyone had been holding their breath. The record player has caught the soldier's eye. He seems impressed. Your pride turns to shame as he insists it's dangerous. He has to confiscate it. You try to argue. You've always stood up for yourself . . . It's yours. But your dad snaps at you to hand it over. The fear in your body. You haven't done anything wrong. But the adults say you have. And the shame mixes with fear as you start to detect the tone of your father's voice. And you realize he's no longer in control. And it's the first time he's made you feel like he can't protect you. And you feel his anger and shame at not being able to protect you. And you hand over the record player and drive off. The car is silent, but the fear rings in your ears as your mother breathes a deep sigh of relief.

Later, I ask her about it. My mother's story is less charged than my imagined one:

Bored teenager in the back seat stuck for hours at the border. She pulled out her record player, a new gift from her father, and a soldier knocked on the window. He asked her to hand it over. My mother, adolescent and defiant, said no. The soldier insisted, saying that they had not registered the device on arrival. Jiddo paid him off to keep it.

The invented memory conjured fears solely my own.

"... believe me, we were all terrified and my parents were pissed off at me. Teenagers are oblivious."

13458 13459 13460
13461 13462 13463 13470
13464 13465 13466
13467 13468 13469
13471 13472 13473
13474 13475 13476
13477 13478 13479
13480 13481 13482
13483 13484 13485
13486 13487 13488
13489 13490 13491
13492 13493 13494
13495 13496 13497
13498 13499 13500
13501 13502 13503
13504 13505 13506
13507 13508 13509
13510 13511 13512
13513 13514 13515
13516 13517 13518
13519 13520 13521
13522 13523 13524
13525 13526 13527 13528
13529 13530 13531
13532 13533 13534
13535 13536 13537 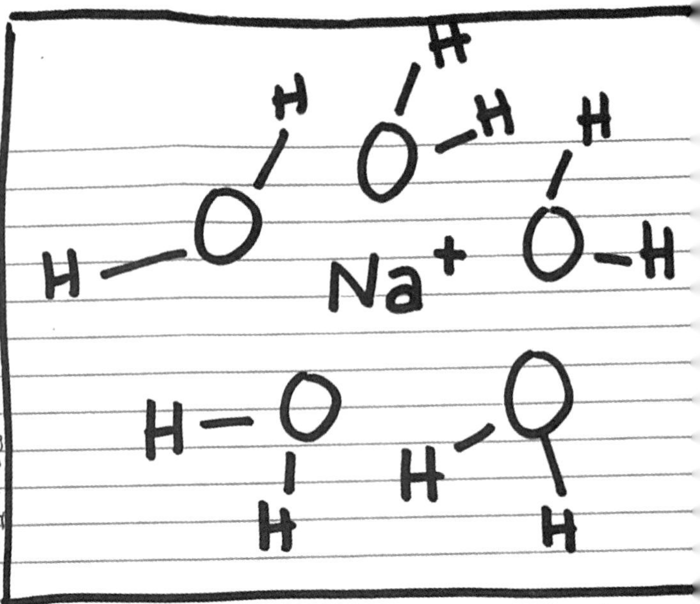
13538 13539 13540 13541 13542 13543 13544 13545 13546 13547 13548 13549 13550
13551 13552 13553 13554 13555 13556 13557 13558 13559 13560 13561 13562 13563
13564 13565 13566 13567 13568 13569 13570 13571 13572 13573 13574
13575 13576 13577 13578 13579 13580 13581 13582 13583 13584 13585 13586

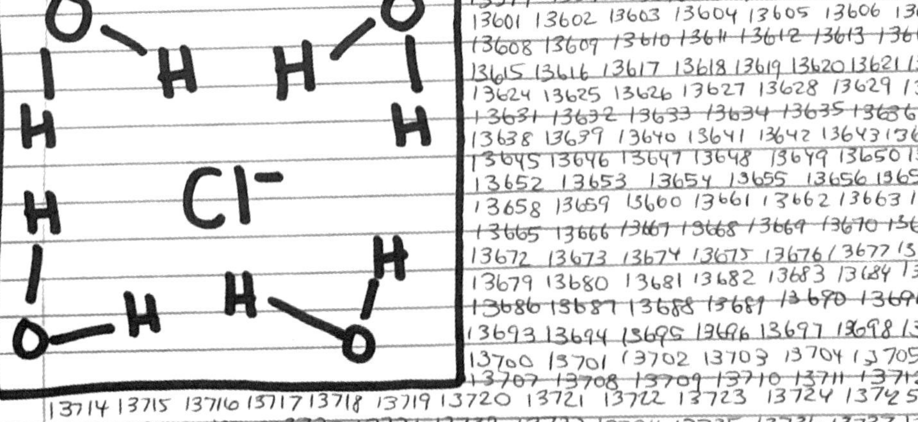

13587 13588 13589 13590 13591 13592 13593
13594 13595 13596 13597 13598 13599 13600
13601 13602 13603 13604 13605 13606 13607
13608 13609 13610 13611 13612 13613 13614
13615 13616 13617 13618 13619 13620 13621 13633
13624 13625 13626 13627 13628 13629 13630
13631 13632 13633 13634 13635 13636 1363
13638 13639 13640 13641 13642 13643 13644
13645 13646 13647 13648 13649 13650 13651
13652 13653 13654 13655 13656 13657
13658 13659 13660 13661 13662 13663 13664
13665 13666 13667 13668 13669 13670 13671
13672 13673 13674 13675 13676 13677 13678
13679 13680 13681 13682 13683 13684 13685
13686 13687 13688 13689 13690 13691 1369
13693 13694 13695 13696 13697 13698 13699
13700 13701 13702 13703 13704 13705 137
13707 13708 13709 13710 13711 13712 137
13714 13715 13716 13717 13718 13719 13720 13721 13722 13723 13724 13725 137
13727 13728 13729 13730 13731 13732 13733 13734 13735 13736 13737 13738
13739 13740 13741 13742 13743 13744 13745 13746 13747 13748 13749 13750
13751 13752 13753 13754 13755 13756 13757 13758 13759 13760 13761 13762 13763
13764 13765 13766 13767 13768 13769 13770 13771 13772 13773 13774
13775 13776 13777 13778 13779 13780 13781 13782 13783 13784 13785 13786
13787 13788 13789 13790 13791 13792 13793 13794 13795 13796 13797 13798
13799 13800 13801 13802 13803 13804 13805 13806 13807 13808 13809 13810
13811 13812 13813 13814 13815 13816 13817 13818 13819 13820 13821 13822 1382
13824 13825 13826 13827 13828 13829 13830 13831 13832 13833 1383
13835 13836 13837 13838 13839 13840 13841 13842 13842 13843 13844 138

Salt water isn't NaCl + H_2O.

Na+ and Cl- ions are suspended in water, constantly pushing and pulling at one another. Two coexisting parties, suspended in the same place, unable to help their volatile chemistry.

Water molecules pull the sodium and chloride ions apart, breaking the ionic bond that held the salt compounds together.

13846 13847 13848 13849 13850 13851 13852 13853 13854 13855 13856 13857 13858 13859

13860 13861 13862 13863 13864 13865 13866 13867 13868 13869 13870 13871 13872 13873 13874 13889 13890

13906 13907 13908 13875 13876 13877 13878 13879 13880 13881 13887 13888 13891 13892 13893 13896 13897

13929 13930 13931 13909 13910 13900 13902 13904 13921

13944 13945 13932 13933 13911 13901 13903 13912 13913 13922 13923 13958

13958 13959 13946 13947 13934 13935 13936 13937 13938 13939 13940 13941 13942 13943

13978 13980 13960 13961 13948 13949 13950 13951 13952 13953 13954 13955 13956 13957

15649 15650 15651 15652 15653 15654 15655 15656 15657 15658 15659 15660

16276 16277 16278 16279 16280 16281 16282 16283 16284 16285

16194 16195 16196 16197 16198 16199 16200 16201 16202 16203 16204 16205

16085 16086 16208 16209 16210 16211 16212 16089 16090 16091 16092 16093 16094 16083 16066 16206

16084 16088 16077 16078 16079 16080 16081 16082 16065 16064 16256 16257 16207

16040 16041 16042 16043 16044 16045 16046 16047 16048 16063 16260 16261 16264 16265 16267 16268 16270 16271 16272 16274 16275

16026 16027 16028 16029 16030 16031 16032 16033 16034 16035 16049 16050 16051 16052 16053

16250 16251 16252 16253 16254 16255 16036 16233 16037 16038 16039

15802 15803 15804 15805 15806 15807 16248 16247 15808 15811 15812 15813 15814 15815 15816 15817 15818

15823 15824 15825 15826 15827 15828 15829 15830 15841 15842 15843 15844 15845 15846 15847 15848 15819 15820 15821 15822 16061 16062

15854 15837 15838 15839 15840 15862 15863 15864 15865 15849 15850 15851

15856 15857 15858 15859 15860 15861 15874 15875 15876 15877 15878 15879 15853

15835 15868 15869 15870 15871 15872 15873 15894 15895 15896 15880 15897 16239 16229

15816 15867 15882 15885 15886 15888 15889 15890 15891 15892 15893 15907 15908 16238 16240 16241 16244

15881 15899 15900 15898 15901 15902 15903 15904 15905 15906 15930 15931 16243 16245 16230

15909 15910 15911 15912 15921 16027 16028 15932 16029

15913 15914 15915 15922 15926 15927 15928 15929 16026 16030 16031 16034 16032 16033

15916 15917 15998 15918 15919 15923 15924 15941 15942 15943 15944 15945 15946

15997 16014 15999 16015 15920 15934 15935 15940 15947 15948 15949 15950 15951 16133

15958 16013 16166 16000 15933 15936 16002 15937 15952 15953 15954 15955 16056

15959 16167 16168 16001 16017 15938 15939

15960 15961 16006 16170 16169 16018 16019 16003 16004 16025 15976 15977 15978 16055

15962 15963 16022 16023 16010 16011 16012 16009 16008 15973 15974 15975 15979 15956 15957

15965 15970 15971 15972 15984 15985 15986 15987 15988 15989 15990 15991 15992 15993 15994 15995 15996 16060

15966 15983 15984 15985 15986 15987 15988 15989 15990 15991 15992 16057 16236 16237 16058 16235 16059

16128 16095 16096 16097 16098 16099 16100 16101 16102 16103 16104 16105 16106 16107 16190

16113 16114 16115 16116 16117 16118 16119 16120 16121 16122 16123 16213 16214 16215 16216 16217 16218 16219 16220 16221 16222 16223 16224 16108 16109 16110 16111 16112 16189

16228 16133 16134 16135 16136 16137 16138 16139 16140 16124 16125 16126 16127 16188

16172 16173 16174 16175 16176 16177 16178 16179 16180 16181 16182 16183 16184 16185 16186 16187 16141 16142 16143 16144 16145 16146 16191 16192

16131 16132 16232 16231

I've always craved the salt. Licked
mounds from my palm. Delighted in
the pucker of sharp salinity, magnetic
pull of particles; salt seeking salt.
A grain, a pinch, a heap. Ions in search
of lost charge. Gravity of ocean pulling
on heartbeat and bloodstreams.

Visits to Uncle Sami on Sundays, sneaking
fistfuls of salt to sate
hunger while stovepots stewed.

I was a child, rapt
as Mom recalled the Dead Sea.
Another universe here on earth.
Sediment of gilded shale, glinting
in sunlight, sandstone, strata
of clay, soft chalk sheet rock.

I wanted to be buoyant, weightless,
held in water so salty it prickles,
pickles skin, rejects
all forms of marine life.

Her daily hajj, summers centered
on the grit of salt and sand,
returning to water like a baby
to the womb. Catacombs in dark pools,
pinpricks abrading smooth skin
scales and stalactites, ossified.

Watching the nightly news I felt like a tide
pool, left behind, full of remnants
and when I cried, each salty
orb: a tiny ecosystem
of dead things.

16923 16924 16925 16926 16927 16928 16929 16930 16931 16932
16933 16934 16935 16936 16937 16938 16939 16940 16941 16942 16943
16944 16945 16946 16947 16948 16949 16950 16951 16952 16953
16954 16955 16956 16957 16958 16959 16960 16961 16962
16964 16965 16966 16967 16968
16969 16970
16972 16973 16974 16975 16976
16977 16978
16980 16981 16982 16983 16984
16985 16986
16988 16989 16990 16991 16992
16993 16994 16995 16996
16997 16998 16999 17000 17001
17002 17003 17004
17005 17006 17007 17008 17009
17010 17011 17012 17013
17014 17015 17016 17017 17018
17019 17020 17021 17022
17023 17024 17025 17026
17027 17028 17029
17030 17031 17032 17033
17034 17035 17036
17037 17038 17039 17040
17041 17042 17043
17044 17045 17046 17047
17048 17049 17050
17051 17052 17053 17054
17055 17056 17057 17058
17059 17060 17061 17062
17063 17064 17065 17066
17067 17068 17069 17070
17071 17072 17073 17074
17075 17076 17077 17078
17079 17080 17081 17082
17083 17084 17085 17086
17087 17088 17089
17090 17091 17092 17093
17095 17096
17097 17098 17099
17100 17101 17102 17103
17104 17105 17106 17107
17111 17112 17113 17114
17119 17120 17121 17122
17118
17127 17128 17129 17130
17126
17135 17136 17137 17138
17139 17140 17141 17142
17147 17148 17149 17150
17155 17156 17157 17158
17159 17160
17163 17164 17165 17166
17171 17172 17173 17174
17175 17176
17179 17180 17181 17182
17183 17184 17185
17188 17189 17190 17191
17192
17196 17197 17198 17199
17200 17201
17204 17205 17206
17207 17208
17211 17212 17213
17215 17217
17218 17219 17220
17225 17226 17227
17232 17333 17234
17224
17239 17240 17241 17242
17231
17247 17248 17249 17250
17238
17255 17256 17257 17258
17246
17263 17264 17265 17266
17254
17271 17273 17274 17275
17262
17279 17280 17281 17282
17270
17287 17288 17289
17278
17290 17291 17292
17286
17296 17297 17298
17302 17303 17304
17309 17310 17311 17312
17313 17314 17315 17316
17317 17318 17319
17320 17321 17322 17323
17324 17325 17326
17327 17328 17329 17323
17331 17332 17333
17334 17335 17336
17337 17338 17339
17340 17341 17342

The Dead Sea is actually a lake. The lowest body of water on Earth, more than 1,400 feet below sea level, sinking 3 feet per year.

The Dead Sea is evaporating, going extinct.

Which leads us back to longing, to scarcity, to imminence.

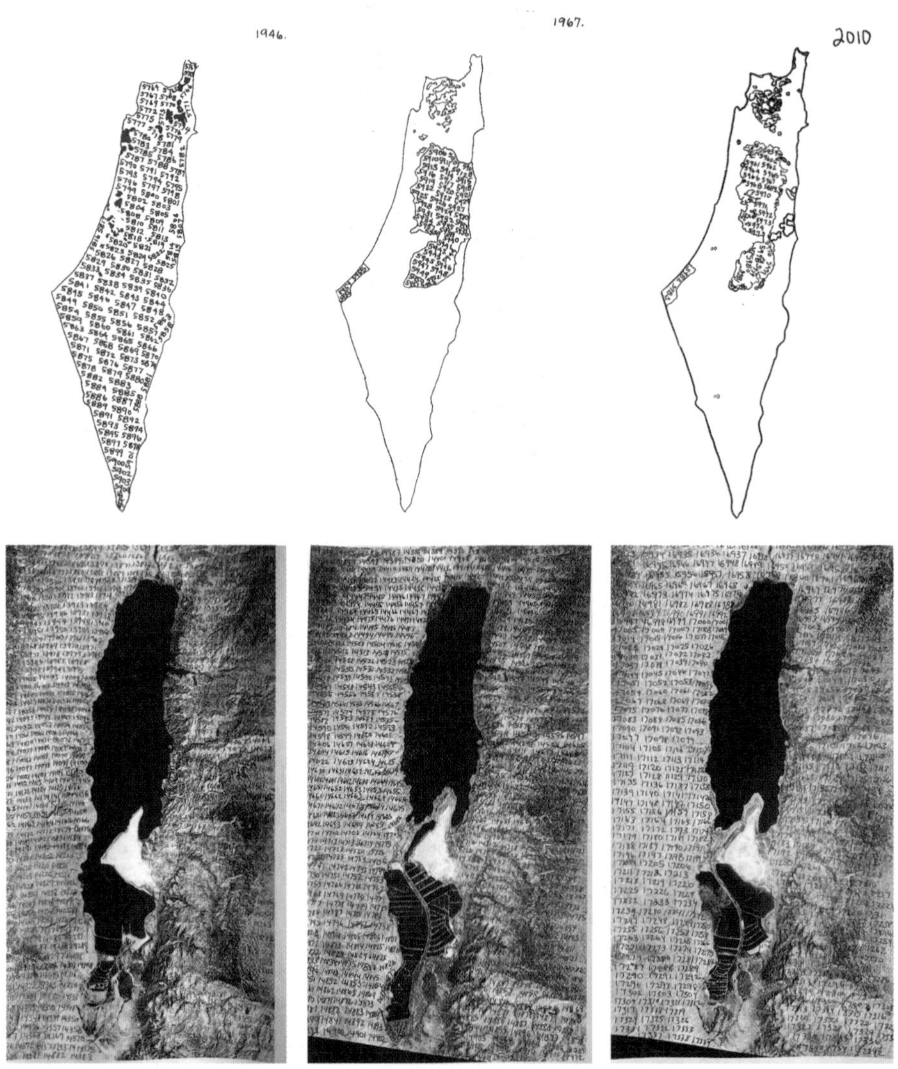

1973 - My parents meet while attending university at AUB in Beirut, Lebanon.

1978 - Israel invades the south of Lebanon with 30,000 troops.

1979 - My parents move to the US.

My mother recounts,
"I almost burst into tears the day I walked into a store on the Upper West Side in Manhattan and a little old Jewish lady behind the counter asked me where I was from and ████ jumped in and said 'Palestine' and she said: 'Palestine? There is no Palestine!' I learnt to keep my mouth shut about my country of origin . . ."

1982 - Israel invades Lebanon and begins bombing schools, orphanages and hospitals in Beirut. More than 30,000 civilians are massacred.[5] Israel cuts off electricity, water, and food in West Beirut.

In Sabra and Shatila, Israeli forces massacre 3,500 Palestinian and Lebanese civilians.[6]

1987 - I'm born in the US.

This is the same year that The First Intifada begins.

Hamas is established as a resistance movement, funded and backed by the state of Israel.

5 "The 1982 Israeli invasion of Lebanon: the casualties." (1983). *Race & Class*, 24(4), 340-343.

6 "Sabra and Shatila massacre: What happened in Lebanon in 1982?" *Al Jazeera*. September 16, 2022.

Thenar eminence: *Lump of flesh. Thumb mound.*

Neck crimped, body seized, gripped shoulder blade, crumpled forearm, crunched wrist. Radius hollow, throbbing. Ulna squeeze. Claw calcified, pseudoarthritic, pre-carpal tunnel. Each bone, a swollen puzzle piece: trapezoid, trapezium, scaphoid, capitate, hamate, pisiform, triquetrum, lunate . . . metacarpals coagulating.

Of salt, pinch
Salt mound on palm
Prick of tongue

Tip of the left thumb
Tip of the pointer finger
Tip of the middle finger
Tip of the ring finger
Tip of the pinky finger

Tip of the right thumb
Tip of the pointer finger
Tip of the middle finger
Tip of the ring finger
Tip of the pinky finger

Wrist joint
Elbow joint
Shoulder joint
Starlike point
of light

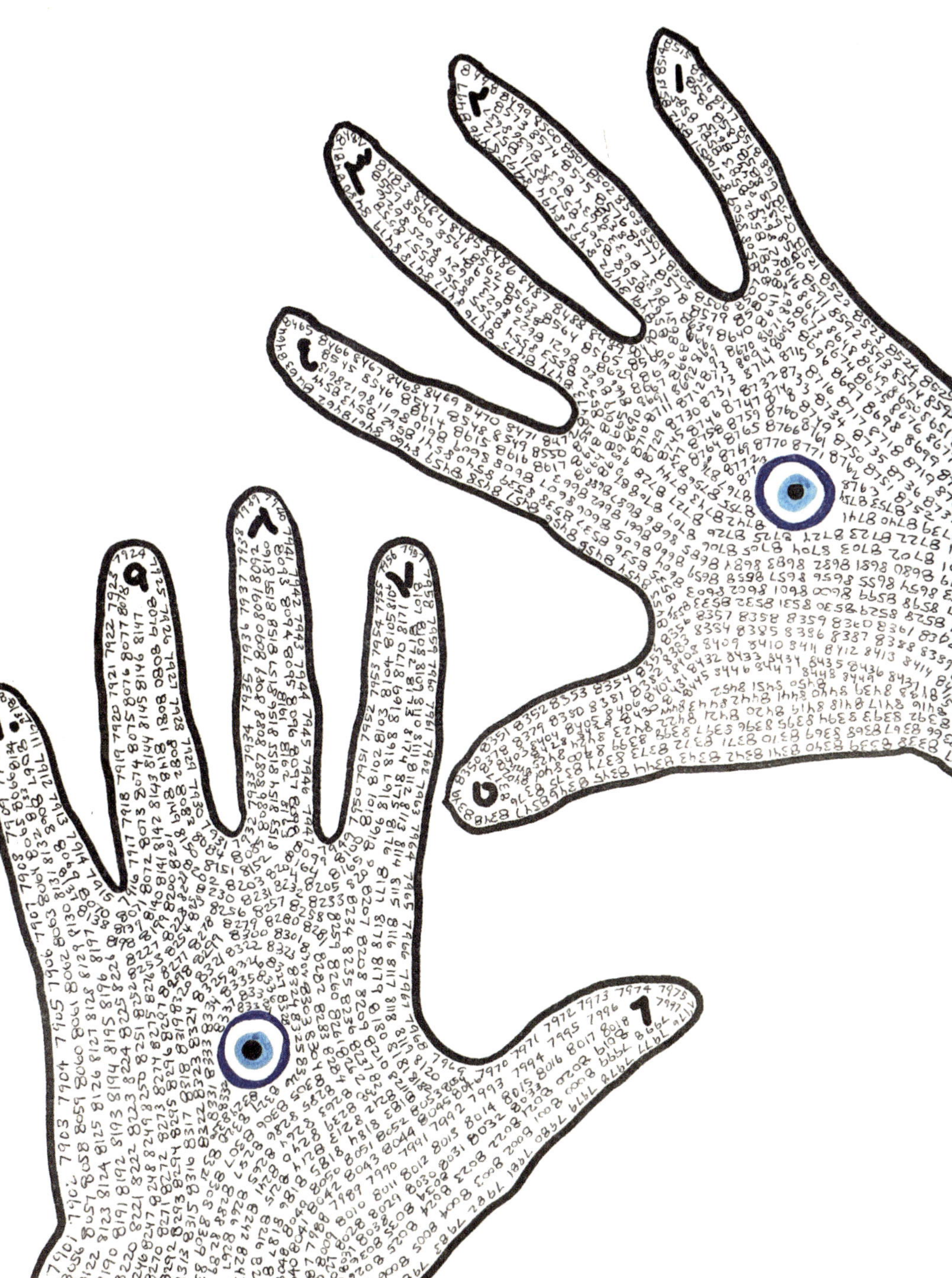

she skimmed my palm
lucent fingers peeled
back to reveal the crinkle
of seed on skin, expose
a story of sparrow, pursuing

إجى يشرب من هوني

little bird lands on the surface
fingertip breadcrumbs
sprinkled on plane of palm
fingers folded in on keepsake

هادا سقا
وهادا طعما

a pearl is born from the grit, the incessant scraping
if I was generous I'd thank the corrosion for my contusions
that grew into luminescence and jewels

وهادا غطّا

lullaby for baby bird
bath of conjured dust

I reach for thread, blues and reds, like the cushions my grandmother kept. Needle nose swooping into fabric like a seagull skimming across ocean surface, gulping fish in its gullet, cross-stitching a silenced story. I conspire to toil with thread like the fallaha who tilled the soil before me. Passed down for 3,000 years, tatreez, delicate motifs embroidered in strands dyed deep red with pomegranate skins, crimson with extracted carminic dye from cochineal insects, and vibrant purple from the powdered shells of snails. And when we were told to take down our flags, we wore, instead, proof of existence.[7]

7 During the first intifada, 1987-1993, "the Israeli army confiscated visible Palestinian symbols such as the national flag. In order to continue to resist and stand in defiance to Israel and its occupation, Palestinian women created what is known as the 'intifada dress.' Cut as a traditional Palestinian 'thobe' or dress, the intifada dress was embroidered with Palestinian flags, maps of Palestine, traditional natural symbols such as olive branches or orange trees, and phrases such as 'We will return', all woven in traditional Palestinian colors." - Erin Quinn, "This is Artful Resistance: The Power of Tatreez" (2019).

The olea are my ancestors, rooted where I was removed,
trunks twisted and gnarled, their elephant rib cages empty.
What would have been imprinted in their carbon rings:
evidence of near permanence, thousands of years and wars.
What would we see inside their hollow chambers?

Athena struck a rock with her spear and sparked the olive tree, offering fruitfulness, prosperity, and peace. Resurrection and hope. Veined wood carved into gods. Branches of industry, growing ovoid fruit, dark purple drupe studded with a thick bony stone. Blunt keel down one side, containing a single seed. Oil that burnt in the sacred lamps of temples and preserved bodies, mummified.

Who are these petrified ghosts, wispy and reaching?
Knots of rough bark, asking little of the land aside
from being. I, too, am hollow, a giving tree, growing
bitter fruit softened by salt.

20063 20064 20065 20066

20371 20372 20373 20374 20375
20376 20377 20378 20379 20380
20381 20382 20383 20384 20385
20386 20387 20388 20389 20390
20391 20392 20393 20394 20395
20396 20397 20398 20399 20400
20401 20402 20403 20404 20405 20406
20407 20408 20409 20410 20411
20412 20413 20414 20415 20416
20417 20418 20419 20420 20421
20422 20423 20424 20425 20426
20427 20428 20429 20430 20431
20432 20433 20434 20435 20436 20437
20438 20439 20440 20441 20442 20443
20444 20445 20446 20447 20448 20449 20450
20451 20452 20453 20454 20455 20456
20457 20458 20459 20460 20461
20462 20463 20464 20465 20466
20467 20468 20469 20470 20471
20472 20473 20474 20475 20476
20477 20478 20479 20480 20481
20482 20483 20484 20485 20486
20487 20488 20489 20490 20491
20492 20493 20494 20495 20496
20497 20498 20499 20500
20501 20502 20503 20504
20505 20506 20507
20508 20509 20510
20511 20512 20513
20514 20515
20516 20517
20518 20519 20520
20521 20522 20523
20524 20525 20526 20527
20528 20529 20530 20531
20532 20533 20534 20536
20537 20538 20539 20540
20541 20542 20543 20544 20545
20546 20547 20548 20549 20550
20551 20552 20553 20554 20555
20556 20557 20558 20559 20560
20561 20562 20563 20564 20565
20566 20567 20568 20569 20570
20571 20572 20573 20574 20575
20576 20577 20578 20579 20580
20581 20582 20583 20584 20585
20586 20587 20588 20589 20590
20591 20592 20593 20594 20595 20596
20597 20598 20599 20600 20601 20602
20603 20604 20605 20606 20607 20608 20609 2061
20611 20612 20613 20614 20615 20616 20617 20618
20619 20620 20621 20622 20623 20624 20625 2062
20627 20628 20629 20630 20631 20632 20633 20634 20635 20636
637 20638 20639 20640 20641 20642 20643 20644
0645 20646 20647

A summer spent rolling Arabic letters around in my mouth.
A sommelier of sound, the velvet thud of the dhal ذ behind
my front teeth, the simmering of ghain غ at the back
of the throat, gurgling. The swallowed echo of qaaf,
a c caught in the throat.

An alphabet of longing, letters curlicued like tendrils
of hair. A malformed mouth full of marbles, clumsy.
An ear tuned to my own ineptitude, the inaccurate
aperture of my throat, letting in too much light,
bleeding light, overexposed, so light I slip by
unnoticed within my own glaring mistake.

SOS.IL

On the news I see them
on the streets of Tel Aviv:
630,000 people in protest.
A moment of validation, solidarity.
A call for democracy—but not for everyone.

To occupy, unflinching.

On the news I see
a response from the president.
"Bibi, I don't agree
with a damn thing you say, but I love you."

On the news, a sea
of suffocating symbols.

Most protesters don't see any irony
in waving a Zionist flag and yelling for democracy,
in protesters who oppose occupation

getting arrested.

I sit with my soon-to-be-in-laws at the Passover table, spill wine for the plight of the Egyptians, temper our joy which came at the expense of others.

I can't help but think of blood.

The child smearing herself in her parents' blood, playing dead under their stiff bodies, a sick game of tag where no one wakes and no one wins.

The child hiding under his bed while his family is lined up against a wall and shot. Dead. Blood spilled over blood.

55 children orphaned and deposited at the Jaffa Gate.

The horrible stories bubble up from inside, spill.

At the table we drink a bottle of wine each, for freedom.

While families are separated by barbed wire at borders. Denied access to water.

I drink my bottle of wine.

Let it dull my tender heart.

2451 22498 22529 22541 22552 22596 22616 22636
2452 22499 22530 22542 22553 22597 22617 22637 22666 22685 22708 22736
2453 22500 22531 22543 22554 22598 22618 22638 22667 22686 22709 22737
2454 22501 22532 22544 22555 22599 22619 22639 22668 22687 22710 22738
2455 22502 22533 22545 22556 22600 22620 22640 22669 22688 22711 22739
2456 22503 22534 22546 22557 22601 22621 22641 22670 22689 22712 22740
2457 22504 22535 22547 22558 22602 22622 22642 22671 22690 22713 22741
22458 22505 22536 22548 22559 22603 22623 22643 22672 22691 22714 22742
22459 22506 22537 22549 22560 22604 22624 22644 22673 22692 22715 22743
22460 22507 22538 22550 22561 22605 22625 22645 22674 22693 22716 22744
22461 22508 22539 22551 22562 22606 22626 22646 22675 22694 22717 22745
22462 22509 22540 22647 22695 22718 22746
22463 22510 22696 22719 22720 22747
22464 22511 22721 22748
22465 22512 22722 22749
22466 22513 22723 22750
22467 22724 22751
22468 22752
22469 22753
2470
2471
2472

481
482
2483 22514
2484 22515
2485 22516
2486 22517 22563
2487 22518 22564
2488 22519 22565 22575
2489 22520 22566 22576 22586
2490 22521 22567 22577 22587 22607 22627 22648 22657 22676 22698 22725 22754
2491 22522 22568 22578 22588 22608 22628 22649 22658 22677 22699 22726 22755
2492 22523 22569 22579 22589 22609 22629 22650 22659 22678 22700 22727 22756
493 22524 22570 22580 22590 22610 22630 22651 22660 22679 22701 22728 22757
494 22525 22571 22581 22591 22611 22631 22652 22661 22680 22702 22729 22758
495 22526 22572 22582 22592 22612 22632 22653 22662 22681 22703 22730 22759
496 22527 22573 22583 22593 22613 22633 22654 22663 22682 22704 22731 22760
497 22528 22574 22584 22594 22614 22634 22655 22664 22683 22705 22732 22761
22585 22595 22615 22635 22656 22665 22684 22706 22733 22762
22707 22734 22763
22735 22764
22765
22766
22767

22768 22769 22770 22771 22772 22773 22774 22775 22776 22777 22778 22779 22780 22781 22782 22783 22784 22785 22786 22787 22788 22789 22790 22791 22792 22793 22794 22795 22796 22797 22798 22799 22800 22801 22802 22803 22804 22805 22806 22807 22808 22809 22810 22811 22812 22813 22814 22815 22816 22817 22818 22819 22820 22821 22822 22823 22824 22825 22826 22827 22828 22829 22830 22831 22832 22833 22834 22835 22836

22837 22838 22839 22840 22841 22842 22843 22844 22845 22846 22847 22848 22849 22850 22851 22852 22853 22854 22855 22856 22857 22858 22859 22860 22861 22862 22863 22864 22865 22866 22867 22868 22869 22870 22871 22872 22873 22874 22875 22876 22877 22878 22879 22880 22881 22882 22883 22884 22885 22886 22887 22888 22889 22890 22891 22892 22893 22894 22895 22896 22897 22898 22899 22900 22901 22902 22903 22904 22905 22906 22907 22908 22909 22910 22911 22912 22913 22914 22915 22916 22917 22918 22919 22920 22921

22922 22923 22924 22925 22926 22927 22928 22929 22930 22931 22932 22933 22934 22935 22936 22937 22938 22939 22940 22941 22942 22943 22944 22945 22946 22947 22948 22949 22950 22951 22952 22953 22954 22955 22956 22957 22958 22959 22960 22961 22962 22963 22964 22965 22966 22967 22968 22969 22970 22971 22972 22973 22974 22975 22976 22977 22978 22979 22980 22981 22982 22983 22984 22985 22986 22987 22988 22989 22990 22991 22992 22993 22994 22995 22996 22997 22998 22999 23000 23001 23002 23003 23004 23005 23006 23007 23008

23009 23010 23011 23012 23013 23014 23015 23016 23017 23018 23019 23020 23021 23022 23023 23024 23025 23026 23027 23028 23029 23030 23031 23032 23033 23034 23035 23036 23037 23038 23039 23040 23041 23042 23043 23044 23045 23046 23047 23048 23049 23050 23051 23052 23053 23054 23055 23056 23057 23058 23059 23060 23061 23062 23063 23064 23065 23066 23067 23068 23069 23070 23071 23072 23073 23074 23075 23076 23077 23078 23079 23080 23081 23082 23083 23084 23085 23086 23087 23088 23089 23090 23091 23092 23093 23094

23095 23096 23097 23098 23099 23100 23101 23102 2303 23104 23105 23106 23107 23108 23109 23110 23111 23112 23113 23114 23115 23116 23117 23118 23119 23120 23121 23122 23123 23124 23125 23126 23127 23128 23129 23130 23131 23132 23133 23134 23135 23136 23137 23138 23139 23140 23141 23142 23143 23144 23145 23146 23147 23148 23149 23150 23151 23152 23153 23154 23155 23156 23157 23158 23159 23160 23161 23162 23163 23164 23165 23166 23167 23168 23169 23170 23171 23172 23173 23174 23175 23176

23177 23178 23179 23180 23181 23182 23183 23184 23185 23186 23187 23188 23189 23190 23191 23192 23193 23194 23195 23196 23197 23198 23199 23200 23201 23202 23203 23204 23205 23206 23207 23208 23209 23210 23211 23212 23213 23214 23215 23216 23217 23218 23219 23220 23221 23222 23223 23224 23225 23226 23227 23228 23229 23230 23231 23232 23233 23234 23235 23236 23237 23238 23239 23240 23241 23242 23243 23244 23245 23246 23247 23248 23249 23250 23251 23252 23253 23254 23255 23256 23257 23258 23259 23260

23261 23262 23263 23264 23265 23266 23267 23268 23269 23270 23271 23272 23273 23274 23275 23276 23277 23278 23279 23280 23281 23282 23283 23284 23285 23286 23287 23288 23289 23290 23291 23292 23293 23294 23295 23296 23297 23298 23299 23300 23301 23302 23303 23304 23305 23306 23307 23308 23309 23310 23311 23312 23313 23314 23315 23316 23317 23318 23319 23320 23321 23322 23323 23324 23325 23326 23327 23328 23329 23330 23331 23332 23333 23334 23335 23336 23337 23338 23339

23340 23341 23342 23343 23344 23345 23346 23347 23348 23349 23350 23351 23352 23353 23354 23355 23356 23357 23358 23359 23360 23361 23362 23363 23364 23365 23366 23367 23368 23369 23370 23371 23372 23373 23374 23375 23376 23377 23378 23379 23380 23381 23382 23383 23384 23385 23386 23387 23388 23389 23390 23391 23392 23393 23394 23395 23396 23397 23398 23399 23400 23401 23402 23403 23404 23405 23406 23407 23408 23409 23410 23411 23412 23413 23414 23415 23416

23417 23418 23419 23420 23421 23422 23423 23424 23425 23426 23427 23428 23429 23430 23431 23432 23433 23434 23435 23436 23437 23438 23439 23440 23441 23442 23443 23444 23445 23446 23447 23448 23449 23450 23451 23452 23453 23454 23455 23456 23457 23458 23459 23460 23461 23462 23463 23464 23465 23466 23467 23468 23469 23470 23471 23472 23473 23474 23475 23476 23477 23478 23479 23480 23481 23482 23483 23484 23485 23486 23487 23488 23489 23490 23491 23492 23493

23494 23495 23496 23497 23498 23499 23500 23501 23502 23503 23504 23505 23506 23507 23508 23509 23510 23511 23512 23513 23514 23515 23516 23517 23518 23519 23520 23521 23522 23523 23524 23525 23526 23527 23528 23529 23530 23531 23532 23533 23534 23535 23536 23537 23538 23539 23540 23541 23542 23543 23544 23545 23546 23547 23548 23549 23550 23551 23552 23553 23554 23555 23556 23557 23558 23559 23560 23561 23562 23563 23564 23565 23566 23567 23568

23569 23570 23571 23572 23573 23574 23575 23576 23577 23578 23579 23580 23581 23582 23583 23584 23585 23586 23587 23588 23589 23590 23591 23592 23593 23594 23595 23596 23597 23598 23599 23600 23601 23602 23603 23604 23605 23606 23607 23608 23609 23610 23611 23612 23613 23614 23615 23616 23617 23618 23619 23620 23621 23622 23623 23624 23625 23626 23627 23628 23629 23630 23631 23632 23633 23634 23635 23636 23637 23638 23639 23640 23641 23642 23643 23644 23645 23646 23647

23648 23649 23650 23651 23652 23653 23654 23655 23656 23657 23658 23659 23660 23661 23662 23663 23664 23665 23666 23667 23668 23669 23670 23671 23672 23673 23674 23675 23676 23677 23678 23679 23680 23681 23682 23683 23684 23685 23686 23687 23688 23689 23690 23691 23692 23693 23694 23695 23696 23697 23698 23699 23700 23701 23702 23703 23704 23705 23706 23707 23708 23709 23710 23711 23712 23713 23714 23715 23716 23717 23718 23719 23720 23721 23722 23723 23724 23725

23726 23727 23728 23729 23730 23731 23732 23733 23734 23735 23736 23737 23738 23739 23740 23741 23742 23743 23744 23745 23746 23747 23748 23749 23750 23751 23752 23753 23754 23755 23756 23757 23758 23759 23760 23761 23762 23763 23764 23765 23766 23767 23768 23769 23770 23771 23772 23773 23774 23775 23776 23777 23778 23779 23780 23781 23782 23783 23784 23785 23786 23787 23788 23789 23790 23791 23792 23793 23794 23795 23796 23797 23798 23799 23800

23801 23802 23803 23804 23805 23806 23807 23808 23809 23810 23811 23812 23813 23814 23815 23816 23817 23818 23819 23820 23821 23822 23823 23824 23825 23826 23827 23828 23829 23830 23831 23832 23833 23834 23835 23836 23837 23838 23839 23840 23841 23842 23843 23844 23845 23846 23847 23848 23849 23850 23857 23852 23853 23854 23855 23856 23857 23858 23859 23860 23861 23862 23863 23864 23865 23866 23867 23868 23869 23870 23871 23872 23873 23874 23875 23876 23877 23878 23879

23880 23881 23882 23883 23884 23885 23886 23887 23888 23889 23890 23841 23892 23893 23894 23895 23896 23897 23898 23899 23900 23901 23902 23903 23904 23905 23906 23907 23908 23909 23910 23911 23912 23913 23914 23915 23916 23917 23918 23919 23920 23921 23922 23923 23924 23925 23926 23927 23928 23929 23930 23931 23932 23933 23934 23935 23936 23937 23938 23939 23940 23941 23942 23943 23944 23945 23946 23947 23948 23949 23950 23951 23952 23953 23954 23955 23956 23957

23958 23959 23960 23961 23962 23963 23964 23965 23966 23967 23968 23969 23970 23971 23972 23973 23974 23975 23976 23977 23978 23979 23980 23981 23982 23983 23984 23985 23986 23987 23988 23989 23990 23991 23992 23993 23994 23995 23996 23997 23998 23999 24000 24001 24002 24003 24004 24005 24006 24007 24008 24009 24010 2404 24012 2403 24014 24015 24016 24017 24018 24019 24020 24021 24022 24023 24024 24025 24026 24027 24028 24029 24030 24031 2403 2403

24034 24035 24036 24037 24038 24039 24040 24041 2404 2404 2404 2404 24046 24047 2404 2404 2404 2405 2405 240 2405 2405 2405 2405 2405 24059 2406 2406 240 2406 2406 2406 2406 2406 2406 2406 2406 2407 2407 2407 2407 2407 24074 24075 2407 2407 2407 24078 24079 24080 24081 2408 240 240 240 240 24 24 24 24 24 24 24 24 24 24 24 24 24 240

24102
24103
24104
24105
24106
24107
24108
24109
24110
24111
24112
24113
24114
24115
24116
24117
24118
24119
24120
24121
24122
24123
24124
24125
24126
24127
24128
24129
24130
24131
24132
24133
24134
24135
24136
24137
24138
24139
24140
24141
24142
24143
24144
24145
24146
24147
24148
24149
24150
24151
24152
24153
24154
24155
24156
24157
24158
24159
24160
24161
24162
24163
24164
24165
24166
24167
24168
24169
24170
24171
24172
24173
24174
24175
24176
24177
24178
24179
24180
24181
24182
24183
24184
24185
24186
24187
24188
24189
24190
24191
24192
24193
24194
24195
24196
24197
24198
24199
24200
24201
24202
24203
24204
24205

24206
24207
24208
24209
24210
24211
24212
24213
24214
24215
24216
24217
24218
24219
24220
24221
24222
24223
24224
24225
24226
24227
24228
24229
24230
24231
24232
24233
24234
24235
24236
24237
24238
24239
24240
24241
24242
24243
24244
24245
24246
24247
24248
24249
24250
24251
24252
24253
24254
24255
24256
24257
24258
24259
24260
24261
24262
24263
24264
24265
24266
24267
24268
24269
24270
24271
24272
24273
24274
24275
24276
24277
24278
24279
24280
24281
24282
24283
24284
24285
24286
24287
24288
24289
24290
24291
24292
24293
24294
24295
24296
24297
24298
24299
24300
24301
24302
24303
24304
24305
24306
24307
24308
24309
24310
24311
24312
24313
24314
24315
24316
24317
24318
24319
24320
24321
24322
24323
24324
24325
24326
24327
24328
24329
24330
24331
24332
24333
24334
24335
24336
24337
24338
24339
24340
24341
24342
24343
24344
24345
24346
24347
24348
24349
24350
24351
24352

24353
24354
24355
24356
24357
24358
24359
24360
24361
24362
24363
24364
24365
24366
24367
24368
24369
24370
24371
24372
24373
24374
24375
24376
24377
24378
24379
24380
24381
24382
24383
24384
24385
24386
24387
24388
24389
24390
24391
24392
24393
24394
24395
24396
24397
24398
24399
24400
24401
24402
24403
24404
24405
24406

24407
24408
24409
24410
24411
24412
24413
24414
24415
24416
24417
24418
24419
24420
24421
24422
24423
24424
24425
24426
24427
24428
24429
24430
24431
24432
24433
24434
24435
24436
24437
24438
24439
24440
24441
24442
24443
24444
24445
24446
24447
24448
24449
24450
24451
24452
24453
24454
24455
24456
24457
24458
24459
24460

24461
24462
24463
24464
24465
24466
24467
24468
24469
24470
24471
24472
24473
24474
24475
24476
24477
24478
24479
24480
24481
24482
24483
24484
24485
24486
24487
24488
24489
24490
24491
24492
24493
24494
24495
24496
24497
24498
24499
24500
24501
24502
24503
24504
24505
24506
24507
24508
24509
24510
24511
24512
24513
24514

24515
24516
24517
24518
24519
24520
24521
24522
24523
24524
24525
24526
24527
24528
24529
24530
24531
24532
24533
24534
24535
24536
24537
24538
24539
24540
24541
24542
24543
24544
24545
24546
24547
24548
24549
24550
24551
24552
24553
24554
24555
24556
24557
24558
24559
24560
24561
24562
24563
24564
24565
24566
24567
24568
24569
24570
24571

24572
24573
24574
24575
24576
24577
24578
24579
24580
24581
24582
24583
24584
24585
24586
24587
24588
24589
24590
24591
24592
24593
24594
24595
24596
24597
24598
24599
24600
24601
24602
24603
24604
24605
24606
24607
24608
24609
24610
24611
24612
24613
24614
24615
24616
24617
24618
24619
24620
24621
24622
24623
24624
24625
24626
24627
24628
24629
24630

24631
24632
24633
24634
24635
24636
24637
24638
24639
24640
24641
24642
24643
24644
24645
24646
24647
24648
24649
24650
24651
24652
24653
24654
24655
24656
24657
24658
24659
24660
24661
24662
24663
24664
24665
24666
24667
24668
24669
24670
24671
24672
24673
24674
24675
24676
24677
24678
24679
24680
24681
24682
24683
24684
24685
24686

24687
24688
24689
24690
24691
24692
24693
24694
24695
24696
24697
24698
24699
24700
24701
24702
24703
24704
24705
24706
24707
24708
24709
24710
24711
24712
24713
24714
24715
24716
24717
24718
24719
24720
24721
24722
24723
24724
24725
24726
24727
24728
24729
24730
24731
24732
24733
24734
24735
24736
24737
24738
24739
24740
24741
24742
24743
24744
24745
24746
24747

24748
24749
24750
24751
24752
24753
24754
24755
24756
24757
24758
24759
24760
24761
24762
24763
24764
24765
24766
24767
24768
24769
24770
24771
24772
24773
24774
24775
24776
24777
24778
24779
24780
24781
24782
24783
24784
24785
24786
24787
24788
24789
24790
24791
24792
24793
24794
24795
24796
24797
24798
24799
24800
24801
24802
24803
24804
24805
24806
24807

24808
24809
24810
24811
24812
24813
24814
24815
24816
24817
24818
24819
24820
24821
24822
24823
24824
24825
24826
24827
24828
24829
24830
24831
24832
24833
24834
24835
24836
24837
24838
24839
24840
24841
24842
24843
24844
24845
24846
24847
24848
24849
24850
24851
24852
24853
24854
24855
24856
24857
24858
24859
24860
24861
24862
24863
24864
24865
24866
24867
24868
24869
24870

24871
24872
24873
24874
24875
24876
24877
24878
24879
24880
24881
24882
24883
24884
24885
24886
24887
24888
24889
24890
24891
24892
24893
24894
24895
24896
24897
24898
24899
24900
24901
24902
24903
24904
24905
24906
24907
24908
24909
24910
24911
24912
24913
24914
24915
24916
24917
24918
24919
24920
24921
24922
24923
24924
24925
24926
24927
24928
24929
24930
24931
24932

24933
24934
24935
24936
24937
24938
24939
24940
24941
24942
24943
24944
24945
24946
24947
24948
24949
24950
24951
24952
24953
24954
24955
24956
24957
24958
24959
24960
24961
24962
24963
24964
24965
24966
24967
24968
24969
24970
24971
24972
24973
24974
24975
24976
24977
24978
24979
24980
24981
24982
24983
24984
24985
24986
24987
24988
24989
24990
24991

24992
24993
24994
24995
24996
24997
24998
24999
25000
25001
25002
25003
25004
25005
25006
25007
25008
25009
25010
25011
25012
25013
25014
25015
25016
25017
25018
25019
25020
25021
25022
25023
25024
25025
25026
25027
25028
25029
25030
25031
25032
25033
25034
25035
25036
25037
25038
25039
25040
25041
25042
25043
25044
25045
25046
25047
25048
25049
25050
25051
25052
25053
25054
25055
25056
25057
25058
25059
25060

250
250
25
25
25
25
250
250
250
250
250
250
250
250
2507
2507
250
2507
2508
2508
250
250
250
25085
2508
2508
2508
2508
2509
2509
2509
2509
250
2509
250
250
250
250
251
251
251
251
251
251
251
251
251
251
251
251
251
251
251
25
25
25
25
25
25
25
25
25
251
25

How to cure an olive

Recipe

SERVES all PREP TIME ≥13 yrs COOK TIME 3-6 weeks

DIRECTIONS

1. Grow an olive tree — Be patient. It takes 12 years & 2 months of rest before they grow fruit.
2. Wait until the fruit has ripened. — Be patient. It takes 6-8 months before they are ripe enough to harvest.
3. Submerge the fruit in saline. — Be patient. It takes 3-6 weeks to cure
   - Combine 1 part salt : 10 parts H_2O
   - Shake once a day
   - Change the brine weekly
4. Scoop fruit into sterile jars. — Season, cover with brine & let soak. Blanket with a layer of olive oil. BE PATIENT

FROM THE KITCHEN OF teta ♡

NOTES: I come from olive:

Tough, resilient, patient creatures. Elders woven in the earth, rough-skinned and silver-haired. Each knot, each snarl, each contortion, proof of adaptability. Each tree lives up to 2,000 years.

Self-pollinating, self-sufficient. Even their fruit takes patience

Bitter, unpalatable. Harvested fruit has to soak in the sea. You may wish to slice our flesh with a knife, or weigh us down to abrade our skin. THIS WILL ONLY MAKE US SWEETER

You may press us/ for oil/ but we'll use it as a protective cloak/ to brace against the elements.

DIRECTIONS

5. Survive.

Survive.

Survive.*

* NOTES: Destroyed in an instant. 800,000 olive trees in Palestine destroyed since 1967. That's the number of trees in Central Park — 33 times over.

NOTES: I come from olive:

Equipped to survive sub-zero temperatures, droughts and fires, with roots that can regrow.

25127 25128 25129 25130 25131 25132 25133 25134 25135 25136 25137 25138 25139 25140 25141 25142 25143 25144 25145 25146 25147 25148 25149 25150 25151 25152 25153 25154 25155 25156 25157 25158 25159 25160 25161 25162 25163 25164 25165 25166 25167 25168 25169 25170 25171 25172 25173 25174 25175 25176 25177 25178 25179 25180

25181 25182 25183 25184 25185 25186 25187 25188 25189 25190 25191 25192 25193 25194 25195 25196 25197 25198 25199 25200 25201 25202 25203 25204 25205 25206 25207 25208 25209 25210 25211 25212 25213 25214 25215 25216 25217 25218 25219 25220 25221 25222 25223 25224 25225 25226 25227 25228 25229 25230

25231 25232 25233 25234 25235 25236 25237 25238 25239 25240 25241 25242 25243 25244 25245 25246 25247 25248 25249 25250 25251 25252 25253 25254 25255 25256 25257 25258 25259 25260 25261 25262 25263 25264 25265 25266 25267 25268 25269 25270 25271 25272 25273 25274 25275 25276 25277 25278 25279 25280 25281 25282 25283 25284 25285 25286 25287 25288 25289 25290 25291 25292 25293 25294

25295 25296 25297 25298 25299 25300 25301 25302 25303 25304 25305 25306 25307 25308 25309 25310 25311 25312 25313 25314 25315 25316 25317

25318 25319 25320 25321 25322 25323 25324 25325 25326 25327 25328 25329

25330 25331 25332 25333 25334 25335 25336 25337 25338 25339 25340 25341 25342 25343 25344

25352 25353 25354 25355 25356 25357 25358 25359 25360 25361 25362 25363 25364 25365

25373 25374 25375 25376 25377 25378 25379 25380 25381 25382 25383 25384 25385 25386

25395 25396 25397 25398 25399 25400 25401 25402 25403 25404 25405 25406 25407 25408 25409

25418 25419 25420 25421 25422 25423 25424 25425 25426 25427 25428 25429 25430 25431

25439 25440 25441 25442 25443 25444 25445 25446 25447 25448 25449 25450 25451 25452 25453 25454 25455 25456 25457 25458 25459 25460 25461 25462 25463 25464 25465 25466 25467 25468 25469 25470 25471 25472 25473 25474 25475 25476 25477 25478 25479 25480 25481 25482 25483 25484 25485 25486 25487 25488 25489 25490 25491 25492 25493 25494 25495 25496 25497

25498 25499 25500 25501 25502 25503 25504 25505 25506 25507 25508 25509 25510 25511 25512 25513 25514 25515 25516 25517 25518 25519 25520 25521 25522 25523 25524 25525 25526 25527 25528 25529 25530 25531 25532 25533 25534 25535 25536 25537 25538 25539 25540 25541 25542 25543 25544 25545 25546 25547 25548 25549 25550 25551 25552 25553 25554 25555 25556

25557 25558 25559 25560 25561 25562 25563 25564 25565 25566 25567 25568 25569 25570 25571 25572 25573 25574 25575 25576 25577 25578 25579 25580 25581 25582 25583 25584 25585 25586 25587 25588 25589 25590 25591 25592 25593 25594 25595 25596 25597 25598 25599 25600 25601 25602 25603 25604 25605 25606 25607 25608 25609 25610 25611 25612 25613 25614 25615 25616

2561 2561 2561 2562 2562 2562 2562 2562 25625 2562 25627 25628 25629 25630 25631 25632 25633 25634 25635 25636 25637 25638 25639 25640 25641 25642 25643 25644 25645 25646 25647 25648 25649 25650 25651 25652 25653 25654 25655 25656 25657 25658 25659 25660 25661 25662 25663 2566 25665 2566 25667 25668 25669 25670 25671 2567 2567 25674

25675 25676 25677 25678 25679 2568

25681 25682 25683 25684 25685 25686

25687 25688 25689 25690 25691 25692 2569

25702 25703 25704 25 706 25707 25701

25345 25346 25347 25348 25349 25350 25351

25366 25367 25368 25369 25370 25371 25372

25387 25388 25389 25390 25391 25392 25393 25394

25410 25411 25412 25413 25414 25415 25416 25417

25432 25433 25434 25435 25436 25437 25438

26144 26145 26146 26147 26148 26149 26150 26151 26152 26153 26154 26155 26156 26157 26158 26159 26160 26161 26162 26163 26164 26165 26166 26167 26168 26169 26170 26171 26172 26173 26174 26175 26176 26177 26178 26179 26180 26181 26182 26183 26184 26185 26186 26187 26188 26189 26190 26191 26192 26193 26194 26195 26196 26197 26198 26199 26200 26201 26202 26203 26204 26205 26206 26207 26208 26209 26210 26211 26212 26213 26214 26215 26216

26217 26218 26219 26220 26221 26222 26223 26224 26225 26226 26227 26228 26229 26230 26231 26232 26233 26234 26235 26236 26237 26238 26239 26240 26241 26242 26243 26244 26245 26246 26247 26248 26249 26250 26251 26252 26253 26254 26255 26256 26257 26258 26259 26260 26261 26262 26263 26264 26265 26266 26267 26268 26269 26270 26271 26272 26273 26274 26275 26276 26277 26278 26279 26280 26281 26282 26283 26284 26285 26286 26287 26288 26289 26290 26291 26292 26293 26294 26295 26296 26297 26298

26299 26300 26301 26302 26303 26304 26305 26306 26307 26308 26309 26310 26311 26312 26313 26314 26315 26316 26317 26318 26319 26320 26321 26322 26323 26324 26325 26326 26327 26328 26329 26330 26331 26332 26333 26334 26335 26336 26337 26338 26339 26340 26341 26342 26343 26344 26345 26346 26347 26348 26349 26350 26351 26352 26353 26354 26355 26356 26357 26358 26359 26360 26361 26362 26363 26364 26365 26366 26367 26368 26369 26370 26371 26372 26373 26374 26375 26376 26377 26378 26379 26380 26381 26382 26383

26384 26385 26386 26387 26388 26389 26390 26391 26392 26393 26394 26395 26396 26397 26398 26399 26400 26401 26402 26403 26404 26405 26406 26407 26408 26409 26410 26411 26412 26413 26414 26415 26416 26417 26418 26419 26420 26421 26422 26423 26424 26425 26426 26427 26428 26429 26430 26431 26432 26433 26434 26435 26436 26437 26438 26439 26440 26441 26442 26443 26444 26445 26446 26447 26448 26449 26450 26451 26452 26453 26454 26455 26456 26457 26458 26459 26460 26461 26462 26463 26464 26465 26466 26467 26468

26469 26470 26471 26472 26473 26474 26475 26476 26477 26478 26479 26480 26481 26482 26483 26484 26485 26486 26487 26488 26489 26490 26491 26492 26493 26494 26495 26496 26497 26498 26499 26500 26501 26502 26503 26564 26565 26566 26567 26568 26569 26570 26571 26572 26573 26574 26575 26576 26577 26578 26579 26580 26581 26582 26583 26584 26585 26586 26587 26588 26589 26590 26591 26592 26593 26544 26545 26546 26547 26548 26549 26550 26551 26552 26553 26554 26555 26556 26557 26558 26559 26560 26561 26562 26563 26569 26570 26571

26572 26573 26574 26575 26576 26577 26578 26579 26580 26581 26582 26583 26584 26585 26586 26587 26588 26589 26600 26601 26602 26603 26604 26605 26606 26607 26608 26609 26610 26611 26612 26613 26614 26615 26616 26617 26618 26619 26620 26621 26622 26623 26624 26625 26626 26627 26628 26629 26630 26631 26632 26633 26634 26635 26636 26637 26638 26639 26640 26641 26642 26643 26644 26645 26646 26647 26648 26649 26650 26651 26652 26653 26654 26655 26656 26657 26658 26659 26660 26661 26662 26663 26664 26665 26666 26667 26668 26669 26670 26671 26672 26673 26674 26675

26676 26677 26678 26679 26680 26681 26682 26683 26684 26685 26686 26687 26688 26689 26690 26691 26692 26693 26694 26695 26696 26697 26698 26699 26700 26701 26702 26703 26704 26705 26706 26707 26708 26709 26710 26711 26712 26713 26714 26715 26716 26717 26718 26719 26720 26721 26722 26723 26724 26725 26726 26727 26728 26729 26730 26731 26732 26733 26734 26735 26736 26737 26738 26739 26740 26741 26742 26743 26744 26745 26746 26747 26748 26749 26750 26751 26752 26753 26754 26755 26756 26757 26758 26759 26760 26761 26762 26763 26764 26765 26766 26767 26768 26769 26770 26771 26772 26773 26774 26775 26776 26777 26778

26779 26780 26781 26782 26783 26784 26785 26786 26787 26788 26789 26790 26791 26792 26793 26794 26795 26796 26797 26798 26799 26800 26801 26802 26803 26804 26805 26806 26807 26808 26809 26810 26811 26812 26813 26814 26815 26816 26817 26818 26819 26820 26821 26822 26823 26824 26825 26826 26827 26828 26829 26830 26831 26832 26833 26834 26835 26836 26837 26838 26839 26840 26841 26842 26843 26844 26845 26846 26847 26848 26849 26850 26851 26852 26853 26854 26855 26856 26857 26858 26859 26860 26861 26862 26863 26864 26865 26866 26867 26868 26869 26890 26891 26892 26893 26894 26895 26896 26897 26898 26899 26900 26901 26902 26903 26904 26905 26906 26907 26908 26909 26910 26911 26912 26913 26914 26915 26916 26917 26918 26919 26920 26921 26922 26923 26924 26925 26926

26927 26928 26929 26930 26931 26932 26933 26934 26935 26936 26937 26938 26939 26940 26941 26942 26943 26944 26945 26946 26947 26948 26949 26950 26951 26952 26953 26954 26955 26956 26957 26958 26959 26960 26961 26962 26963 26964 26965 26966 26967 26968 26969 26970 26971 26972 26973 26974 26975 26976 26977 26978 26979 26980 26981 26982 26983 26984 26985 26986 26987 26988 26989 26990 26991 26992 26993 26994 26995 26996 26997 26998 26999 27000 27001 27002 27003 27004 27005 27006 27007 27008 27009 27010 27011 27012 27013 27014 27015 27016 27017 27018 27019 27020 27021 27022 27023 27024 27025 27026 27027 27028 27029 27030 27031 27032 27033 27034 27035 27036 27037 27038 27039 27040 27041 27042

27043 27044 27045 27046 27047 27048 27049 27050 27051 27052 27053 27054 27055 27056 27057 27058 27059 27060 27061 27062 27063 27064 27065 27066 27067 27068 27069 27070 27071 27072 27073 27074 27075 27076 27077 27078 27079 27080 27081 27082 27083 27084 27085 27086 27087 27088 27089 27090 27091 27092 27093 27094 27095 27096 27097 27098 27099 27100 27101 27102 27103 27104 27105 27106 27107 27108 27109 27110 27111 27112 27113 27114 27115 27116 27117 27118 27119 27120 27121 27122 27123 27124 27125 27126 27127 27128 27129 27130 27131 27132 27133 27134 27135 27136 27137 27138 27139 27140 27141 27142 27143 27144 27145 27146 27147 27148 27149

27150 27151 27152 27153 27154 27155 27156 27157 27158 27159 27160 27161 27162 27163 27164 27165 27166 27167 27168 27169 27170 27171 27172 27173 27174 27175 27176 27177 27178 27179 27180 27181 27182 27183 27184 27185 27186 27187 27188 27189 27190 27191 27192 27193 27194 27195 27196 27197 27198 27199 27200 27201 27202 27203 27204 27205 27206 27207 27208 27209 27210 27211 27212 27213 27214 27215 27216 27217 27218 27219 27220 27221 27222 27223 27224 27225 27226 27227 27228 27229 27230 27231 27232 27233 27234 27235 27236 27237 27238 27239 27240 27241 27242

27243 27244 27245 27246 27247 27248 27249 27250 27251 27252 27253 27254 27255 27256 27257 27258 27259 27260 27261 27262 27263 27264 27265 27266 27267 27268 27269 27270 27271 27272 27273 27274 27275 27276 27277 27278 27279 27280 27281 27282 27283 27284 27285 27286 27287 27288 27289 27290 27291 27292 27293 27294 27295 27296 27297 27298 27299 27300 27301 27302 27303 27304 27305 27306 27307 27308 27309 27310 27311 27312 27313 27314 27315 27316 27317 27318 27319 27320 27321 27322 27323 27324 27325 27326 27327 27328 27329 27330 27331 27332

27333 27334 27335 27336 27337 27338 27339 27340 27341 27342 27343 27344 27345 27346 27347 27348 27349 27350 27351 27352 27353 27354 27355 27356 27357 27358 27359 27360 27361 27362 27363 27364 27365 27366 27367 27368 27369 27370 27371 27372 27373 27374 27375 27376 27377 27378 27379 27380 27381 27382 27383 27384 27385 27386 27387 27388 27389 27390 27391 27392 27393 27394 27395 27396 27397 27398 27399 27400 27401 27402 27403 27404 27405 27406 27407 27408 27409 27410 27411 27412 27413 27414 27415

27416 27417 27418 27419 27420 27421 27422 27423 27424 27425 27426 27427 27428 27429 27430 27431 27432 27433 27434 27435 27436 27437 27438 27439 27440 27441 27442 27443 27444 27445 27446 27447 27448 27449 27450 27451 27452 27453 27454 27455 27456 27457 27458 27459 27460 27461 27462 27463 27464 27465 27466 27467 27468 27469 27470 27471 27472 27473 27474 27475 27476 27477 27478 27479 27480 27481 27482 27483 27484 27485 27486 27487 27488 27489 27490 27491 27492 27493 27494

27495 27496 27497 27498 27499 27500 27501 27502 27503 27504 27505 27506 27507 27508 27509 27510 27511 27512 27513 27514 27515 27516 27517 27518 27519 27520 27521 27522 27523 27524 27525 27526 27527 27528 27529 27530 27531 27532 27533 27534 27535 27536 27537 27538 27539 27540 27541 27542 27543 27544 27545 27546 27547 27548 27549 27550 27551 27552 27553 27554 27555 27556 27557 27558 27559 27560 27561 27562 27563 27564

27565 27566 27567 27568 27569 27570 27571 27572 27573 27574 27525 27526 27527 27528 27529 27530 27531 27532 27533 27534 27535 27536 27537 27538 27539 27540 27541 27542 27543 27544 27545 27546 27547 27548 27549 27550 27551 27552 27553 27554 27555 27556 27557 27558 27559 27560 27561 27562 27563 27564 27565 27566 27567 27568 27569 27570 27571 27572 27573 27574 27575 27576 27577 27578 27579 27580 27581 27582 27583 27584 27585 27586 27587 27588 27589

27590 27591 27592 27593 27594 27595 27596 27597 27598 27599 27600 27601 27602 27603 27604 27605 27606 27607 27608 27609 27610 27611 27612 27613 27614 27615 27616 27617 27618 27619 27620 27621 27622 27623 27624 27625 27626 27627 27628 27629 27630 27631 27632 27633 27634 27635 27636 27637 27638 27639 27640 27641 27642 27643 27644 27645 27646 27647 27648 27649 27650 27651 27652 27653 27654 27655 27656 27657 27658 27659 27660 27661 27662 27663 27664 27665 27666

27667 27668 27669 27670 27671 27672 27673 27674 27675 27676 27677 27678 27679 27680 27681 27682 27683 27684 27685 27686 27687 27688 27689 27690 27691 27692 27693 27694 27695 27696 27697 27698 27699 27700 27701 27702 27703 27704 27705 27706 27707 27708 27709 27710 27711 27712 27713 27714 27715 27716 27717 27718 27719 27720 27721 27722 27723 27724 27725 27726 27727 27728 27729 27730 27731 27732 27733 27734 27735 27736 27737 27738 27739 27740 27741 27742 27743 27744

27745 27746 27747 27748 27749 27750 27751 27752 27753 27754 27755 27756 27757 27758 27759 27760 27761 27762 27763 27764 27765 27766 27767 27768 27769 27770 27771 27772 27773 27774 27775 27776 27777 27778 27779 27780 27781 27782 27783 27784 27785 27786 27787 27788 27789 27790 27791 27792 27793 27794 27795 27796 27797 27798 27799 27800 27801 27802 27803 27804 27805 27806 27807 27808 27809 27810 27811 27812 27813 27814 27815 27816

Missing (verb):

_______ *me manque(s)*

In French, when you say you miss someone or something, it translates to

_______*is missing from me.*

In the above example, what is missing from me?
Fill in the blank:

a. Land
b. Home
c. Community
d. Identity
e. Belonging

What is the word to say *I am missing from*_______?

Home:

(noun)

1. A place ~~of permanence~~
2. A place ~~where one lives~~

(verb)

1. (of an animal) Return by instinct to its territory after leaving it

Homesickness (noun):

A separation anxiety from ground(ing).
A condition of longing for a place of belonging,
while absent from it.

Symptoms:

- ✔ Feeling lonely or (isolated)
- ✔ Tearfulness
- ✔ Headaches
- ✔ Difficulty concentrating
- ✔ Brain fog
- ✔ Overwhelm
- ✔ Nostalgia
- ✔ Anxiety, panic
- ✔ Feeling nervous or sad
- ✔ Nausea
- ✔ Suicidal thoughts
- ✔ Disturbed sleep
- ✔ Fatigue
- ✔ Body aches
- ✔ Withdrawal
- ✔ Grief

Use of the word "homesick" over time[8]

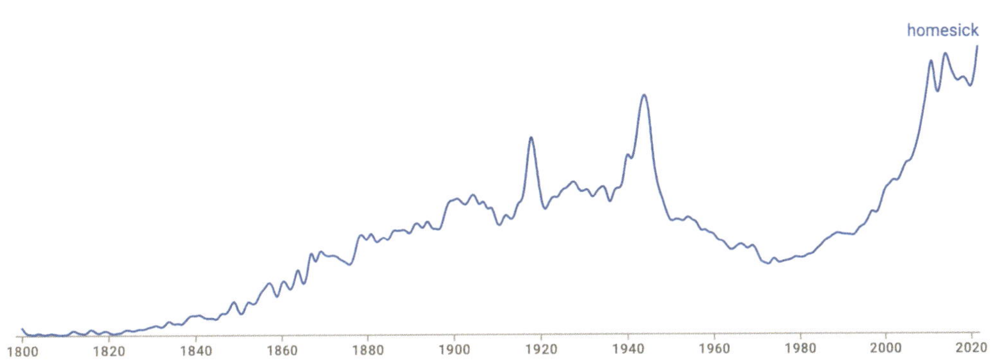

8 Source: Google Ngram viewer, which searches for appearances in a corpus of scanned books.

The legacy of diaspora is:

always longing for an avoidant lover

a pinch of table salt when you're hungry for ocean

trying to leave footprints, but rain licks the sidewalk clean

an overcooked yolk, paralyzed

an eyeball without a socket

the ghost of your joy in the bathtub[9]

your own voice on the answering machine, disembodied,
unfamiliar, resonating in your chest, an echo, returning

becoming a time capsule, some sad photocopy
of a 1940s dreamscape, a relic from a place with a name
that no longer exists, a house without a face

an unfamiliar alphabet, a spectrum of language
in colors my eye can't decipher

waking, tongue carpeted with bone dust
traces of ash and freshly fallen snow

the textile surface of my body worn thin
corrugated where anxious fingers rake in

a culture pieced together from scraps
off the editing room floor

---

9 Noor Hindi, "The World's Loneliest Whale Sings the Loudest Song," *Split This Rock (2023).*

the taste of burnt
hair, frizz crackling over birthday flame

an armchair, leather skin broken in

teta's fingerprints bleached smooth

my mother's wrists, brittle like
fishbones on Sundays

returning to an open door, unable to cross
the threshold while strangers come
and go as they please

28713 28714 28715
28716 28717 28718
28729 28730 28731
28738 28739 28740 28741 28742
28732 28733 28734 28735 28736 28737
28725 28726 28727 28728

How to cure homesickness

1. Gather artifacts. Remnants
   of home. An altar. A black
   and white photograph: ancestors
   on the beach in their homeland,
   movie star smiles and '40s swim
   suits, froth licking ankles;
   a seashell, a diamond ring,
   a pumice stone, a key without
   a lock.

2. Strike a match. Self-hypnotize
   in the fire. Let the flame
   summon—

3. In a kettle, mobilize bubbles;
   listen to their rumors roil.

4. Steep herbs for tea: maryamiyah chamomile myrrh yansoon za'atar. Nature
   is generous. We grow what we need. The yansoon's bitter perfume warm and
   sweetened for a midnight tummy ache. Chamomile to calm the nerves: the
   symptoms of longing quelled by elements from the land
   from which one was removed.

Warm between cupped palms.
Sip, savor till sleep comes.
Reunite in dreams.

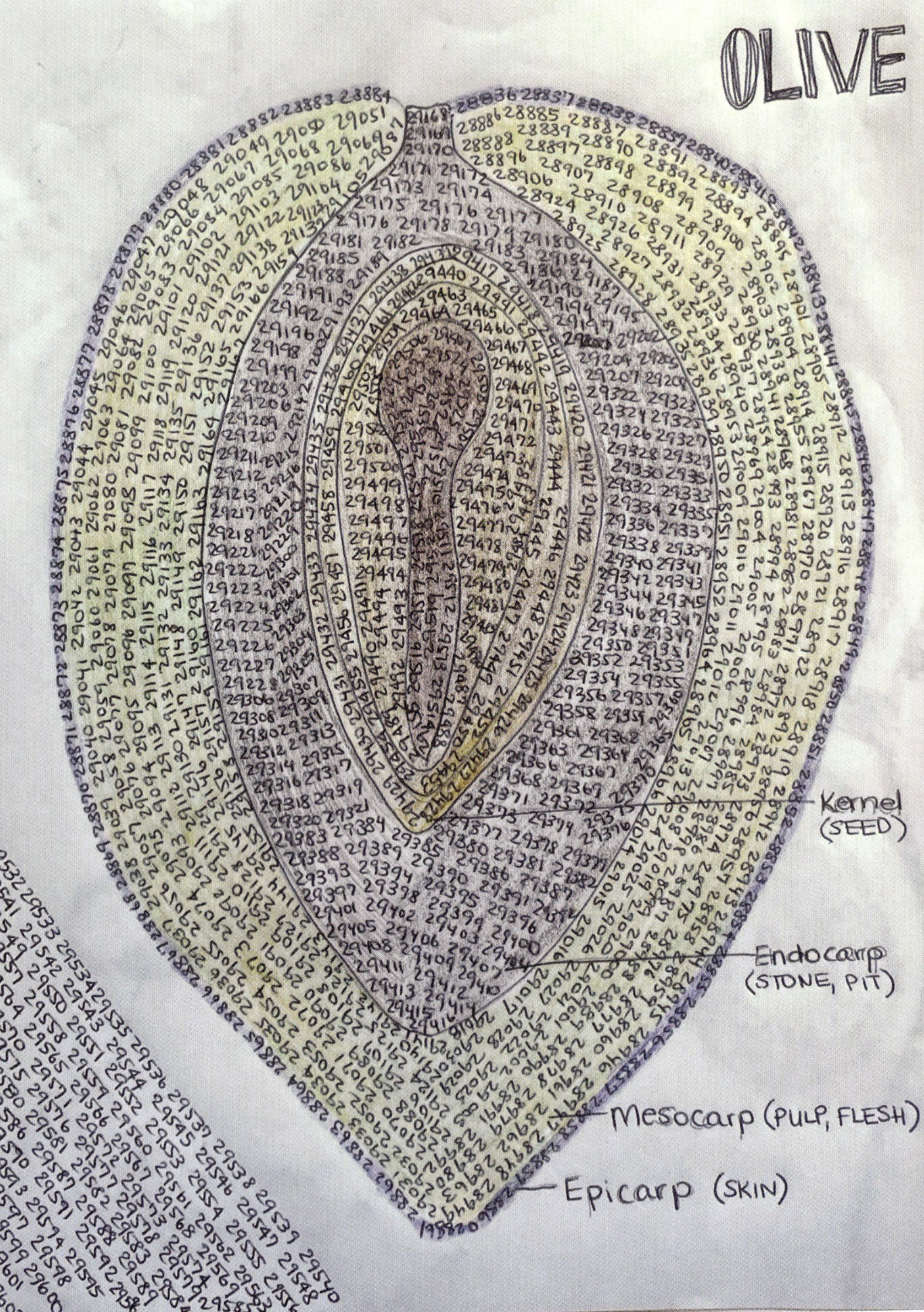
OLIVE
Kernel (SEED)
Endocarp (STONE, PIT)
Mesocarp (PULP, FLESH)
Epicarp (SKIN)

di·as·po·ra

You come upon a copse, unlocked, holding
vigil. Enter and listen to coded whispers,
thirsty to tap root systems like phone lines.
We are one single tree, standing separate
but connected beneath, we reach toward
each other with raw wires, nerve endings
and beginnings and never endings. I am

impulse.

I stretch,

I yawn,

I shade.

I choose.

I bend,

I break.

I make

shadows.

My achy roots renewed
dig fingertips in dirt, claw soil
under fingernails. Shake me. Listen
for the thud of fruit jumping onto
damp ground. Petrichor calls your
name, says, *you are alive.*

No wonder they want
us dead.

30047 30048 30049 30050 30051 30052 30053 30054 30055 30056 30057 30058 30059 30060 30061 30062 30063 30064 30065 30066 30067 30068 30069 30070 30071 30072 30073 30074 30075 30076 30077 30078 30079 30080 30081 30082 30083 30084 30085 30086 30087 30088 30089 30090 30091 30092 30093 30094 30095 30096 30097 30098 30099 30100 30101 30102 30103 30104 30105 30106 30107 30108 30109 30110 30111 30112 30113 30114 30115 30116 30117 30118 30119 30120 30121 30122

30123 30124 30125 30126 30127 30128 30129 30130 30131 30132 30133 30134 30135 30136 30137 30138 30139 30140 30141 30142 30143 30144 30145 30146 30147 30148 30149 30150 30151 30152 30153 30154 30155 30156 30157 30158 30159 30160 30161 30162 30163 30164 30165 30166 30167 30168 30169 30170 30171 30172 30173 30174 30175 30176 30177 30178 30179 30180 30181 30182 30183 30184 30185 30186 30187 30188 30189 30190 30191 30192 30193

30194 30195 30196 30197 30198 30199 30200 30201 30202 30203 30204 30205 30206 30207 30208 30209 30210 30211 30212 30213 20214 30215 30216 30217 30218 30219 30220 30221 30222 30223 30224 30225 30226 30227 30228 30229 30230 30231 30232 30233 30234 30235 30236 30237 30238 30239 30240 30241 30242 30243 30244 30245 30246 30247 30248 30249 30250 30251 30252 30253 30254 30255 30256 30257 30258 30259

30260 30261 30262 30263 30264 30265 30266 30267 30268 30269 30270 30271 30272 30273 30274 30275 30276 30277 30278 30279 30280 30281 30282 30283 30284 30285 30286 30287 30288 30289 30290 30291 30292 30293 30294 30295 30296 30297 30298 30299 30300 30301 30302 30303 30304 30305 30306 30307 30308 30309 30310 30311 30312 30313 30314 30315 30316 30317 30318 30319 30320 30321 30322 30323 30324 30325 30326

30327 30328 30329 30330 30331 30332 30333 30334 30335 30336 30337 30338 30339 30340 30341 30342 30343 30344 30345 30346 30347 30348 30349 30350 30351 30352 30353 30354 30355 30356 30357 30358 30359 30360 30361 30362 30363 30364 30365 30366 30367 30368 30369 30370 30371 30372 30373 30374 30375 30376 30377 30378 30379 30380 30381 30382 30383 30384 30385 30386 30387 30388 30389 30390

30391 30392 30393 30394 30395 30396 30397 30398 30399 30400 30401 30402 30403 30404 30405 30406 30407 30408 30409 30410 30411 30412 30413 30414 30415 30416 30417 30418 30419 30420 30421 30422 30423 30424 30425 30426 30427 30428 30429 30430 30431 30432 30433 30434 30435 30436 30437 30438 30439 30440 30441 30442 30443 30444 30445 30446 30447 30448 30449 30450 30451 30452 30453 30454

30455 30456 30457 30458 30459 30460 30461 30462 30463 30464 30465 30466 30467 30468 30469 30470 30471 30472 30473 30474 30475 30476 30477 30478 30479 30480 30481 30482 30483 30484 30485 30486 30487 30488 30489 30490 30491 30492 30493 30494 30495 30496 30497 30498 30499 30500 30501 30502 30503 30504 30505 30506 30507 30508 30509 30510 30511 30512 30513 30514 30515 30516

30517 30518 30519 30520 30521 30522 30523 30524 30525 30526 30527 30528 30529 30530 30531 30532 30533 30534 30535 30536 30537 30538 30539 30540 30541 30542 30543 30544 30545 30546 30547 30548 30549 30550 30551 30552 30553 30554 30555 30556 30557 30558 30559 30560 30561 30562 30563 30564 30565 30566 30567 30568 30569 30570 30571 30572 30573 30574 30575 30576 30577 30578 30579 30580

30581 30582 30583 30584 30585 30586 30587 30588 30589 30590 30591 30592 30593 30594 30595 30596 30597 30598 30599 30600 30601 30602 30603 30604 30605 30606 30607 30608 30609 30610 30611 30612 30613 30614 30615 30616 30617 30618 30619 30620 30621 30622 30623 30624 30625 30626 30627 30628 30629 30630 30631 30632 30633 30634 30635 30636 30637 30638 30639 30640 30641 30642 30643

30644 30645 30646 30647 30648 30649 30650 30651 30652 30653 30654 30655 30656 30657 30658 30659 30660 30661 30662 30663 30664 30665 30666 30667 30668 30669 30670 30671 30672 30673 30674 30675 30676 30677 30678 30679 30680 30681 30682 30683 30684 30685 30686 30687 30688 30689 30690 30691 30692 30693 30694 30695 30696 30697 30698 30699 30700 30701 30702 30703 30704

30705 30706 30707 30708 30709 30710 30711 30712 30713 30714 30715 30716 30117 30718 30719 30720 30721 30722 30723 30724 30725 30726 30727 30728 30729 30730 30731 30732 30733 30734 30735 30736 30737 30738 30739 30740 30741 30742 30743 30744 30745 30746 30747 30748 30749 30750 30751 30752 30753 30754 30755 30756 30757 30758 30759 30760 30761 30762 30763 30764

30765 30766 30767 30768 30769 30770 30771 30772 30773 30774 30775 30776 30777 30778 30779 30780 30781 30782 30783 30784 30785 30786 30787 30788 30789 30790 30791 30792 30793 30794 30795 30796 30797 30798 30799 30800 30801 30802 30803 30804 30805 30806 30807 30808 30809 30810 30811 30812 30813 30814 30815 30816 30817 30818 30819 30820 30821 3082

30823
30824
30825
30826
30827
30828
30829
30830
30831
30832
30833
30834
30835
30836
30837
30838
30839
30840
30841
30842
30843
30844
30845
30846
30847
30848
30849
30850
30851
30852
30853
30854
30855
30856
30857
30858
30859
30860
30861
30862
30863
30864
30865
30866
30867
30868
30869
30870
30871
30872
30873
30874
30875
30876
30877
30878
30879
30880
30881
30882
30883
30884
30885
30886
30887
30888
30889
30890
30891
30892
30893
30894
30895
30896
30897
30898
30899
30900
30901
30902
30903
30904
30905
30906
30907
30908
30909
30910
30911
30912
30913
30914
30915
30916
30917
30918
30919
30920
30921
30922
30923
30924
30925
30926
30927
30928
30929
30930
30931
30932
30933
30934
30935
30936
30937
30938
30939
30940
30941
30942
30943
30944
30945
30946
30947
30948
30949
30950
30951
30952
30953
30954
30955
30956
30957
30958
30959
30960
30961
30962
30963
30964
30965
30966
30967
30968
30969
30970
30971
30972
30973
30974
30975
30976
30977
30978
30979
30980
30981
30982
30983
30984
30985
30986
30987
30988
30989
30990
30991
30992
30993
30994
30995
30996
30997
30998
30999
31000
31001
31002
31003
31004
31005
31006
31007
31008
31009
31010
31011
31012
31013
31014
31015
31016
31017
31018
31019
31020
31021
31022
31023
31024
31025
31026
31027
31028
31029
31030
31031
31032
31033
31034
31035
31036
31037
31038
31039
31040
31041
31042
31043
31044
31045
31046
31047
31048
31049
31050
31051
31052
31053
31054
31055
31056
31057
31058
31059
31060
31061
31062
31063
31064
31065
31066
31067
31068
31069
31070
31071
31072
31073
31074
31075
31076
31077
31078
31079
31080
31081
31082
31083
31084
31085
31086
31087
31088
31089
31090
31091
31092
31093
31094
31095
31096
31097
31098
31099
31100
31101
31102
31103
31104
31105
31106
31107
31108
31109
31110
31111
31112
31113
31114
31115
31116
31117
31118
31119
31120
31121
31122
31123
31124
31125
31126
31127
31128
31129
31130
31131
31132
31133
31134
31135
31136
31137
31138
31139
31140
31141
31142
31143
31144
31145
31146
31147
31148
31149
31150
31151
31152
31153
31154
31155
31156
31157
31158
31159
31160
31161
31162
31163
31164
31165
31166
31167
31168
31169
31170
31171
31172
31173
31174
31175
31176
31177
31178
31179
31180
31181
31182
31183
31184
31185
31186
31187
31188
31189
31190
31191
31192
31193
31194
31195
31196
31197
31198
31199
31200
31201
31202
31203
31204
31205
31206
31207
31208
31209
31210
31211
31212
31213
31214
31215
31216
31217
31218
31219
31220
31221
31222
31223
31224
31225
31226
31227
31228
31229
31230
31231
31232
31233
31234
31235
31236
31237
31238
31239
31240
31241
31242
31243
31244
31245
31246
31247
31248
31249
31250
31251
31252
31253
31254
31255
31256
31257
31258
31259
31260
31261
31262
31263
31264
31265
31266
31267
31268
31269
31270
31271
31272
31273
31274
31275
31276
31277
31278
31279
31280
31281
31282
31283
31284
31285
31286
31287
31288
31289
31290
31291
31292
31293
31294
31295
31296
31297
31298
31299
31300
31301
31302
31303
31304
31305
31306
31307
31308
31309
31310
31311
31312
31313
31314
31315
31316
31317
31318
31319
31320
31321
31322
31323
31324
31325
31326
31327
31328
31329
31330
31331
31332
31333
31334
31335
31336
31337
31338
31339
31340
31341
31342
31343
31344
31345
31346
31347
31348
31349
31350
31351
31352
31353
31354
31355
31356
31357
31358
31359
31360
31361
31362
31363
31364
31365
31366
31367
31368
31369
31370
31371
31372
31373
31374

De(ad) **S**(ea) **ire**

So little left of the sea (dead).   Cordoned / off / and / doled / out,

Sea wants :   ((((((expanse))))))   (((to spread her wings wide)))

& make ? angels   winking across crystalline surface

Sea wants :   open-mouthed howl,   gulps of land,
engulf the holy,   to see her Mediterranean cousin.

Sea wants :   to be   whole, engorged   a massive salty beast,

killing any fish that dare cross her   sharp-tongued, prickly

Sea wants : her rock underneath   to rock babies
like   tree   tops

Sea wants: to yell and expel the bodies
Sea wants: to hold, to be beheld, but not held

Sea wants: to keep all her names
and belong only to herself

Sea wants: to belong,   to be

(((((((to be long)))))))   ((((((((and wide))))))))

& f r e e   (((((((t o s p r e a d))))))) limbs long

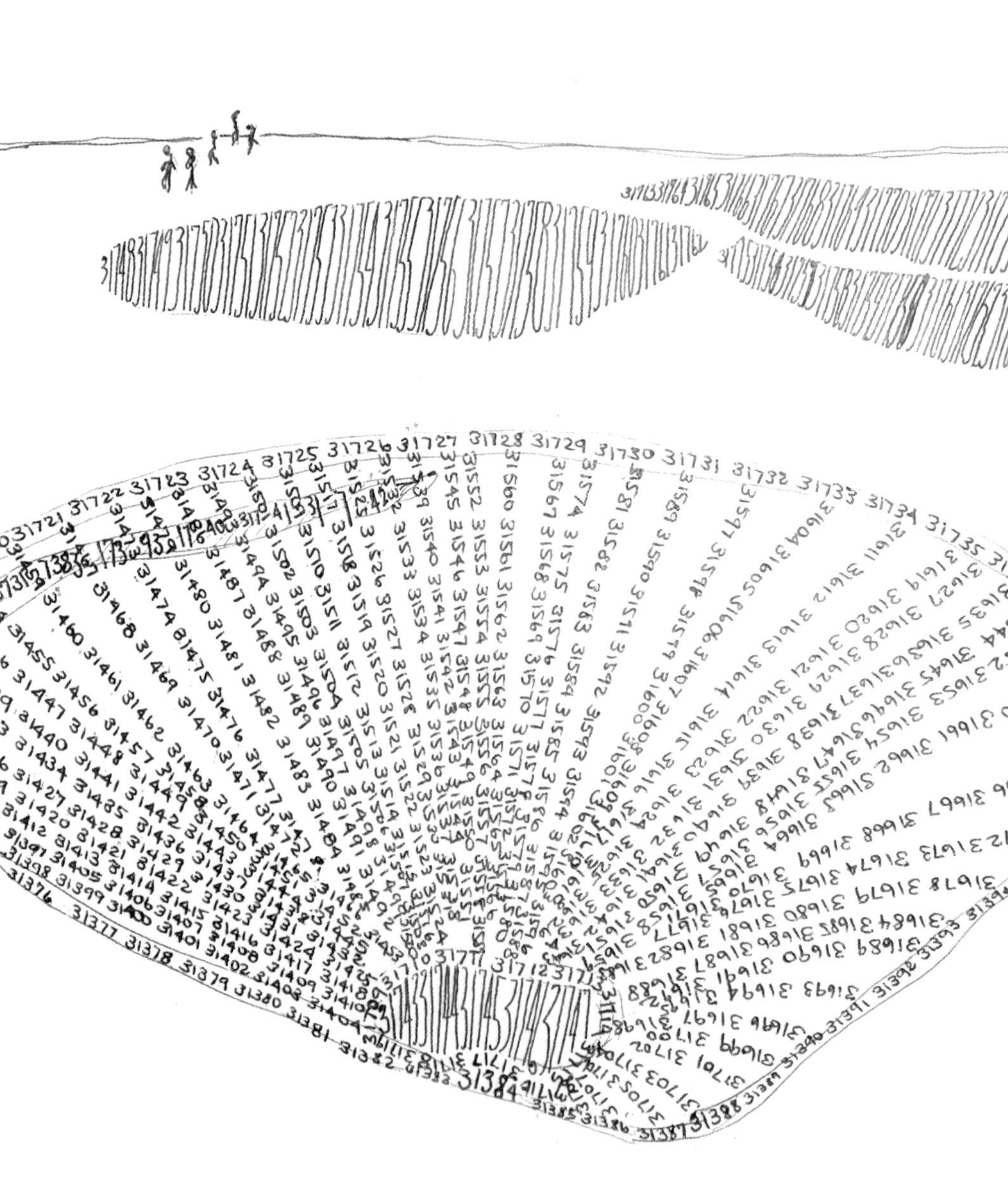

When the flag
was banned, they carried
watermelons.

Thirsty for red,
green, black, and white
juicy resistance—

so those too were deemed
forbidden.

How far they'll go
to erase us
that they'll give up
something so sweet.

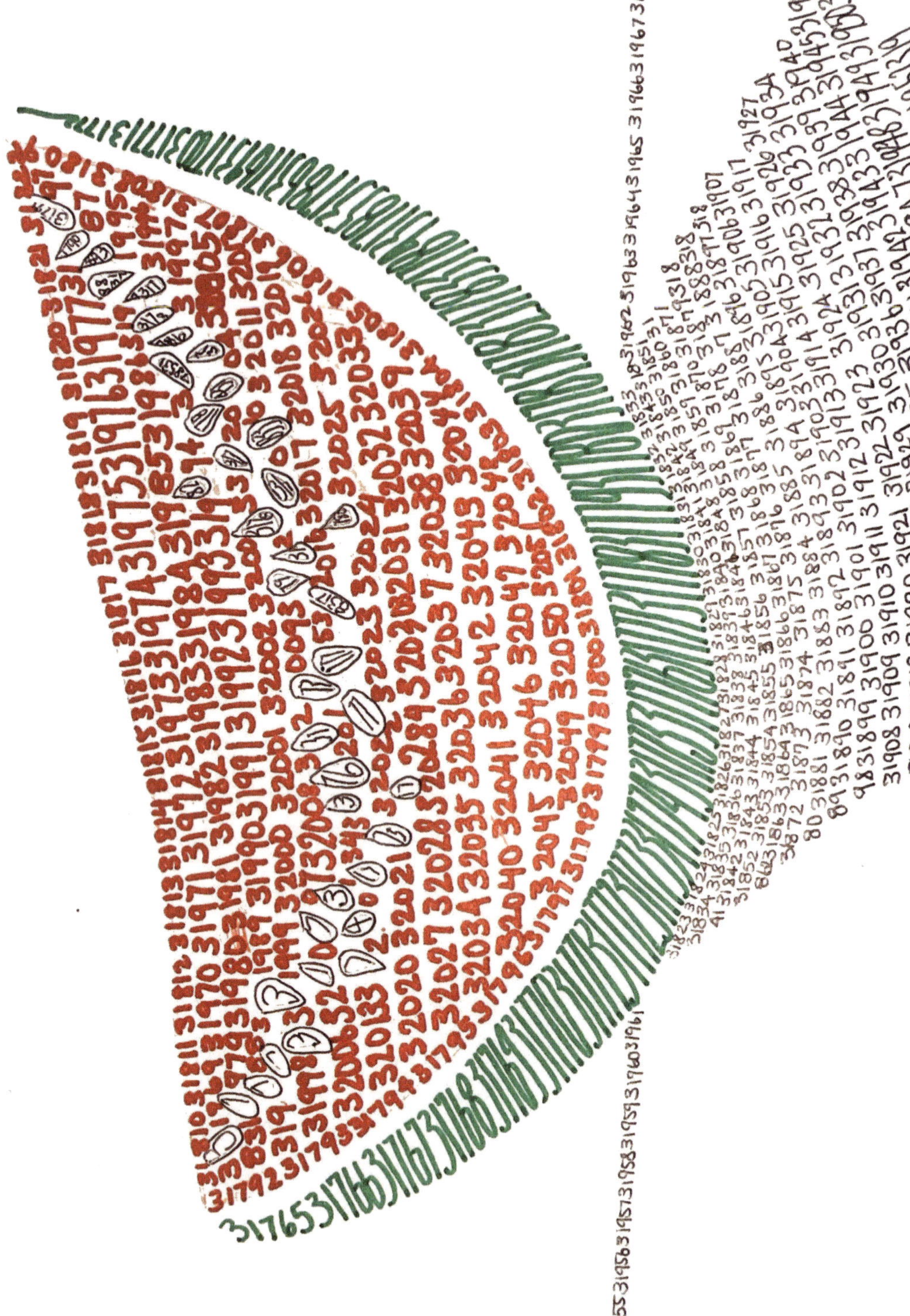

watermelon × بطيخ
ˈwôdərˌmelən batikh

I imagine

D
R
O
P
P
I
N
G

RI
PE WATER
MELONS -WAT juice
ER BALL
OON Slosh-

S ing
B ST liquid
UR

resonant thud

a hollow drum

Batikh

Batikh

Batikh

A field,

vast and open;

the sky stretched wide;

the pregnant

bellies of melons suckling

from umbilical vine,

coiled and curled, creeping

across soil,   sediment,   dust.

Taut canvas of sky clear-luminous over

head, blue ink pooled ominous on the other end;

another climate just out of reach.

Maybe I'm a basking watermelon,

sun-tender and tethered

by vine to the storm melons.

I am not a terrorist.
I will not yell, I will not die.
I paint my face, try
to blend armed and armored
camouflage skin, I appraise
each exterior for fit.

The vellum of me: tremoring,
translucent. I belong
in a box my boundaries blurred I am
estranged, cast aside I search for
kin far and wide I muddy each
surface with my blood weave
webs of DNA across
the globe and hope home
will call.

I am not a terrorist.
I will not yell, I will not die.
Dream to detonate my cells
in your biome to lace your lips
with my saliva to stain each surface
with blood leave strands in the back
seat so if someone ever comes
looking, I've left a trace.

32363 32364 32365 32366 32367 32368 32369 32370 32371 32372 32373 32374 32375 32376 32377 32378 32379 32380 32381 32382 32383 32384 32385 32386 3287 32388 32389 32390 32391 32392 32393 32394 32395 32396 32397 32398 32399 32400 32401 32902 32403 32404 32405 32406 32407 32408 32409 32410 32411 32412 32413 32414 32415 32416 32417 32418 32419 32420 32421 32422 32423 32424 32425 32426 32427 32428 32429 32430 32431 32482 32433 32434 32435 32436 32437 32438 32439 32440 32441 32442 32443 32444

32445 32446 32447 32448 32449 32450 32451 32452 32453 32454 32455 32456 32457 32458 32459 32460 32461 32462 32463 32464 32465 32466 32467 32468 32469 32470 32471 32472 32473 32474 32475 32476 32477 32478 32479 32480 32481 32482 32483 32484 32485 32486 32487 32488 32489 32490 32491 32492 32493 32494 32495 32496 32497 32498 32499 32500 32501 32502 32503 32504 32505 32506 32507 32508 32509 32510 32511 32512 32513 32514 32515 32516 32517 32518 32519 32520 32521 32522 32523 32524 32525

32526 32527 32528 32529 32530 32531 32532 32533 32534 32535 32536 32537 32538 32539 32540 32541 32542 32543 32544 32545 32546 32547 32548 32549 32550 32551 32552 32553 32554 32555 32556 32557 32558 32559 32560 32561 32562 32563 32564 32565 32566 32567 32568 32569 32570 32571 32572 32573 32574 32575 32576 32577 32578 32579 32580 32581 32582 32583 32584 32585 32586 32587 32588 32589 32590 32591 32592 32593 32594 32595 32596 32597 32598 32599 32600 32601 32602

32603 32604 32005 32606 32607 32608 32609 32610 32611 32612 32613 32614 32615 32616 32617 32618 32619 32620 32621 32622 32623 32624 32625 32626 32627 32628 32629 32630 32631 32632 32633 32634 32635 32636 32637 32638 32639 32640 32641 32642 32643 32644 32645 32646 32647 32648 32649 32650 32651 32652 32653 32654 32655 32656 32657 32658 32659 32660 32661 32662 32663 32664 32665 32666 32667 32668 32669 32670 32671

32672 32673 32674 32675 32676 32677 32678 32679 32680 32681 32682 32683 32684 32685 32686 32687 32688 32689 32610 32691 32692 3267 32694 32695 32696 32697 32698 32699 32700 32701 32702 32703 32704 32705 32706 32707 32708 32709 32710 32711 32712 32713 32714 32715 32716 32717 32718 32719 32720 32721 32722 32723 32724 32725 32726 32727 32728 32729 32730 32731 32732 32733 32734 32735 32736 32737 32738 32739

32740 32741 32742 32743 32744 32745 32746 32747 32748 32749 32750 32751 32752 32753 32754 32755 32756 32757 32758 32759 32760 32761 32762 32763 32764 32765 32766 32767 32768 32769 32770 32771 32772 32773 32774 32775 32776 32777 32778 32779 32780 32781 32782 32783 32784 32785 32786 32787 32788 32789 32790 32791 32792 32793 32794 32795 32796 32797 32798 32799 32800 32801 32802 32803 32804 32805 32806 32807 32808

32809 32810 32811 32812 32813 32814 32815 32816 32817 32818 32819 32820 32821 32822 32823 32824 32825 32826 32827 32828 32829 32830 32831 32832 32833 32834 32835 32836 32837 32838 32839 32840 32841 32842 32843 32844 32845 32846 32847 32848 32849 32850 32851 32852 32853 32854 32855 32856 32857 32858 32859 32860 32861 32862 32863 32864 32865 32866 32867 32868 32869 32870 32871 32872 32873 32874 32875 32876 32877 32878 32879 32880

32881 32882 32883 32884 32885 32886 32887 32888 32889 32890 32891 32892 32893 32894 32895 32896 32897 32898 32899 32900 32901 32902 32903 32904 32905 32906 32907 32908 32909 32910 32911 32912 32913 32914 32915 32916 32917 32918 32919 32920 32921 32922 32923 32924 32925 32926 32927 32928 32929 32930 32931 32932 32933 32934 32935 32936 32937 32938 32959 32940 32941 32942 32943 32944 32945 32946 32947 32948 32949 32950 32951 32952 32953 32954 32955 32956

32957 32958 32959 32960 32961 32962 32963 32964 32965 32966 32967 32968 32969 32970 32971 32972 32973 32974 32975 32976 32977 32978 32979 32980 32981 32982 32983 32984 32985 32986 32987 32988 32989 32990 32991 32992 32993 32994 32995 32996 32997 32998 32999 33000 33001 33002 33003 33004 33005 33006 33007 33008 33009 33010 33011 33012 33013 33014 33015 33016 33017 33018 33019 33020 33021 33022

33023 33024 33025 33026 33027 33028 33029 33030 33031 33032 33033 33034 33035 33036 33037 33038 33039 33040 33041 33042 33043 33044 33045 33046 33047 33048 33049 33050 33051 33052 33053 33054 33055 33056 33057 33058 33059 33060 33061 33062 33063 33064 33065 33066 33067 33068 33069 33070 33071 33072 33073 33074 33075 33076 33077 33078 33079 33080 33081 33082 33083 33084 33085 33086 33087 33088 33089 33090 33091 33092 33093 33094 33095 33096

33097 33098 33099 33100 33101 33102 33103 33104 33105 33106 33107 33108 33109 33110 33111 33112 33113 33114 33115 33116 33117 33118 33119 33120 33121 33122 33123 33124 33125 33126 33127 33128 33129 33130 33131 33132 33133 33134 33135 33136 33137 33138 33139 33140 33141 33142 33143 33144 33145 33146 33147 33148 33149 33150 33151 33152 33153 33154 33155 33156 33157 33158 33159 33160 33161 33162 33163 33164

33165 33166 33167 33168 33169 33170 33171 33172 33173 33174 33175 33176 33177 33178 33179 33180 33181 33182 33183 33184 33185 33186 33187 33188 33189 33190 33191 33192 33193 33194 33195 33196 33197 33198 33199 33200 33201 33202 33203 33204 33205 33206 33207 33208 33209 33210 33211 33212 33213 33214 33215 33216 33217 33218 33219 33220 33221 33222 33223 33224 33225 33226 33227 33228 33229 33230 33231 33232 33233

33234 33235 33236 33237 33238 33239 33240 33241 33242 33243 33244 33245 33246 33247 33248 33249 33250 33251 33252 33253 33254 33255 33256 33257 33258 33259 33260 33261 33262 33263 33264 33265 33266 33267 33268 33269 33270 33271 33272 33273 33274 33275 33276 33277 33278 33279 33280 33281 33282 33283 33284 33285 33286 33287 33288 33289 33290 33291 33292 33293 33294 33295 33296 33297 33298 33299 33300 33301 33302 33303

33304 33305 33306 33307 33308 33309 33310 33311 33312 33313 33314 33315 33316 33317 33318 33319 33320 33321 33322 33323 33324 33325 33326 33327 33328 33329 33330 33331 33332 33333 33334 33335 33336 33337 33338 33339 33340 33342 33343 33344 33345 33346 33347 33348 33349 33350 33351 33352 33353 33354 33355 33356 33357 33358 33359 33360 33361 33362 33363 33364 33365 33366 33367 33368 33369 33370 33371 33372 33373 33374 33375 33376

I AM
SO
TIRED

4298 4299 4300 4301 4302 4303 4304 4305 4306 4307 34308 34309 34310 34311 34312 34313 34314 34315 34316 34317 34318 34319 34320 34321 34322 34323 34324 34325 34326 34327 34328 34329 34330 34331 34332 34333 34334 34335 34336 34337 34338 34339 34340 34341 34342 34343 34344 34345 34346 34347 34348 34349 34350 34351 34352 34353 34354 34355 34356 34357 34358 34359 34360 34361 34362 34363 34364 34365 34366 34367 34368 34369 34370 34371

34372 34373 34374 34375 34376 34377 34378 34379 34380 34381 34382 34383 34384 34385 34386 34387 34388 34389 34390 34391 34392 34393 34394 34395 34396 34397 34398 34399 34400 34401 34402 34403 34404 34405 34406 34407 34408 34409 34410 34411 34412 34413 34414 34415 34416 34417 34418 34419 34420 34421 34422 34423 34424 34425 34426 34427 34428 34429 34430 34431 34432 34433 34434 34435 34436 34437 34438 34439 34440 34441 34442 34443 34444 34445 34446 34447 34448 34449

34450 34451 34452 34453 34454 34455 34456 34457 34458 34459 34460 34461 34462 34463 34464 34465 34466 34467 34468 34469 34470 34471 34472 34473 34474 34475 34476 34477 34478 34479 34450 34451 34452 34453 34454 34455 34456 34457 34458 34459 34460 34461 34462 34463 34464 34465 34466 34467 34468 34469 34470 34471 34472 34473 34474 34475 34476 34477 34478 34479 34450 34451 34452 34453 34454 34455 34456

34487 34488 34489 34490 34491 34492 34493 34494 34495 34496 34497 34498 34499 34500 34501 34502 34503 34504 34505 34506 34507 34508 34509 34510 34511 34512 34513 34514 34515 34516 34517 34518 34519 34520 34521 34522 34523 34524 34525 34526 34527 34528 34529 34530 34531 34532 34533 34534 34535 34536 34537 34538 34539 34540 34541 34542 34543 34544 34545 34546 34547 34548 34549 34550 34551 34552 34553 34554 34555 34556 34557 34558 34559 34560 34561 34562

34563 34564 34565 34566 34567 34568 34569 34570 34571 34572 34573 34574 34575 34576 34577 34578 34579 34580 34581 34582 34583 34584 34585 34586 34587 34588 34589 34590 34591 34592 34593 34594 34595 34596 34597 34598 34599 34600 34601 34602 34603 34604 34605 34606 34607 34608 34609 34610 34611 34612 34613 34614 34615 34616 34617 34618 34619 34620 34621 34622 34623 34624 34625 34626 34627 34628 34629 34630 34631 34632 34633 34634 34635 34636

34637 34638 34639 34640 34641 34642 34643 34644 34645 34646 34647 34648 34649 34650 34651 34652 34653 34654 34655 34656 34657 34658 34659 34660 34661 34662 34663 34664 34665 34666 34667 34668 34669 34670 34671 34672 34673 34674 34675 34676 34677 34678 34679 34680 34681 34682 34683 34684 34685 34686 34687 34688 34689 34690 34691 34692 34693 34694 34695 34696 34697 34698 34699 34700 34701 34702 34703 34704 34705 34706 34707 34708

34709 34710 34711 34712 34713 34714 34715 34716 34717 34718 34719 34720 34721 34722 34723 34724 34725 34726 34727 34728 34729 34730 34731 34732 34733 34734 34735 34736 34737 34738 34739 34740 34741 34742 34743 34744 34745 34746 34747 34748 34749 34750 34751 34752 34753 34754 34755 34756 34757 34758 34759 34760 34761 34762 34763 34764 34765 34766 34767 34768 34769 34770 34771 34772 34773 34774

34775 34776 34777 34778 34779 34780 34781 34782 34783 34784 34785 34786 34787 34788 34789 34790 34791 34792 34793 34794 34795 34796 34797 34798 34799 34800 34801 34802 34803 34804 34805 34806 34807 34808 34809 34810 34811 34812 34813 34814 34815 34816 34817 34818 34819 34820 34821 34822 34823 34824 34825 34826 34827 34828 34829 34830 34831 34832 34833 34834 34835 34836 34837 34838 34839 34840 34841 34842 34843

34844 34845 34846 34847 34848 34849 34850 34851 34852 34853 34854 34855 34856 34857 34858 34859 34860 34861 34862 34863 34864 34865 34866 34867 34868 34869 34870 34871 34872 34873 34874 34875 34876 34877 34878 34879 34880 34881 34882 34883 34884 34885 34886 34887 34888 34889 34890 34891 34892 34893 34894 34895 34896 34897 34898 34899 34900 34901 34902 34903 34904 34905 34906 34907 34908 34909

34910 34911 34912 34913 34914 34915 34916 34917 34918 34919 34920 34921 34922 34923 34924 34925 34926 34927 34928 34929 34930 34931 34932 34933 34934 34935 34936 34937 34938 34939 34940 34941 34942 34943 34944 34945 34946 34947 34948 34949 34950 34951 34952 34953 34954 34955 34956 34957 34958 34959 34960 34961 34962 34963 34964 34965 34966 34967 34968 34969 34970 34971 34972 34973

34974 34975 34976 34977 34978 34979 34980 34981 34982 34983 34984 34985 34986 34987 34988 34989 34990 34991 34992 34993 34994 34995 34996 34997 34998 34999 35000 35001 35002 35003 35004 35005 35006 35007 35008 35009 35010 35011 35012 35013 35014 35015 35016 35017 35018 35019 35020 35021 35022 35023 35024 35025 35026 35027 35028 35029 35030 35031 35032 35033 35034 35035 35036 35037 35038

35039 35040 35041 35042 35043 35044 35045 35046 35047 35048 35049 35050 35051 35052 35053 35054 35055 35056 35057 35058 35059 35060 35061 35062 35063 35064 35065 35066 35067 35068 35069 35070 35071 35072 35073 35074 35075 35076 35077 35078 35079 35080 35081 35082 35083 35084 35085 35086 35087 35088 35089 35090 35091 35092 35093 35094 35095 35096 35097 35098 35099 35100 35101 35102 35103 35104 35105 35106

35107 35108 35109 35110 35111 35112 35113 35114 35115 35116 35117 35118 35119 35120 35121 35122 35123 35124 35125 35126 35127 35128 35129 35130 35131 35132 35133 35134 35135 35136 35137 35138 35139 35140 35141 35142 35143 35144 35145 35146 35147 35148 35149 35150 35151 35152 35153 35154 35155 35156 35157 35158 35159 35160 35161 35162 35163 35164 35165 35166 35167

35168 35169 35170 35171 35172 35173 35174 35175 35176 35177 35178 35179 35180 35181 35182 35183 35184 35185 35186 35187 35188 35189 35190 35191 35192 35193 35194 35195 35196 35197 35198 35199 35200 35201 35202 35203 35204 35205 35206 35207 35208 35209 35210 35211 35212 35213 35214 35215 35216 35217 35218 35219 35220 35221 35222 35223 35224 35225 35226 35227 35228 35229 35230

35231 35232 35233 35234 35235 35236 35237 35238 35239 35240 35241 35242 35243 35244 35245 35246 35247 35248 35249 35250 35251 35252 35253 35254 35255 35256 35257 35258 35259 35260 35261 35262 35263 35264 35265 35266 35267 35268 35269 35270 35271 35272 35273 35274 35275 35276 35277 35278 35279 35280 35281 35282 35283 35284 35285 35286 35287 35288 35289 35290 35291 35292 35293 35294 35295 35296 35297

35298 35299 35300 35301 35302 35303 35304 35305 35306 35307 35308 35309 35310 35311 35312 35313 35314 35315 35316 35317 35318 35319 35320 35321 35322 35323 35324 35325 35326 35327 35328 35329 35330 35331 35332 35333 35334 35335 35336 35337 35338 35339 35340 35341 35342 35343 35344 35345 35346 35347 35348 35349 35350 35351 35352 35353 35354 35355 35356 35357 35358 35359 35360 35361 35362 35363 35364

35365 35366 35367 35368 35369 35310 35311 35312 35313 35314 35315 35316 35317 35318 35319 35320 35321 35322 35323 35324 35325 35326 35327 35328 35329 35330 35331 35332 35333 35334 35335 35336 35337 35338 35339 35340 35341 35342 35343 35344 35345 35346 35347 35348 35349 35350 35351 35352 35353 35354 35355 35356 35357 35358 35359 35360 35361 35362 35363 35364 35365 35366 35367

35368 35369 35370 35371 35372 35373 35374 35375 35376 35377 35378 35379 35380 35381 35382 35383 35384 35385 35386 35387 35388 35389 35390 35391 35392 35393 35394 35395 35396 35397 35398 35399 35400 35401 35402 35463 35464 35465 35466 35467 35468 35469 35470 35471 35472 35473 35474 35475 35476 35477 35478 35479 35480 35481 35482 35483 35484 35485 35486 35487 35488 35489

35490 35491 35492 35493 35494 35495 35496 35497 35498 35499 35500 35501 35502 35503 35504 35505 35506 35507 35508 35509 35510 35511 35512 35513 35514 35515 35516 35517 35518 35519 35520 35521 35522 35523 35524 35525 35526 35527 35528 35529 35530 35531 35532 35533 35534 35535 35536 35537 35538 35539 35540 35541 35542 35543 35544 35545 35546 35547 35548 35549 35550 35551 35552

35553 35554 35555 35556 35557 35558 35559 35560 35561 35562 35563 35564 35565 35566 35567 35568 35569 35570 35571 35572 35573 35574 35575 35576 35577 35578 35579 35580 35581 35582 35583 35584 35585 35586 35587 35588 35589 35590 35591 35592 35593 35594 35595 35596 35597 35598 35599 35600 35601 35602 35603 35604 35605 35606 35607 35608 35609 35610 35611 35612 35613 35614 35615

35616 35617 35618 35619 35620 35621 35622 35623 35624 35625 35626 35627 35628 35629 35630 35631 35632 35633 35634 35635 35636 35637 35638 35639 35640 35641 35642 35643 35644 35645 35646 35647 35648 35649 35650 35651 35652 35653 35654 35655 35656 35657 35658 35659 35660 35661 35662 35663 35604 35605 35606 35607 35608 35609 35610 35611 35612 35613 35614 35615 35616 35617 35618 35619

35620 35621 35622 35623 35624 35625 35626 35627 35628 35629 35630 35631 35632 35633 35634 35635 35636 35637 35638 35639 35640 35641 35642 35643 35644 35645 35646 35647 35648 35649 35650 35651 35652 35653 35654 35655 35656 35657 35658 35659 35660 35661 35662 35663 35664 35665 35666 35667 35668 35669 35670 35671 35672 35673 35674 35675 35676 35677 35678 35679 35680 35681 35682

35683 35684 35685 35686 35687 35688 35689 35690 35691 35692 35693 35694 35695 35696 35697 35698 35699 35700 35701 35702 35703 35704 35705 35706 35707 35708 35709 35710 35711 35712 35713 35714 35715 35716 35717 35718 35719 35720 35721 35722 35723 35724 35725 35726 35727 35728 35729 35730 35731 35732 35733 35734 35735 35736 35737 35738 35739 35740 35741 35742 35743 35744 35745 35746

35747 35748 35749 35750 35751 35752 35753 35754 35755 35756 35757 35758 35759 35760 35761 35762 35763 35764 35765 35766 35767 35768 35769 35770 35771 35772 35773 35774 35775 35776 35777 35778 35779 35780 35781 35782 35783 35784 35785 35786 35787 35788 35789 35790 35791 35792 35793 35794 35795 35796 35797 35798 35799 35800 35801 35802 35803 35804 35805 35806 35807 35808 35809 35810 35811

35812 35813 35814 35815 35816 35817 35818 35819 35820 35821 35822 35823 35824 35825 35826 35827 35828 35829 35830 35831 35832 35833 35834 35835 35836 35837 35838 35839 35840 35841 35842 35843 35844 35845 35846 35847 35848 35849 35850 35851 35852 35853 35854 35855 35856 35857 35858 35859 35860 35861 35862 35863 35864 35865 35866 35867 35868 35869 35870 35871 35872 35873 35874 35875 35876

35877 35878 35879 35880 35881 35882 35883 35684 35885 35886 35887 35888 35889 35890 35891 35892 35893 35894 35895 35896 35897 35898 35899 35900 35901 35902 35903 35904 35905 35906 35907 35908 35909 35910 35911 35912 35913 35914 35915 35916 35917 35918 35919 35920 35921 35922 35923 35924 35925 35926 35927 35928 35929 35930 35931 35932 35933 35934 35935 35936 35937 35938 35939

35940 35941 35942 35943 35944 35945 35946 35947 35948 35949 35950 35951 35952 35953 35954 35955 35956 35957 35958 35959 35960 35961 35962 35963 35964 35965 35966 35967 35968 35969 35970 35971 35972 35973 35974 35975 35976 35977 35978 35979 35980 35981 35982 35983 35984 35985 35986 35987 35988 35989 35990 35991 35992 35993 35994 35995 35996 35997 35998 35999

36000 36001 36002 36003 36004 36005 36006 36007 36008 36009 36010 36011 36012 36013 36014 36015 36016 36017 36018 36019 36020 36021 36022 36023 36024 36025 36026 36027 36028 36029 36030 36031 36032 36033 36034 36035 36036 36037 36038 36039 36040 36041 36042 36043 36044 36045 36046 36047 36048 36049 36050 36051 36052 36053 36054 36055 36056 36057 36058 36059 36060 36061 36062 36063 36064

36065 36066 36067 36068 36069 36070 36071 36072 36073 36074 36075 36076 36077 36078 36079 36080 36081 36082 36083 36084 36085 36086 36087 36088 36089 36090 36091 36092 36093 36094 36095 36096 36097 36098 36099 36100 36101 36102 36103 36104 36105 36106 36107 36108 36109 36110 36111 36112 36113 36114 36115 36116 36117 36118 36119 36120 36121 36122 36123 36124 36125 36126 36127

36128 36129 36130 36131 36132 36133 36134 36135 36136 36137 36138 36139 36140 36141 36142 36143 36144 36145 36146 36147 36148 36149 36150 36151 36152 36153 36154 36155 36156 36157 36158 36159 36160 36161 36162 36163 36164 36165 36166 36167 36168 36169 36170 36171 36172 36123 36174 36175 36176 36177 36178 36179 36180 36181 36182 36183 36184 36185 36186 36187 36188 36189

Nerves.—All the muscles of this group are supplied by the eighth cervical nerve through the ulnar nerve.

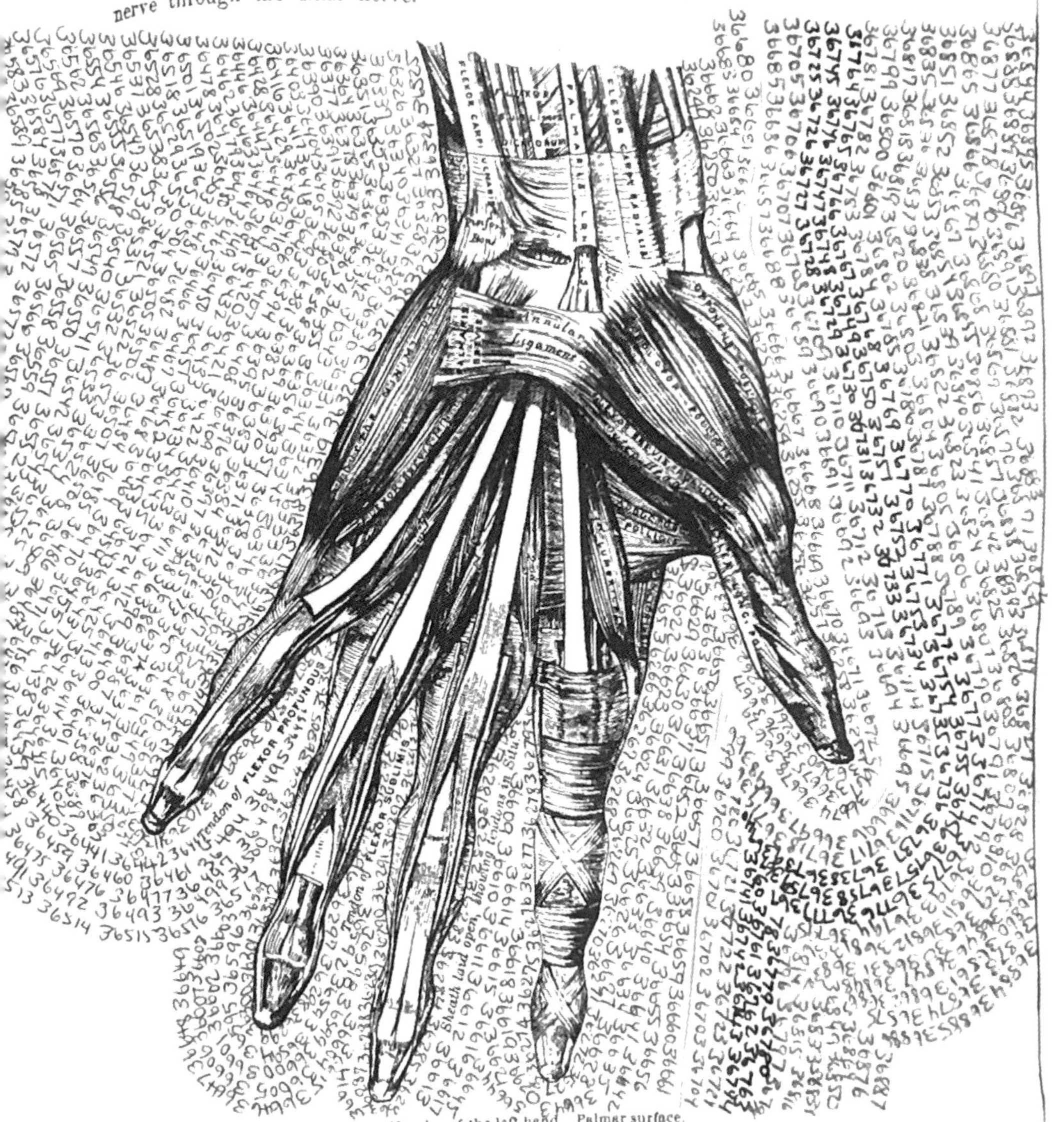

FIG 243.—Muscles of the left hand. Palmar surface.

Actions.—The Abductor minimi digiti abducts the little finger from the middle line of the hand. It corresponds to a dorsal interosseous muscle. It also assists in flexing the proximal phalanx. The Flexor brevis minimi digiti abducts the little finger from the middle line of the hand. It also assists in flexing the proximal phalanx. The Opponens minimi digiti draws forward the fifth metacarpal bone, so as to deepen the hollow of the palm. The Palmaris brevis corrugates the skin on the inner side of the palm of the hand.

KEY : Villages of Jaffa District

al Abbasiyya (36916)
Abu Kishk (36903)
Bayt Dajan (36919)
Biyar Adas (36901)
Fajja (36910)
al Haram (36898)
Ijlil al-Qibliyya (36900)
Ijlil al-Shamaliyya (36899)
al Jammasin al Gharbi (36907)
Jarisha (36908)
Kafr Ana (36917)
al Khayriyya (36914)
al Mas'udiyya (36911)
al Mirr (36905)
al Muwaylih (36904)
Rantiya (36913)
al Safiriyya (36920)
Salama (36912)
Saqiya (36915)
al Sawalima (36902)
al Shaykh Muwannis (36906)
Yazur (36918)

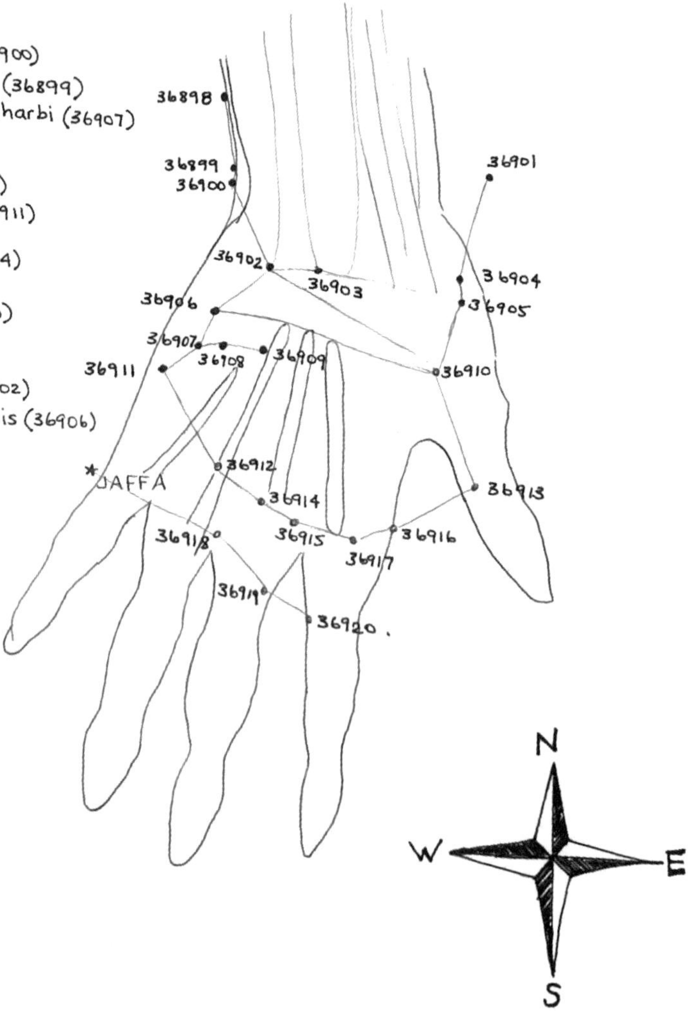

aifa and Joffa are at our mercy. We can starve them out. -Ben-Gurion to Sharett

37538 37539 37540 37541 37542 37543 37544 37545 37546 37547 37548 37549 37550 37551 37552 37553 37554 3
37556 37557 37558 37559 37560 37561 37562 37563 37564 37565 37566 37567 37568 37569 37570 37571 37572 375
37574 37575 37576 37577 37578 37579 37580 37581 37582 37583 37584 37585 37586 37587 37588 37589 37590
37591 37592 37593 37594 37595 37596 37597 37598 37599 37600 37601 37602 37603 37604 37605 37606 37607
37608 37609 37610 37611 37612 37613 37614 37615 37616 37617 37618 37619 37620 37621 37622 37623 3762
37624 37625 37626 37627 37628 37629 37630 37631 37632 37633 37634 37635 37636 37637 37638 37639 3764
37641 37642 37643 37644 37645 37646 37647 37648 37649 37650 37651 37652 37653 37654 37655 37656 37657
37658 37659 37660 37661 37662 37663 37664 37665 37666 37667 37668 37669 37670 37671 37672 37673 3767
37675 37676 37677 37678 37679 37680 37681 37682 37683 37684 37685 37686 37687 37688 37689 37690 376
37692 37693 37694 37695 37696 37697 37698 37699 37700 37701 37702 37703 37704 37705 37706 37707
37708 37709 37710 37711 37712 37713 37714 37715 37716 37717 37718 37719 37720 37721 37722 37723 37724 3772
37726 37727 37728 37729 37730 37731 37732 37733 37734 37735 37736 37737 37738 37739 37740 37741 377
37743 37744 37745 37746 37747 37748 37749 37750 37751 37752 37753 37754 37755 37756 37757 37758 377
37760 37761 37762 37763 37764 37765 37766 37767 37768 37769 37770 37771 37772 37773 37774 3777
37776 37777 37778 37779 37780 37781 37782 37783 37784 37785 37786 37787 37788 37789 37790 37791
37792 37793 37794 37795 37796 37797 37798 37799 37800 37801 37802 37803 37804 37805 37806 37807 378
37809 37810 37811 37812 37813 37814 37815 37816 37817 37818 37819 37820 37821 37822 37823 37824 37825 37826 37
37828 37829 37830 37831 37832 37833 37834 37835 37836 37837 37838 37839 37840 37841 37842 37843 37844 37845 3784
37847 37848 37849 37850 37851 37852 37853 37854 37855 37856 37857 37858 37859 37860 37861 37862 37863 37864 37865 3786
37867 37868 37869 37870 37871 37872 37873 37874 37875 37876 37877 37878 37879 37880 37881 37882 37883 37884 37885 37886
37887 37888 37889 37890 37891 37892 37893 37894 37895 37896 37897 37898 37899 37900 37901 37902 37903 37904 37905
37906 37907 37908 37909 37910 37911 37912 37913 37914 37915 37916 37917 37918 37919 37920 37921 37922 37923 37924 37925 37926
37927 37928 37929 37930 37931 37932 37933 37934 37935 37936 37937 37938 37939 37940 37941 37942 37943 37944 37945
37946 37947 37948 37949 37950 37951 37952 37953 37954 37955 37956 37957 37958 37959 37960 37961 37962 37963 37964
37965 37966 37967 37968 37969 37970 37971 37972 37973 37974 37975 37976 37977 37978 37979 37980 37981 37982 37983 3
37985 37986 37987 37988 37989 37990 37991 37992 37993 37994 37995 37996 37997 37998 37999 38000 38001 38002 38003
38004 38005 38006 38007 38008 38009 38010 38011 38012 38013 38014 38015 38016 38017 38018 38019 38020 38021 38022 38023 38024 38
38026 38027 38028 38029 38030 38031 38032 38033 38034 38035 38036 38037 38038 38039 38040 38041 38042 380
38044 38045 38046 38047 38048 38049 38050 38051 38052 38053 38054 38055 38056 38057 38058 38059 38060 38061
38062 38063 38064 38065 38066 38067 38068 38069 38070 38071 38072 38073 38074 38075 38076 38077 3807
38079 38080 38081 38082 38083 38084 38085 38086 38087 38088 38089 38090 38091 38092 38093 38094 38
38096 38097 38098 38099 38100 38101 38102 38103 38104 38105 38106 38107 38108 38109 38110 38111 38112 38113 381
38120 38121 38122 38123 38124 38125
38115 38116 38117 38118 38119 38120 38121 38122 38123 38124 38125 38126 38126 38127 38128 38129 38130 3813
38133 38134 38135 38136 38137 38138 38139 38140 38141 38142 38143 38144 38127 38128 38129 38130 38131 38132
38149 38150 38151 38152 38153 38154 38155 38156 38157 38158 3159 38160 38146 3815 38146 38147 38148
38161 38162 38163 38164 38165
38466 38467 38468 38469 38470 38471 38472 38473 38474 38475 38476 38477 38478 38479 3848
38481 38482 38483 38484 38485 38486 38487 38488 38489 38490 38491 38492 38493 38494 38495 384
38497 38498 38499 38500 38501 38502 38503 38504 38505 38506 38507 38508 38509 38510 38511 38512
38513 38514 38515 38516 38517 38578 38579 38880 38881 38882 38883 38884 38928 38929 38930
38887 38888 38889 38890 38891 38892 38893 38894 38894 38895 38896 38884 38885 38886
38901 38902 38903 38904 38905 38907 38908 38909 38910 38911 38912 38913 38914 38915 38897 38925 38926 389
38925 38926 38927 38928 38929 39141 39142 39143 39144 39145 39146 39147 38916 38898 38899 38
38936 38937 38138 38939 38940 38941 39148 39149 39150 39151 39152 39153 39 38920 38921 38917 38918 38919
38942 38943 38944 38945 38946 39155 39156 39157 39158 39159 39160 39 38930 38931 38932 38922 38933 38923 38924
38947 38948 38949 38950 38951 39162 39163 39164 39165 39166 39167 39008 39009 39010 39011 39012 38934 38
38952 38953 38954 38955 38956 39168 39169 39170 39171 39172 39173 39014 39015 39016 39017 39018 3901
38957 38958 38959 38960 38961 39174 39175 39176 39177 39178 39179 39020 39021 39022 39023 39024 390
38962 38963 38964 38965 38966 39180 39181 39182 39183 39184 39185 39026 39027 39028 39029 39030 3903
38966 38967 38968 38969 39186 39187 39188 39189 39190 39191 39032 39033 39034 39035 39036 39037
38971 38972 38973 38974 39192 39193 39194 39195 39196 39197 39038 39039 39040 39041 39042 39043
38975 38976 38977 38978 39198 39199 39200 39201 39202 39203 39044 39045 39046 39047 39048 39049 3905
38979 38980 38981 38982 39204 39205 39206 39207 39208 39209 39051 39052 39053 39054 39055 39056 3905
38984 38985 38986 38987 39210 39211 39212 39213 39214 39215 39058 39059 39060 39061 39062 39063 3906
38988 38989 38990 38991 39215 39216 39217 39218 39219 39065 39066 39067 39068 39069 39070 3907
38992 38993 38994 38995 39221 39222 39223 39224 39225 39071 39078 39079 39080 39081 39082 39083 3908
38996 38997 38998 39000 39226 39227 39228 39229 39230 39085 39086 39087 39088 39089 39090 39091 3909
38999 39000 39001 39230 39231 39232 39233 39234 39093 39094 39095 39096 39097 39098 39099 39
39002 39003 39004 39235 39236 39237 39238 39239 39101 39102 39103 39104 39105 39106 39107 39
39004 39005 39 39240 39241 39242 39243 39244 39109 39110 39111 39112 39113 39114 39115 39116 39
39246 39247 39248 39249 39118 39119 39120 39121 39122 39123 39124 3912
39249 39250 39251 39126 39127 39128 39129 39130 39131 39132
9252 39133 39134 39135 39136 39137 39138

"The destruction of Jaffa, the city and the port, will happen and it will be for the best. This city [...] is asking for destruction. [...] When Jaffa falls into hell I will not be among the mourners." - Ben-Gurion.

"every response to our dealing a hard blow at the [Palestinian] Arabs with many casualties is a blessing. This will increase the Arabs' fear [...] Haifa and Jaffa will be evacuated [by the Palestinians] because of hunger." - Ben-Gurion.

"I believe we should prevent their return ... We must settle Jaffa, Jaffa will become a Jewish city ... We must prevent at all costs their return."
- Ben-Gurion.

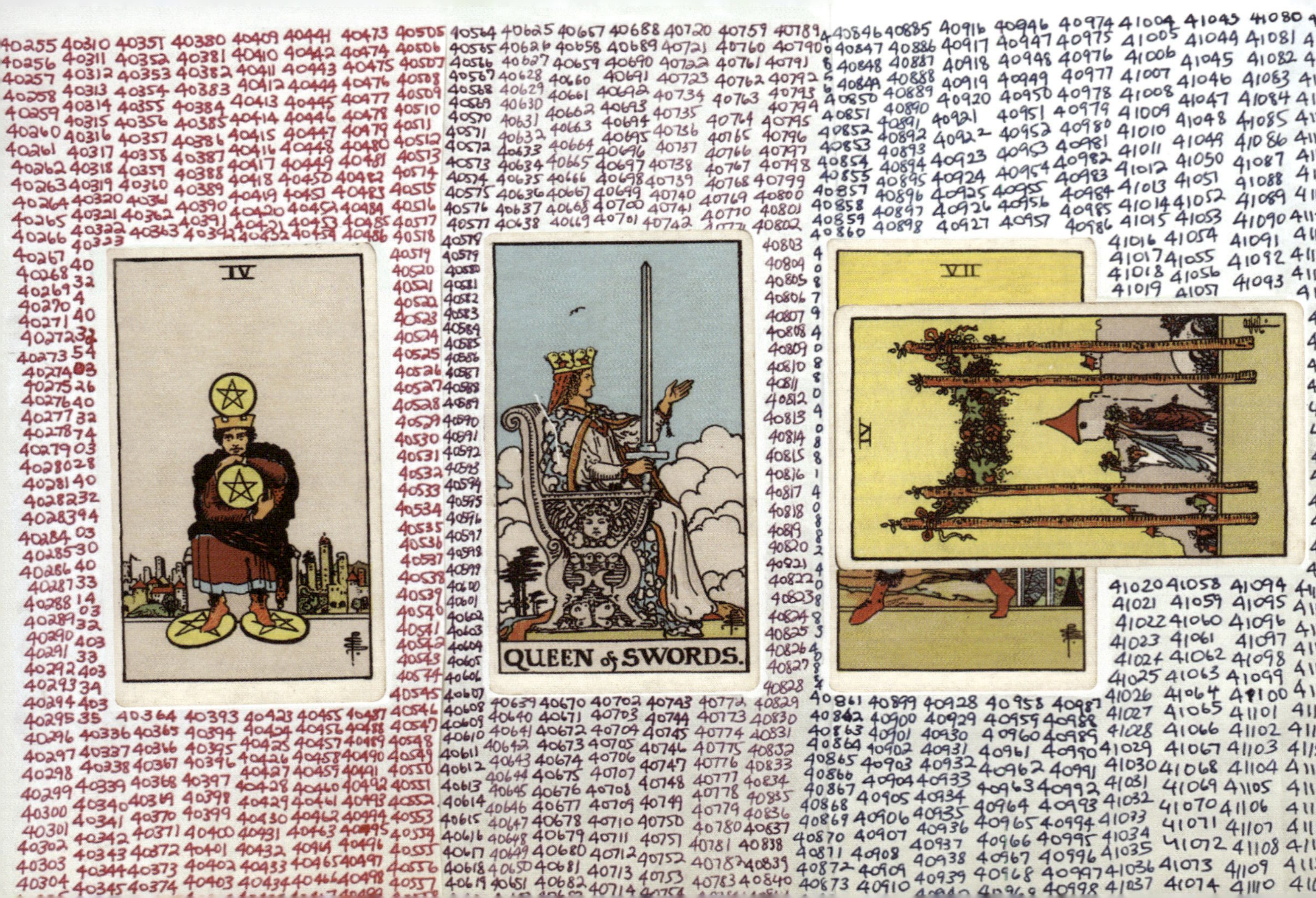
QUEEN of SWORDS.

In my last tarot reading, the ancestors show up.

Go back to the land, they say,
so that you can heal, so that we can heal.
They say it's not safe, to be discreet, to be careful.

We'll protect you. But you must go.

I build an altar.
Teta's diaries, their tiny mundanities,
letters to jiddo. Seashells and a wooden
box inlaid with mother-of-pearl,
her wedding ring in its mouth.
I ask the ancestors for guidance,
bring out the ouija board.

All they offer is "G-O."

I book a flight.

I find a direct flight.
Leaving on my grandparents' wedding anniversary,
arriving on 11/11: Make a wish.
It feels destined.

41163 41211 41266 41314 41331 41348 41366 41383 41402 41421 41441 41497 41549 41566 41583 41601 41620 41639 41658 41678 41728
41164 41212 41267 41315 41332 41349 41367 41384 41403 41422 41442 41498 41550 41567 41584 41602 41621 41640 41659 41679 41729
41165 41213 41268 41316 41333 41350 41308 41385 41404 41423 41443 41499 41551 41568 41585 41603 41622 41641 41660 41680 41730
41166 41214 41269 91317 41334 41351 41369 41386 41405 41424 41444 41500 41552 41569 41586 41604 41623 41642 41661 41681 41731
41167 41215 41270 41318 41335 41352 41270 41387 41406 41425 41445 41501 41553 41570 41587 41605 41624 41643 41662 41682 41732
41168 41216 41271 41319 41336 41353 41388 41407 41426 41446 41502 41554 41571 41588 41606 41625 41644 41663 41683 41733
41169 41217 41272 41320 41337 41354 41371 41389 41408 41427 41447 41503 41555 41572 41589 41607 41626 41645 41664 41684 41734
41170 41218 41273 41448 41504 41608 41627 41646 41665 41685 41735
41171 41219 41274 41449 41505 41686 41736
41172 41220 41275 41450 41506 41687 41737
41173 41221 41276 41451 41507 41688 41738
41174 41222 41277 41452 41508 41689 41739
41175 41223 41278 41453 41509 41690 41740
41176 41224 41279 41454 41510 41691 41741
41177 41225 41280 41455 41511 41692 41742
41178 41226 41281 41456 41512 41693 41743
41179 41227 41282 41457 41513 41694 41744
41180 41228 41283 41458 41514 41695 41745
41181 41229 41284 41459 41515 41696 41746
41182 41230 41285 41460 41516 41697 41747
41183 41231 41286 41461 41517 41698 41748
41184 41232 41287 41462 41518 41699 41749
41185 41233 41288 41463 41519 41700 41750
41186 41234 41289 41464 41520 41701 41751
41187 41235 41290 41465 41521 41702 41752
41188 41236 41291 41466 41522 41703 41753
41189 41237 41292 41467 41523 41704 41754
41190 41238 41293 41468 41524 41705 41755
41191 41239 41294 41469 41525 41706 41756
41192 41240 41295 41470 41526 41707 41757
41193 41241 41296 4471 41527 41708 41758
41194 41242 41297 41472 41528 41709 41759
41195 41243 41298 41473 41529 41710 41760
41196 41244 41299 41474 41530 4171 41761
41197 41245 41300 41475 41531 41712 41762
41198 41246 41301 41476 41532 41713 41763
41199 41247 41302 41477 41533 41714 41764
41200 41248 41303 41478 41534 41715 41765
41479 41535 41716 41766
41480 41536
41481 41537
41482
41483
4148A

أجداد
ANCESTORS

الحائكة
THE
WEAVER

41201 41249 41303 41485
41202 41250 41304 41321 41338 41355 41372 41390 41409 41428 41486 41538 41556 41573 41590 41609 41628 41647 41666 41717 41767
41203 41257 41305 41322 41339 41356 41373 41391 41410 41429 41487 41539 41557 41574 41591 41610 41629 41648 41667 41718 41768
41204 41258 41306 41323 41340 41357 41374 41392 41411 41430 41488 41540 41558 41575 41592 41611 41630 41649 41668 41719 41769
41205 41259 41307 41324 41341 41358 41375 41393 41412 41431 41489 41541 41559 41576 41593 41612 41631 41650 41669 41720 41710
41206 41260 41308 41325 41342 41359 41376 41394 41413 41432 41490 41542 41560 41577 41594 41613 41632 41651 41670 41721 41711
41207 41261 41309 41326 41343 41360 41371 41395 41414 41434 41491 41543 41561 41578 41595 41614 41633 41652 41671 41722 41712
41208 41262 41310 41327 41344 41361 41378 41396 41415 41435 41492 41544 41562 41579 41596 41665 41634 41653 41672 41723 41713
41263 41311 41328 41345 41362 41379 41397 41416 41436 41493 41545 41563 41580 41597 41616 41635 41654 41673 41724 41714
41264 41329 41346 41363 41380 41398 41417 41437 41494 41546 41564 41581 41598 41617 41636 41655 41674 41725 41715

41718 41719 41720 41721 41722 41723 41724 41725 41726 41727 41728 41729 41730 41731 41732 41733 41734 41735 41736 41737 41738 41739 41740 41741 41742 41743 41744 41745 41746 41747 41748 41749 41750 41751 41752 41753 41754

41755 41756 41757 41758 41759 41760 41761 41762 41763 41764 41765 41766 41767 41768 41769 41770 41771 41772 41773 41774 41775 41776 41777 41778 41779 41780 41781 41782 41783 41784 41785 41786 41787 41788 41789 41790

41791 41792 41793 41794 41795 41796 41797 41798 41799 41800 41801 41802 41803 4804 41805 41806 41807 41808 41809 41810 41811 41812 41813 41814 41815 41816 41817 41818 41819 41820 41821 41822 41823 41824 41825 41826

41827 41828 41829 41830 41831 41832 41833 41834 41835 41836 41837 41838 41839 41840 41841 41842 41843 41844 41845 41846 41847 41848 41849 41850 41851 41852 41853 41854 41855 41856 41857 41858 41859 41860 41861 41862

41863 41864 41865 41866 41867 41868 41869 41870 41871 41872 41873 41874 41875 41876 41877 41878 41879 41880 41881 41882 41883 41884 41885 41886 41887 41888 41889 41890 41891 41892 41893 41894 41895 41896 41897 41898 41899

41900 41901 41902 41903 41904 41905 41906 41907 41908 41909 41910 41911 41912 41913 41914 41915 41916 41917 41918 41919 41920 41921 41922 41923 41924 41925 41926 41927 41928 41929 41930 41931 41932 41933 41934 41935

41936 41937 41938 41939 41940 41941 41942 41943 41944 41945 41946 41947 41948 41949 41950 41951 41152 41953 41954 41955 41956 41957 41958 41959 41960 41961 41962 41963 41964 41965 41966 41967 41968 41969 41970 41971

41972 41973 41974 41975 41976 41977 41978 41979 41980 41981 41982 41983 41984 41985 41986 41987 41988 41989 41990 41991 41992 41993 41994 41995 41996 41997 41998 41999 42000 42001 42002 42003 42004 42005 42006 42007

42008 42009 42010 42011 42012 42013 42014 42015 42016 42017 42018 42019 42020 42021 42022 42023 42024 42025 42026 42027 42028 42029 42030 42031 42032 42033 42034 42035 42036 42037 42038 42039 42040 42041 42042 42043 42044

42045 42046 42047 42048 42049 42050 42051 42052 42053 42054 42055 42056 42057 42058 42059 42060 42061 42062 42063 42064 42065 42066 42067 42068 42069 42070 42071 42072 42073 42074 42075 42076 42077 42078 42079

42080 42081 42082 42083 42084 42085 42086 42087 42088 42089 42090 42091 42092 42093 42094 42095 42096 42097 42098 42099 42100 42101 42102 42103 42104 42105 42106 42107 42108 42109 42110 42111 42112 42113 42114 42115 42116

42117 42118 42119 42120 42121 42122 42123 42124 42125 42126 42127 42128 42129 42130 42131 42132 42133 42134 42135 42136 42137 42138 42139 42140 42141 42142 42143 42144 42145 42146 42147 42148 42149 42150 42151 42152 42153

42154 42155 42156 42157 42158 42159 42160 42161 42162 42163 42164 42165 42166 42167 42168 42169 42170 42171 42172 42173 42174 42175 42176 42177 42178 42179 42180 42181 42182 42183 42184 42185 42186 42187 42188 42189

42190 42191 42192 42193 42194 42195 42196 42197 42198 42199 42200 42201 42202 42203 42204 42205 42206 42207 42208 42209 42210 42211 42212 42213 42214 42215 42216 42217 42218 42219 42220 42221 42222 42223 42224 42225 42226 42227 42228

42229 42230 42231 42232 42233 42234 42235 42236 42237 42238 42239 42240 42241 42242 42243 42244 42245 42246 42247 42248 42249 42250 42251 42252 42253 42254 42255 42256 42257 42258 42259 42260 42261 42262 42263 42264 42265 42266

42267 42268 42269 42270 42271 42272 42273 42274 42275 42276 42277 42278 42279 42280 42281 42282 42283 42284 42285 42286 42287 42288 42289 42290 42291 42292 42293 42294 42295 42296 42297 42298 42299 42300 42301 42302 42303 42304

42305 42306 42307 42308 42309 42310 42311 42312 42313 42314 42315 42316 42317 42318 42319 42320 42321 42322 42323 42324 42325 42326 42327 42328 42329 42330 42331 42332 42333 42334 42335 42336 42337 42338 42339

العدد ٨١ - ٣٢٧٢

« السنة العشرون »

Vol. XX No 81 - 3272

صاحب الجريدة
عيسى داود العيسى
محرر الجريدة
يوسف حنا
مدير ادارة الجريدة
داود بندلي العيسى

فلسطين
FALASTIN

جريدة ، يومية سياسية ، اخبارية ، ادبية ، مصورة

الاشتراك
في يافا جنيه ودربع في فلسطين وشرق الاردن جنيه ونصف وفي الخارج عشرة دولارات اميركية

الاعلانات
اجرة السطر ٥٠ ملا . الاعلانات الشهرية والسنوية يتفق عليها مع الادارة

مركز ادارة وتحرير الجريدة
العجمي (البوابة) تلفون ٩٤ صندوق البريد ١٩٤

يافا الخميس في ١٨ حزيران سنة ١٩٣٦
Jaffa Thursday 18 June 1936
٢٩ ربيع الاول سنة ١٣٥٥

لا كان التحسين ولا التجميل اذا كانت هذه اساليبه !!

تزعم الحكومة لتبرير اقدامها على تشريد قسم كبير من سكان المدينة القديمة في يافا ، انها « تنوي القيام بمشروع لاجل فتح طرق ، وادخال تحسينات في المدينة القديمة » ... ولكن كل ظروف وملابسات الاقدام على هذا المشروع ينفي زعم الحكومة ، ويثبتين ان الغاية منه هو تحدي العرب ، وارهاقهم ، لا القيام بفتح طرق وادخال تحسينات .

فالظروف القاسية التي تجتازها البلاد لا تتسع لمشاريع اصلاح طرق ... وتحسين مدن ... لا سيما في المدينة القديمة .

ولم يسمع انسان من قبل ، ولعله سوف لا يوجد من يسمع من بعد ، ان اعمال اصلاح وتجميل المدن يشرع فيها بانذار ينزل على الاهالي من عال ... بواسطة الطيارات الحربية ، ويكون اول الانذار كما ذكرنا في مستهل كلامنا ، وآخره كما يلي :

« ان سكان المدينة القديمة المحافظين على القانون سوف لا يصيبهم ضرر ، ولكن اذا حصلت مقاومة فان العسكرية تستعمل القوة للقيام بالعمل » .

والبديهي يعهده الناس ان اعمال اصلاح وتجميل المدن لا يقاومها احد فما شأن مشروع تجميل ... المدينة القديمة وهذا التهديد العسكري ؟

وفي يافا حكومة محلية على رأسها المستر كروسبي ، اخصب عقلية عرفتها حكومة فلسطين ، واوسعها خبرة بشؤون البلاد فلماذا لم يصدر هذا الانذار من حكومة يافا ، وصدر من مطبعة .. الحكومة بالقدس خلواً من اي امضاء ؟ وحين تقوم الحكومات باشباه هذه المشاريع تمهد بها في العادة البلديات وهذه تتفاوض مع اصحاب البيوت المختصة في رفق ولين ، وفي تبادل مساومة واتفاق ، حتى اذا انتهوا الى قرار امهلتهم مدة تكفي لاخلاء المنازل وايجاد غيرها للأوام ، اما سكان ٢٤٠ منزلا في المدينة القديمة فقد انذرتهم الطيارات الحربية في الصباح الباكر ثم حددت لهم ميعاداً فقل لا يتجاوز الساعة السابعة مساء ، واخيراً وبعد ابتهالات وتضرعات مد الميعاد قليلا الى صباح اليوم .

بل ، لقد تحدثت الحكومة في انذارها عن التعويضات .. ولكننا لسنا نبحث مشكلة اصحاب البيوت والتعويض عليهم وانما نحن معنيون بمئات العائلات التي تسكن هذه المنطقة والتي يطلب منها اخلاء دورها ثم ايجاد غيرها في ساعات ثم يمتد الزمن الى يومين ويكون ذلك في ظرف اجمعت فيه البلاد على الاضراب العام الشامل فلا سبيل للتفاوض لايجار دور ولا لاستئجار وسائل النقل ومعظم سكان هذه المنازل بعد هذا كله من طبقة كريمة من الناس تتجمل على العيش بالقليل الذي تكد للحصول عليه وتلقى في ذلك عنتا لا يعلمه غير الله وليس بالسهل على هؤلاء حتى ان وجدوا دوراً ان يدفعوا ايجارها

يجب ان لا يفوت القارئ هذه البدعة الجديدة التي اصطنعتها حكومة فلسطين في مشاريع تحسين ... المدن وتجميلها ... والتي جعلتها تنذر سكان يافا وتل ابيب بترك نوافذ دورهم الزجاجية مفتوحة لان رجال الجيش سيتعهدون بانفسهم القيام باعمال التحسين والتجميل نسفا ... بالديناميت ... ونحن نترك للقارئ تقدير اثر استعمال الديناميت في المدينة القديمة التي تتلاصق دورها ، ويستند بعضها البعض ، فاذا نسف واحد منها ، جر معه

الديلي ميل تنتصر لعرب فلسطين
اوقفوا الهجرة وصونوا حقوق العرب

جاء من لندن ان جريدة الديلي ميل الشهورة عقدت في عددها الاخير مقالا عن شؤون فلسطين قالت فيه ما يلي :

لا يمكن السلام ان يخيم على فلسطين اذا بقي العرب يعتقدون ان الفناء يهددهم وكل مطلع على قضية فلسطين لا يستطيع ان ينكر حق العرب وان لهم حقوقا لا يمكن نكرانها وان السير هنري مكماهون قد تعهد لهم باسم الحكومة البريطانية سنة ١٩١٥ بجعل فلسطين لهم

وقد زارت فلسطين سنة ١٩٢٠ محكمة عسكرية درست اسباب الاضطرابات التي وقعت اذ ذاك وكتبت في تقريرها ما يلي : يعتقد العرب على العموم ان بريطانيا تريد ان تنشىء لهم مملكة عربية مستقلة تكون فلسطين داخلة فيها ولما مرت سنتان على منح الوعد للعرب جاء اللورد بلفور ومنح اليهود وعدا بانشاء وطن قومي لهم في فلسطين وكان الواجب عليه ان يذكر لهم الوعد الذي منح العرب فكان عمله لا ادب فيه ولا كياسة

ان العرب يرون انفسهم مضطرين الى النزوح من وطنهم امام المهاجرين اليهود فقد دخل فلسطين في ١٤ عاما اي الى سنة ١٩٣١ ما يقرب من ١٠٠ الف مهاجر واعلن المندوبون السامون ان هذا هو العدد الذي تمكنت البلاد من استيعابه اما في السنوات الاربع الاخيرة فقد دخل البلاد ٢٠٠ الف مهاجر اي ضعف ما تمكنت البلاد من استيعابه في ١٤ سنة من اجل هذا حمل العرب السلاح واذا سارعت حكومتنا الوطنية الى ادراك هذا السبب رأت ضرورة اجراء تعديل اساسي في سياستها الحاضرة في فلسطين وهذا خير عمل يمكننا ان نقوم به ان هذه السياسة غير عادلة لا لليهود ولا للعرب لانها تدفع اليهود الى زيادة هجرتهم مع ان الحالة لا تتطلب ذلك وسيصبح مستقبل فلسطين مظلما جداً .

لماذا لا تجيب الحكومة رغبة الزعماء العرب فتوقف الهجرة اليهودية الى ان تعلن اللجنة الملكية نتيجة بحثها في قضية فلسطين ؟

•••

The moment the confirmation comes in,
my creative floodgates open.

I feel the surge return. The urge to return.

I recite my script over and over like an incantation:

My Jewish husband, his birthright trip,

my father-in-law's kibbutz.

... Do I buy a burner phone?

Deactivate social media? Erase my hard drive?

Can I deprogram myself, encrypt my identity?

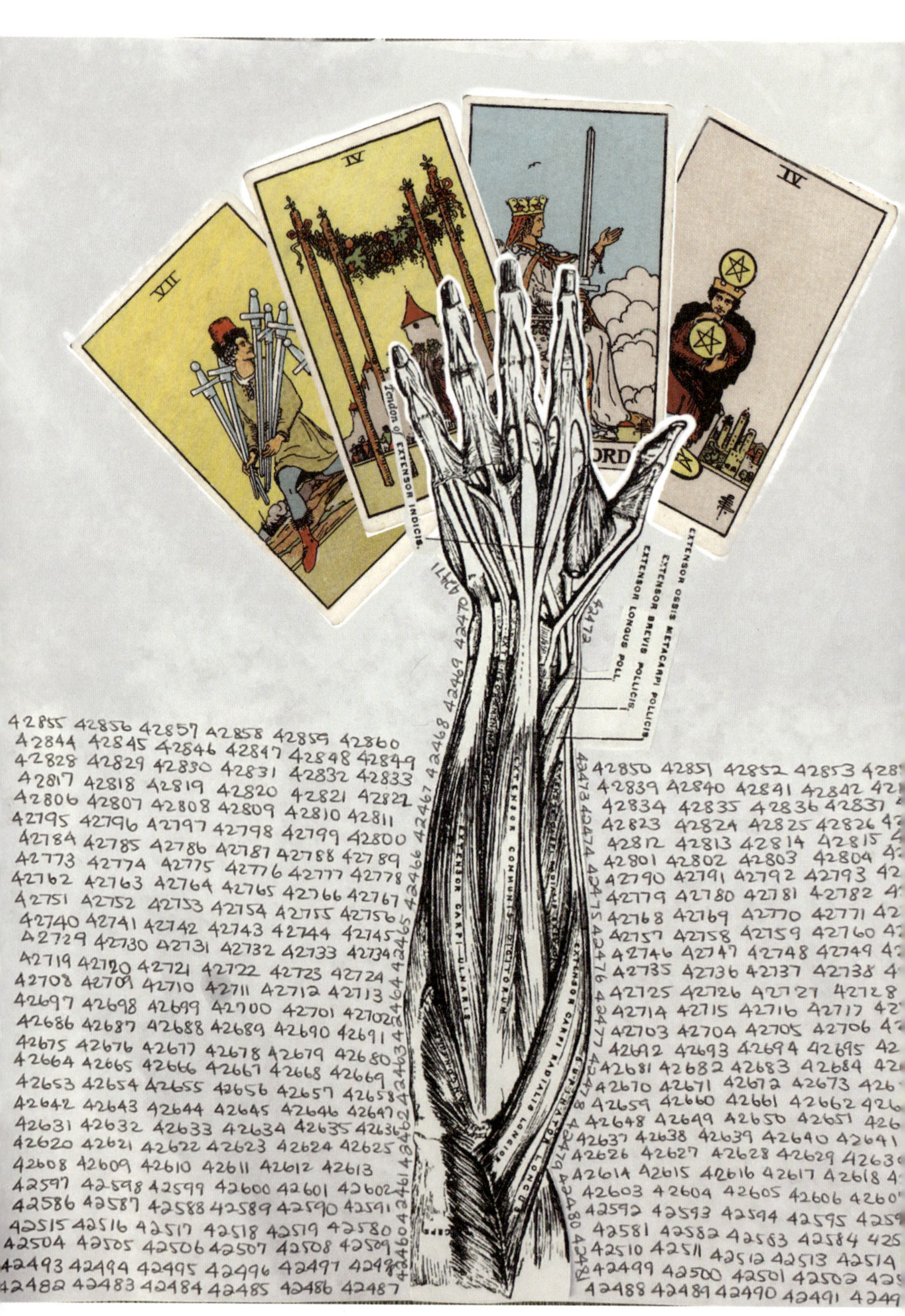

Tendon of EXTENSOR INDICIS.
EXTENSOR OSSIS METACARPI POLLICIS.
EXTENSOR BREVIS POLLICIS.
EXTENSOR LONGUS POLL.
EXTENSOR COMMUNIS DIGITORUM
EXTENSOR CARPI ULNARIS
EXTENSOR CARPI RADIALIS LONGIOR

61 42862 42863 42864 42865 42866 42867 42868 42869 42870
71 42872 42873 42874 42875 42876 42877 42878 42879 4288
81 42882 42883 42884 42885 42886 42887 42888 42889 42890
91 42892 42893 42894 42895 42896 42897 42898 42899
00 42901 42902 42903 42904 42905 42906 42907 42908 4290
910 42911 42912 42913 42914 42915 42916 42917 42918 42919
920 42921 42922 42923 42924 42925 42926 42927 42928 4
30 42931 42932 42933 42934 42935 42936 42937 42938
39 42940 42941 42942 42943 42944 42945 42946 42947
948 42949 42950 42951 42952 42953 42954 42955
56 42957 42958 42959 42960 42961 42962 42963 42964
965 42966 42967 42968 42969 42970 42971 42972
73 42974 42975 42976 42977 42978 42979 42980 42981 42982
83 42984 42985 42986 42987 42988 42989 42990 42991
92 42993 42994 42995 42996 42997 42998 42999 43000 43001
02 43003 43004 43005 43006 43007 43008 43009 43010 43011
12 43013 43014 43015 43016 43017 43018 43019 43020 43021 43022
23 43024 43025 43026 43027 43028 43029 43030 43031 43032
33 43034 43035 43036 43037 43038 43039 43040 43041 43042
43 43044 43045 43046 43047 43048 43049 43050 43051 43052
053 43054 43055 43056 43057 43058 43059 43060 43061 43062 43063 43064 43065 43066 43067 43068
069 43070 43071 43072 43073 43074 43075 43076 43077 43078 43079 43080 43081 43082 43083 43084
085 43086 43087 43088 43089 43090 43091 43092 43093 43094 43095 43096 43097 43098 43099 43100
01 43102 43103 43104 43105 43106 43107 43108 43109 43110 43111 43112 43113 43114 43115 43116 43117 43118
19 43120 43121 43122 43123 43124 43125 43126 43127 43128 43129 43130 43131 43132 43133 43134 43135 43136
137 43138 43139 43140 43141 43142 43143 43144 43145 43146 43147 43148 43149 43150 43151 43152 43153
54 43155 43156 43157 43158 43159 43160 43161 43162 43163 43164 43165 43166 43167 43168 43169 43170
71 43172 43173 43174 43175 43176 43177 43178 43179 43180 43181 43182 43183 43184 43185 43186 431
88 43189 43190 43191 43192 43193 43194 43195 43196 43197 43198 43199 43200 43201 43202 43203 43204
205 43206 43207 43208 43209 43210 43211 43212 43213 43214 43215 43216 43217 43218 43219 43220 43221
222 43223 43224 43225 43226 43227 43228 43229 43230 43231 43232 43233 43234 43235 43236 43237
38 43239 43240 43241 43242 43243 43244 43245 43246 43247 43248 43249 43250 43251 43252 43253 43254
255 43256 43257 43258 43259 43260 43261 43262 43263 43264 43265 43266 43267 43268 43269 43270 43271
72 43273 43274 43275 43276 43277 43278 43279 43280 43281 43282 43283 43284 43285 43286 43287 43288
89 43290 43291 43292 43293 43294 43295 43296 43297 43298 43299 43300 43301 43302 43303 43304 43305 43306
07 43308 43309 43310 43311 43312 43313 43314 43315 43316 43317 43318 43319 43320 43321 43322 43323 43324
325 43326 43327 43328 43329 43330 43331 43332 43333 43334 43335 43336 43337 43338 43339 43340 43341
342 43343 43344 43345 43346 43347 43348 43349 43350 43351 43352 43353 43354 43355 43356 43357
358 43359 43360 43361 43362 43363 43364 43365 43366 43367 43368 43369 43370 43371 43372
373 43374 43375 43376 43377 43378 43379 43380 43381 43382 43383 43384 43385 43386 43387
88 43389 43390 43391 43392 43393 43394 43395 43396 43397 43398 43399 43400 43401 4
403 43404 43405 43406 43407 43408 43409 43410 43411 43412 43413 43414 43415 43416 43417
18 43419 43420 43421 43422 43423 43424 43425 43426 43427 43428 43429 43430 43431
432 43433 43434 43435 43436 43437 43438 43439 43440 43441 43442 43443 43444 43445

September 13, 2023

30 years after the Oslo Accord was signed in 1993.

At the time there were just over 110,000 Jewish settlers living in the West Bank. Now there are more than 700,000.

Settlements are seen as illegal under international law.[10]

September 21, 2023

I tell my friend about the trip. In many years of friendship, it might be the first time I've had the courage to express my desire to visit.

10 Yolande Knell, "Oslo Accords: 30 years of lost Palestinian hopes," BBC.com, Sep. 12, 2023.

Hamas launched incendiary balloons into Israeli occupied land, killing over 200 people and injuring over 1,000.[11]

It is being reported as "unprovoked."

Hamas, in turn, claimed this attack was in response to an attack on worshippers at a historically and culturally significant mosque on a holy day—in which Israeli soldiers:

threw stun grenades,

shot sponge-tipped bullets,

tear-gassed,

abducted,

indiscriminately beat Muslim worshippers

—including elderly people and women—

with batons and rifle butts[12]

and then blocked medical professionals from providing aid.

Question: Does Palestine have a right to defend itself?

11 Yaniv Kubovich, "IDF Ordered Hannibal Directive on October 7 to Prevent Hamas Taking Soldiers Captive," Haaretz, July 7, 2024. Robert Inlakesh, "How Israel Killed Its Own Soldiers, Blamed Hamas and Violated the Ceasefire Again," *The Palestine Chronicle,* October 21, 2025.

12 "Israel: UN expert condemns brutal attacks on Palestinians at Al-Aqsa Mosque," United Nations, April 6, 2023.

I wonder what provocation would look like if not decades of:

Threats

Gaslighting

Blocking trade

Destruction of property

Discrimination

Land theft

Destroying crops

Assault

Bombing

Air raids

Imprisonment

Apartheid

Genocide

Blocking access to roads, supplies, food, medical aid, jobs, free movement, free speech, clean water, electricity, media coverage, voting rights

October 7, 2023

October 8, 2023

My friend asks what I'm planning on doing about my trip. I say I'll likely have to cancel it, but I've pushed it back to December and will see how the next few months play out. She doesn't respond.

This is the last time I speak with her.

October 10, 2023

My friend changes her profile picture on social media to feature an Israeli flag. She has kept it there since.

Israel has declared “war”—

As if there could be a war between a country and the people within it.

As if there could be a war between one army and the people—

and already Israel has matched the body count, killing and injuring just as many Palestinians in Gaza.

An eye for an eye.

:

A body for a body.

Biden announced that the US will “not ever fail to have her [Israel’s] back.”[13]

As if that wasn’t clear by the billions of dollars in arms supplied to Israel by the US.[14]

Does Israel have the right to defend itself
against the people it is oppressing?

What does it mean to defend oneself on occupied land?

---

13 Alistair Bunkall, “Hostages taken as Hamas launches biggest attack on Israel in years - with strikes hitting Gaza in response,” *Sky News,* Oct. 8, 2023.

14 Brendan Rascius, “US aircraft carrier sent toward Israel is world’s largest warship. What can it do?” *Miami Herald,* Oct. 12, 2023.

Netanyahu vows to turn Gaza into 'rubble'[15]

15 James Clark Reynolds and Gina Kalsi, "Netanyahu vows to turn Gaza into 'rubble': Israeli PM tells Palestinians to 'leave now' and says Hamas will pay an 'unprecedented price' after they kidnapped grans and launched shocking attack that has left hundreds dead on both sides," *Daily Mail*, Oct. 10, 2023.

463
66
463 463
67 70
463 463 463
68 71 73
463 463 463 463
69 72 74 75
463
76
463 463 463 463
77 81 84 86
463 463 463
78 82 85
463 463
79 83
463
80

463
87
463 463
88 91
463 463 463
89 92 94
463 463 463 463
90 93 95 96
463
97
463 464 464 464
98 02 05 07
463 464 464
99 03 06
464 464
00 04
464
01

464
08
464 464
09 12
464 464 464
10 13 15
464 464 464 464
11 14 16 17
464
18
464 464 464 464
19 23 26 28
464 464 464
20 24 27
464 464
21 25
464
22

464
29
464 464
30 33
464 464 464
31 34 36
464 464 464 464
32 35 37 38
464
39
464 464 464 464
40 44 47 49
464 464 464
41 45 48
464 464
42 46
464
43

464
50
464 464
51 54
464 464 464
52 55 57
464 464 464 464
53 56 58 59
464
60
464 464 464 464
61 65 68 70
464 464 464
62 66 69
464 464
63 67
464
64

464
71
464 464
72 75
464 464 464
73 76 78
464 464 464 464
74 77 79 80
464
81
464 464 464 464
82 86 89 91
464 464 464
83 87 90
464 464
84 88
464
85

464
92
464 464
93 96
464 464 464
94 97 99
464 464 465 465
95 98 00 01
465
02
465 465 465 465
03 07 10 12
465 465 465
04 08 11
465 465
05 09
465
06

465
13
465 465
14 17
465 465 465
15 18 20
465 465 465 465
16 19 21 22
465
23
465 465 465 465
24 28 31 33
465 465 465
25 29 32
465 465
26 30
465
27

465
34
465 465
35 38
465 465 465
36 39 41
465 465 465 465
37 40 42 43
465
44
465 465 465 465
45 49 52 54
465 465 465
46 50 53
465 465
47 51
465
48

465
55
465 465
56 59
465 465 465
57 60 62
465 465 465 465
58 61 63 64
465
65
465 465 465 465
66 70 73 75
465 465 465
67 71 74
465 465
68 72
465
69

465
76
465 465
77 80
465 465 465
78 81 83
465 465 465 465
79 82 84 85
465
86
465 465 465 465
87 91 94 96
465 465 465
88 92 95
465 465
89 93
465
90

465
97
465 466
98 01
465 466 466
99 02 04
466 466 466 466
00 03 05 06
466
07
466 466 466 466
08 12 15 17
466 466 466
09 13 16
466 466
10 14
466
11

466
18
466 466
19 22
466 466 466
20 23 25
466 466 466 466
21 24 26 27
466
28
466 466 466 466
29 33 36 38
466 466 466
30 34 37
466 466
31 35
466
32

466
39
466 466
40 43
466 466 466
41 44 46
466 466 466 466
42 45 47 48
466
49
466 466 466 466
50 54 57 59
466 466 466
51 55 58
466 466
52 56
466
53

466
60
466 466
61 64
466 466 466
62 65 67
466 466 466 466
63 66 68 69
466
70
466 466 466 466
71 75 78 80
466 466 466
72 76 79
466 466
73 77
466
74

466
81
466 466
82 85
466 466 466
83 86 88
466 466 466 466
84 87 89 90
466
91
466 466 466 467
92 96 99 01
466 466 467
93 97 00
466 466
94 98
466
95

467
02
467 467
03 06
467 467 467
04 07 09
467 467 467 467
05 08 10 11
467
12
467 467 467 467
13 17 20 22
467 467 467
14 18 21
467 467
15 19
467
16

467
23
467 467
24 27
467 467 467
25 28 30
467 467 467 467
26 29 31 32
467
33
467 467 467 467
34 38 41 43
467 467 467
35 39 42
467 467
36 40
467
37

467
34
467 467
35 38
467 467 467
36 39 41
467 467 467 467
37 40 42 43
467
44
467 467 467 467
45 49 52 54
467 467 467
46 50 53
467 467
47 51
467
48

467
55
467 467
56 59
467 467 467
57 60 62
467 467 467 467
58 61 63 64
467
65
467 467 467 467
66 70 73 75
467 467 467
67 71 74
467 467
68 72
467
69

467
76
467 467
77 80
467 467 467
78 81 83
467 467 467 467
79 82 84 85
467
86
467 467 467 467
87 91 94 96
467 467 467
88 92 95
467 467
89 93
467
90

467
97
467 468
98 01
467 468 468
99 02 04
468 468 468 468
00 03 05 06
468
07
468 468 468 468
08 12 15 17
468 468 468
09 13 16
468 468
10 14
468
11

468
18
468 468
19 22
468 468 468
20 23 25
468 468 468 468
21 24 26 27
468
28
468 468 468 468
29 33 36 38
468 468 468
30 34 37
468 468
31 35
468
32

468
39
468 468
40 43
468 468 468
41 44 46
468 468 468 468
42 45 47 48
468
49
468 468 468 468
50 54 57 59
468 468 468
51 55 58
468 468
52 56
468
53

468
60
468 468
61 64
468 468 468
62 65 67
468 468 468 468
63 66 68 69
468
70
468 468 468 468
71 75 78 80
468 468 468
72 76 79
468 468
73 77
468
74

468
81
468 468
82 85
468 468 468
83 86 88
468 468 468 468
84 87 89 90
468
91
468 468 468 469
92 96 99 01
468 468 469
93 97 00
468 468
94 98
468
95

469
02
469 469
03 06
469 469 469
04 07 09
469 469 469 469
05 08 10 11
469
12
469 469 469 469
13 17 20 22
469 469 469
14 18 21
469 469
15 19
469
16

469
23
469 469
24 27
469 469 469
25 28 30
469 469 469 469
26 29 31 32
469
33
469 469 469 469
34 38 41 43
469 469 469
35 39 42
469 469
36 40
469
37

469
44
469 469
45 48
469 469 469
46 49 51
469 469 469 469
47 50 52 53
469
54
469 469 469 469
55 59 62 64
469 469 469
56 60 63
469 469
57 61
469
58

469
65
469 469
66 69
469 469 469
67 70 72
469 469 469 469
68 71 73 74
469
75
469 469 469 469
76 80 83 85
469 469 469
77 81 84
469 469
78 82
469
79

469
76
469 469
77 80
469 469 469
78 81 83
469 469 469 469
79 82 84 85
469
86
469 469 469 469
87 91 94 96
469 469 469
88 92 95
469 469
89 93
469
90

469
97
469 470
98 01
469 470 470
99 02 04
470 470 470 470
00 03 05 06
470
07
470 470 470 470
08 12 15 17
470 470 470
09 13 16
470 470
10 14
470
11

470
18
470 470
19 22
470 470 470
20 23 25
470 470 470 470
21 24 26 27
470
28
470 470 470 470
29 33 36 38
470 470 470
30 34 37
470 470
31 35
470
32

470
39
470 470
40 43
470 470 470
41 44 46
470 470 470 470
42 45 47 48
470
49
470 470 470 470
50 54 57 59
470 470 470
51 55 58
470 470
52 56
470
53

470
60
470 470
61 64
470 470 470
62 65 67
470 470 470 470
63 66 68 69
470
80
470 470 470 470
70 74 77 79
470 470 470
71 75 78
470 470
72 76
470
73

<<frozen>>

<<checked out>>

<<doom scrolling>> >>>

>>remind your body that you are safe:

- Drink a glass of water
- Make eye contact with someone
- Interlace your fingers behind your head and lean back, move your eyes to the right and hold for 15 seconds, move your eyes to the left and hold for 15 seconds
- Stand barefoot in grass
- Sit in a sunny spot and breathe slowly
- Move your body
- Eat a crunchy snack
- Hum low for one minute, feel the vibration in your chest
- Lengthen your exhale by breathing out through pursed lips, like you're blowing out a candle

Sometimes our bodies need reminding we're safe.

Sometimes our minds need encouragement to come back to the body.

Sometimes the things we are witnessing are too much to bear.

47540 47541 47542 47543 47544 47545 47546 47547 47548 47549 47550 47551 47552 47553 47554

47508 47509 47510 47511 47512 47513 47514 47515 47516 47517 47518 47519 47520 47521 47522 4752

47477 47478 47479 47480 47481 47482 47483 47484 47485 47486 47487 47488 47489 47490 47491

47446 47447 47448 47449 47450 47451 47452 47453 47454 47455 47456 47457 47458 47459 47460

47414 47415 47416 47418 47419 47420 47421 47422 47423 47424 47425 47426 47427 47428 4742

47367 47368 47369 47370 47371 47372 47373 47374 47375 47376 47377 47378 47379 47380 47381

47336 47337 47338 47339 47340 47341 47342 47343 47344 47345 47346 47347 47348 47349 4735

47304 47305 47306 47307 47308 47309 47310 47311 47312 47313 47314 47315 47316 47317 4731

47273 47274 47275 47276 47277 47278 47279 47280 47281 47282 47283 47284 47285 47286 4728

47243 47244 47245 47246 47247 47248 47249 47250 47251 47252 47253 47254 47255 47256 47

47211 47212 47213 47214 47215 47216 47217 47218 47219 47220 47221 47222 47223 47224 47225 47226

47178 47179 47180 47181 47182 47183 47184 47185 47186 47187 47188 47189 47190 47191 47192 47193

47146 47147 47148 47149 47150 47151 47152 47153 47154 47155 47156 47157 47158 47159 47160 47161

47112 47113 47114 47115 47116 47117 47118 47119 47120 47121 47122 47123 47124 47125 47126 47127 4712

47081 47082 47083 47084 47085 47086 47087 47088 47089 47090 47091 47092 47093 4709

47095 47096 47097 47098 47099 47100 47101 47102 47103 47104 47105 47106 47107 47108 47109 47110 4

47129 47130 47131 47132 47133 47134 47135 47136 47137 47138 47139 47140 47141 47142 47143 47144 4714

47162 47163 47164 47165 47166 47167 47168 47169 47170 47171 47172 47173 47174 47175 47176 47177

47194 47195 47196 47197 47198 47199 47200 47201 47202 47203 47204 47205 47206 47207 47208 47209 47

47227 47228 47229 47230 47231 47232 47233 47234 47235 47236 47237 47238 47239 47240 4724 1472

47258 47259 47260 47261 47262 47263 47264 47265 47266 47267 47268 47269 47270 47271 47272

47288 47289 47290 47291 47292 47293 47294 47295 47296 47297 47298 47299 47300 47301 47302 473

47319 47320 47321 47322 47323 47324 47325 47326 47327 47328 47329 47330 47331 47332 47333 47335

47351 47352 47353 47354 47355 47356 47357 47358 47359 47360 47361 47362 47363 47364 47365 47366

47382 47383 47384 47385 47386 47387 47388 47389 47390 47391 47392 47393 47394 47395 47396 47397

47398 47399 47400 47401 47402 47403 47404 47405 47406 47407 47408 47409 47410 47411 47412 47413

47430 47431 47432 47433 47434 47435 47436 47437 47438 47439 47440 47441 47442 47443 47444 47445

7461 47462 47463 47464 47465 47466 47467 47468 47469 47470 47471 47472 47473 47474 47475 474

7492 47493 47494 47495 47496 47497 47498 47499 47500 47501 47502 47503 47504 47505 47506 47507

7524 47525 47526 47527 47528 47529 47530 47531 47532 47533 47534 47535 47536 47537 47538 47539

871 47872 47873 47874 47875 47876 47877 47878 47879 47880 47881 47882 47883 47884 47885 47886 47887
840 47841 47842 47843 47844 47845 47846 47847 47848 47849 47850 47851 47852 47853 47854
808 47809 47810 47811 47812 47813 47814 47815 47816 47817 47818 47819 47820 47821 47822 47823
777 47778 47779 47780 47781 47782 47783 47784 47785 47786 47787 47788 47789 47790 47791
746 47747 47748 47749 47750 47751 47752 47753 47754 47755 47756 47757 47758 47759 47760 47761
713 47714 47715 47716 47717 47718 47719 47720 47721 47722 47723 47724 47725 47726 47727 47728 4772
680 47681 47682 47683 47684 47685 47686 47687 47688 47689 47690 47691 47692 47693 47694 47695
649 47650 47651 47652 47653 47654 47655 47656 47657 47658 47659 47660 47661 47662 47663
617 47618 47619 47620 47621 47622 47623 47624 47625 47626 47627 47628 47629 47630 47631 47632
584 47585 47586 47587 47588 47589 47590 47591 47592 47593 47594 47595 47596 47597 47598 47599
555 47556 47557 47558 47559 47560 47561 47562 47563 47564 47565 47566 47567 47568 47569

7570 47571 47572 47573 47574 47575 47576 47577 47578 47579 47580 47581 47582 47582 47583
600 47601 47602 47603 47604 47605 47606 47607 47608 47609 47610 47611 47612 47613 47614 47615 47616
633 47634 47635 47636 47637 47638 47639 47640 47641 47642 47643 47644 47645 47646 47647 47648
664 47665 47666 47667 47668 47669 47670 47671 47672 47673 47674 47675 47676 47677 47678 47679
696 47697 47698 47699 47700 47701 47702 47703 47704 47705 47706 47707 47708 47709 47710 47711 47712
730 47731 47732 47733 47734 47735 47736 47737 47738 47739 47740 47741 47742 47743 47744 47745
762 47763 47764 47765 47766 47767 47768 47769 47770 47771 47772 47773 47774 47775 47776
792 47793 47794 47795 47796 47797 47798 47799 47800 47801 47802 47803 47804 47805 47806 47807
824 47825 47826 47827 47828 47829 47830 47831 47832 47833 47834 47835 47836 47837 47838 47839
855 47856 47857 47858 47859 47860 47861 47862 47863 47864 47865 47866 47867 47868 47869 47870
888 47889 47890 47891 47892 47893 47894 47895 47896 47897 47898 47899 47900 47901 47902 47903 47904

When 45 people in your family are killed,
when your bloodline is obliterated,
when 850 bloodlines are obliterated
with weapons your taxes bought,
what can I say except, I'm *lucky*
to have been removed
from my homeland.
Protected from ever returning
to the houses lost, the family fractured;
from the language that would have me labeled,
fired, arrested;
from the resources that would certainly
be used against me; from the land full
of mines and skies of phosphorus clouds.

It's terrible what's happening, they say,
and when they ask, *Do you have family
there?* I can say, *No, I'm lucky.*

They're all dead.

Prop. and Responsible Editor

I. D. Elissa

Jaffa

P. O. B. 194

Tel. No. 94

فلسطين
La Palestine

صاحب الجريدة ومديرها المسؤول

عيسى داود العيسى

يافا

صندوق البريد ١٩٤

التلفون ٩٤

Jaffa, March 25th, 1925. — Wednesday — الاربعا — يافا في ٢٥ آذار سنة ١٩٢٥

— J'ACCUSE !

"FOR WE WRESTLE NOT AGAINST FLESH AND BLOOD, BUT AGAINST PRINCIPALITIES AND POWERS,
T THE RULERS OF THE DARKNESS OF THIS WORLD, AGAINST SPIRITUAL WICKEDNESS IN HIGH PLACES"

Ephesians VI. 12.

The British Parliament, the people of the British Empire, and the League of Nations, to demand of the Government of Palestine, that the words of the ROYAL PROCLAMATION read in Jerusalem and Haifa in July 1920 by the High Commissioner for Palestine; and those of the ANGLO-FRENCH DECLARATION of November 1918, issued in Palestine by Lord Allenby, shall be respected, viz :-

a. THE ROYAL PROCLAMATION

"TO THE PEOPLE OF PALESTINE"

« I desire to assure you of the absolute imprtiality with which the duties of the Mandatory Power will be carried out, and of the determination of My Government to respect the rights of every race and every creed represented among you.....»

GEORGE R. and I.

b. THE ANGLO-FRENCH DECLARATION

Britain into its service so as to assure world control for itself... We are actually facing a gigantic effort on the part of Jewish international imperialism to win the game; it is the victorious undertaking of pan-Judaism. Far from being favoured, as England has secretly imagined, she is the first to be menaced....

To attain that general confidence without which success cannot be reached, Zionism should have the courage to disavow and rid itself of certain adherents... whose secret aim is to make Palestine the headquarters of International pan-Judaism.... the aim is to establish a national home to serve as an effective center from which the movements and evolution of Jewish imperialism - economic and Messianic - can be directed.

Saint Germain guaranteed the Jews of Oriental Europe the RIGHT to form national minorities and recognised the RIGHT to form a State within a State...

If the reconstitulated Jewish people wishes to be ranked as a nation among nations, it is the duty and interest of all to help; if it intends to organise internationally so as to ruin and dominate other nations, it is the duty of these to arise and not permit it to do so ».

(From " Le problème Juif " by Georges Batault, Paris.)

Zionist Colonisation

In spite of Zionist attempts to acquire large tracts of land, it is open to doubt if these will be successfully colonised. Zionist propaganda has created the legend of the Jew going back to the land in Palestine. It is not generally known that the

them on their fields they wi succeed in living the life of in deni persons. (1)

The Balfour (1) Declaration

We now know that the four Declaration was mer modified version of a for decided upon and drafte the Zionist Committee. C dering all things, it is h surprising that the Arab trust both the origin and i tion of the Balfour Declara and refuse to recognis binding upon them a pact tered into between the R Government and the Zio and to which the Arabs not a party.

(1) Fortnightly Review Jan. 19 Captain Chisholm Dunbar Bro

sraeli evacuation order of 1.1 million
in northern Gaza will cause chao
Imagine The Terror & Horror Jaffa Palestinians Must Have F
When They Were PUSHED INTO THE SEA, May 1948

The call to prayer resonates in my joints,
a sound my body knew in another life.
I call to my grandparents, great
grandparents, feel them hold my feet
to the earth, heavy, their blood
courses through my corps.

Inherited trauma may be real in my body,
but so is inherited resilience.
I've never prayed but find myself
kneeling in the grass. Ancestral
wisdom sun-baked into my bones,
mournful wail that escapes my mouth,
the support of the earth beneath my forehead,
third eye buzzing with the voices of thousands

thousands
thousands thousands
thousands thousands thousands thousands
thousands thousands thousands thousands

thousands thousands thousands thousands
thousands thousands thousands thousands thousands
thousands thousands thousands thousands thousands
thousands thousands thousands thousands thousands thousands thou
thousandssands thousands thousands thousands thousands thousands
thousands thousands thousands thousands thousands thousands

thousands thousands thousands thousands thousands thousands

thousands thousands thousands thousands thousands thousands
thousands thousands thousands thousands thousands thousands
thousands thousands thousands thousands thousands thousands

thousands thousands thousands thousands thousands thousands

48151 48152 48153 48154 48155 48156 48157 48158 48159 48160 48161 48162 48163 48164 48165 48166 48167 48168 48169 48170 48171 48172 48173 48174 48175 48176 48177 48178 48179 48180 48181 48182 48183 48184 48185 48186 48187 48188 48189 48190 48191

48192 48193 48194 48195 48196 48197 48198 48199 48200 48201 48202 48203 48204 48205 48206 48207 48208 48209 48210 48211 48212 48213 48214 48215 48216 48217 48218 48219 48220 48221 48222 48223 48224 48225 48226 48227 48228 48229 48230 48231 48232 48233

48234 48235 48236 48237 48238 48239 48240 48241 48242 48243 48244 48245 48246 48247 48248 48249 48250 48251 48252 48253 48254 48255 48256 48257 48258 48259 48260 48261 48262 48263 48264 48265 48266 48267 48268 48269 48270 48271 48272 48273 48274

48275 48276 48277 48278 48279 48280 48281 48282 48283 48284 48285 48286 48287 48288 48289 48290 48291 48292 48293 48294 48295 48296 48297 48298 48299 48300 48301 48302 48303 48304 48305 48306 48307 48308 48309 48310 48311 48312 48313 48314 48315

48316 48317 48318 48319 48320 48321 48322 48323 48324 48325 48326 48327 48328 48329 48330 48331 48332 48333 48334 48335 48336 48337 48338 48339 48340 48341 48342 48343 48344 48345 48346 48347 48348 48349 48350 48351 48352 48353 48354 48355 48356 48357 48358

48359 48360 48361 48362 48363 48364 48365 48366 48367 48368 48369 48370 48371 48372 48373 48374 48375 48376 48377 48378 48379 48380 48381 48382 48383 48384 48385 48386 48387 48388 48389 48390 48391 48392 48393 48394 48395 48396 48397 48398 48399 48400

48401 48402 48403 48404 48405 48406 48407 48408 48409 48410 48411 48412 48413 48414 48415 48416 48417 48418 48419 48420 48421 48422 48423 48424 48425 48426 48427 48428 48429 48430 48431 48432 48433 48434 48435 48436 48437 48438 48439 48440 48441 48442 48443

48444 48445 48446 48447 48448 48449 48450 48451 48452 48453 48454 48455 48456 48457 48458 48459 48460 48461 48462 48463 48464 48465 48466 48467 48468 48469 48470 48471 48472 48473 48474 48475 48476 48477 48478 48479 48480 48481 48482 48483

48484 48485 48486 48487 48488 48489 48490 48491 48492 48493 48494 48495 48496 48497 48498 48499 48500 48501 48502 48503 48504 48505 48506 48507 48508 48509 48510 48511 48512 48513 48514 48515 48516 48517 48518 48519 48520 48521

48522 48523 48524 48525 48526 48527 48528 48529 48530 48531 48532 48533 48534 48535 48536 48537 48538 48539 48540 48541 48542 48543 48544 48545 48546 48547 48548 48549 48550 48551 48552 48553 48554 48555 48556 48557 48558 48559 48560 48561 48562 48563 48564

48565 48566 48567 48568 48569 48570 48571 48572 48573 48574 48575 48576 48577 48578 48579 48580 48581 48582 48583 48584 48585 48586 48587 48588 48589 48590 48591 48592 48593 48594 48595 48596 48597 48598 48599 48600 48601 48602 48603 48604 48605

48606 48607 48608 48609 48610 48611 48612 48613 48614 48615 48616 48617 48618 48619 48620 48621 48622 48623 48624 48625 48626 48627 48628 48629 48630 48631 48632 48633 48634 48635 48636 48637 48638 48639 48640 48641 48642 48643 48644 48645 48646 48647 48648 48649 48650 48651 48652

48653 48654 48655 48656 48657 48658 48659 48660 48661 48662 48663 48664 48665 48666 48667 48668 48669 48670 48671 48672 48673 48674 48675 48676 48677 48678 48679 48680 48681 48682 48683 48684 48685 48686 48687 48688 48689 48690 48691 48692 48693 48694 48695 48696 48697 48698 48699

48700 48701 48702 48703 48704 48705 48706 48707 48708 48709 48710 48711 48712 48713 48714 48715 48716 48717 48718 48719 48720 48721 48722 48723 48724 48725 48726 48727 48728 48729 48730 48731 48732 48733 48734 48735 48736 48737 48738 48739 48740 48741 48742 48743 48744 48745 48746

48747 48748 48749 48750 48751 48752 48753 48754 48755 48756 48757 48758 48759 48760 48761 48762 48763 48764 48765 48766 48767 48768 48769 48770 48771 48772 48773 48774 48775 48776 48777 48778 48779 48780 48781 48782 48783 48784 48785 48786 48787 48788 48789 48790 48791 48792 48793 48794 48795 48796

48797 48798 48799 48800 48801 48802 48803 48804 48805 48806 48807 48808 48809 48810 48811 48812 48813 48814 48815 48816 48817 48818 48819 48820 48821 48822 48823 48824 48825 48826 48827 48828 48829 48830 48831 48832 48833 48834 48835 48836 48837 48838 48839 48840 48841 48842 48843

48844 48845 48846 48847 48848 48849 48850 48851 48852 48853 48854 48855 48856 48857 48858 48859 48860 48861 48862 48863 48864 48865 48866 48867 48868 48869 48870 48871 48872 48873 48874 48875 48876 48877 48878 48879 48880 48881 48882 48883 48884 48885 48886

48887 48888 48889 48890 48891 48892 48893 48894 48895 48896 48897 48898 48899 48900 48901 48902 48903 48904 48905 48906 48907 48908 48909 48910 48911 48912 48913 48914 48915 48916 48917 48918 48919 48920 48921 48922 48923 48924 48925 48926 48927 48928 48929 48930 48931

48932 48933 48934 48935 48936 48937 48938 48939 48940 48941 48942 48943 48944 48945 48946 48947 48948 48949 48950 48951 48952 48953 48954 48955 48956 48957 48958 48959 48960 48961 48962 48963 48964 48965 48966 48967 48968 48969 48970 48971 48972 48973 48974 48975 48976 48977

48978 48979 48980 48981 48982 48983 48984 48985 48986 48987 48988 48989 48990 48991 48992 48993 48994 48995 48996 48997 48998 48999 49000 49001 49002 49003 49004 49005 49006 49007 49008 49009 49010 49011 49012 49013 49014 49015 49016 49017 49018 49019 49020 49021 49022

49023 49024 49025 49026 49027 49028 49029 49080 49081 49032 49033 49034 49035 49036 49037 49038 49039 49040 49041 49042 49043 49044 49045 49046 49047 49048 49049 49050 49051 49052 49053 49054 49055 49056 49057 49058 49059 49060 49061 49062 49063 49064 49065 49066 49067 49068 49069 49070

49071 49072 49073 49074 49075 49076 49077 49078 49079 49080 49081 49082 49083 49084 49085 49086 49087 49088 49089 49090 49091 49092 49093 49094 49095 49096 49097 49098 49099 49100 49101 49102 49103 49104 49105 49106 49107 49108 49109 49110 49111 49112 49113 49114 49115 49116

49117 49118 49119 49120 49121 49122 49123 49124 49125 49126 49127 49128 49129 49130 49131 49132 49133 49134 49135 49136 49137 49138 49139 49140 49141 49142 49143 49144 49145 49146 49147 49148 49149 49150 49151 49152 49153 49154 49155 49156 49157 49158 49159 49160

49161 49206 49353 4939
49162 49207 November 22, 2023 49354 4940
49163 49355 4940
49164 49208 more than 13,000 people 49356 4940
49165 49209 Killed in the past 7 weeks 49357 4940
49166 49210 49358 4940
49167 49359 4940
49168 49211 We are more than numbers 49360 4940
49169 49212 more than a death toll 49361 4940
49170
49171 49213 1 in every 200 people 49362 494
49172 49214 in Gaza Killed 49363 494
49173 49215 49364
49174 49216 49365 4941
49175 49217 my heart is breaking 49366 4941
49176 49218 49367 494
49177 49219 49368 494
49178 49220 We went to a vigil and took 49369 494
49179 49221 turns reading names of the 49370 4941
49180 49222 children who were killed, 49371 4941
49181 49223 starting with those under the 49372 4941
49182 49224 49373 4941
49183 49225 age of one. We left when 49374 4941
49184 49226 49375 4942
49185 49227 we could no longer stand 49376 4942
49186 49228 49377 4942
49229
49187 49378 4942
49188 49230 we had not yet finished
49189 49231 reading names of the 49379 4942
49190 49232 3 year olds. 49380 4942
49191 49233 49381 4942
49192 49234 49249 49263 49278 49293 49308 49322 49337 49382 4942
49193 49235 49250 49264 49279 49294 49309 49323 49338 49383 4942
49194 49236 49251 49265 49280 49295 49310 49324 49339 49384 49385 4942
49195 49237 49252 49266 49281 49296 49311 49325 49340 49386 4943
49196 49238 49253 49267 49282 49297 49312 49326 49341 49387 4943
49197 49239 49254 49268 49283 49298 49313 49327 49342 49388 4943
49198 49240 49255 49269 49284 49299 49314 49328 49343 49389 4943
49199 49241 49256 49270 49285 49300 49315 49329 49344 49390 4943
49200 49242 49257 49271 49286 49301 49316 49330 49345 49391 4943
49201 49243 49258 49272 49287 49302 49317 49331 49346 49392 4943
49202 49244 49259 49273 49288 49303 49318 49332 49347 49393 4943
49203 49245 49260 49274 49289 49304 49319 49333 49348 49394 4943
49204 49246 49261 49275 49290 49305 49320 49334 49349 49395 4943
49205 49247 49262 49276 49291 49306 49321 49335 49350 49396 4943
49248 49277 49292 49307 49336 49351 49397 4944
49352 49398 4944

49806 49807 49808 49809 49810 49811 49812 49813 49814 49815 49816 49817 49818 49819 49820 49821 49822 49823 49824 49825 49826 49827 49828 49829 49830 49831 49832 49833 49834 49835 49836 49837 49838 49839 49840 49841 49842 49843 49844 49845 49846 49847 49848 49849

49850 49851 49852 49853 49854 49855 49856 49857 49858 49859 49860 49861 49862 49863 49864 49865 49866 49867 49868 49869 49870 49871 49872 49873 49874 49875 49876 49877 49878 49879 49880 49881 49882 49883 49884 49885 49886 49887 49888 49889 49890 49891 49892 49893 49894

49895 49896 49897 49898 49899 49900 49901 49902 49903 49904 49905 49906 49907 49908 49909 49910 49911 49912 49913 49914 49915 49916 49917 49918 49919 49920 49921 49922 49923 49924 49925 49926 49927 49928 49929 49930 49931 49932 49933 49934 49935 49936 49937 49938

49939 49940 49941 49942 49943 49944 49945 49946 49947 49948 49949 49950 49951 49952 49953 49954 49955 49956 49957 49958 49959 49960 49961 49962 49963 49964 49965 49966 49967 49968 49969 49970 49971 49972 49973 49974 49975 49976 49977 49978 49979 49980 49981 49982 49983

49984 49985 49986 49987 49988 49989 49990 49991 49992 49993 49994 49995 49996 49997 49998 49999 50000 50001 50002 50003 50004 50005 50006 50007 50008 50009 50010 50011 50012 50013 50014 50015 50016 50017 50018 50019 50020 50021 50022 50023 50024 50025 50026 50027 50028 50029

50030 50031 50032 50033 50034 50035 50036 50037 50038 50039 50040 50041 50042 50043 50044 50045 50046 50047 50048 50049 50050 50051 50052 50053 50054 50055 50056 50057 50058 50059 50060 50061 50062 50063 50064 50065 50066 50067 50068 50069 50070 50071 50072 50073 50074

50075 50076 50077 50078 50079 50080 50081 50082 50083 50084 50085 50086 50087 50088 50089 50090 50091 50092 50093 50094 50095 50096 50097 50098 50099 50100 50101 50102 50103 50104 50105 50106 50107 50108 50109 50110 50111 50112 50113 50114 50115 50116 50117 50118 50119 50120 50121

50122 50123 50124 50125 50126 50127 50128 50129 50130 50131 50132 50133 50134 50135 50136 50137 50138 50139 50140 50141 50142 50143 50144 50145 50146 50147 50148 50149 50150 50151 50152 50153 50154 50155 50156 50157 50158 50159 50160 50161 50162 50163 50164 50165

50166 50167 50168 50169 50170 50171 50172 50173 50174 50175 50176 50177 50178 50179 50180 50181 50182 50183 50184 50185 50186 50187 50188 50189 50190 50191 50192 50193 50194 50195 50196 50197 50198 50199 50200 50201 50202 50203 50204 50205 50206 50207 50208 50209 50210

50211 50212 50213 50214 50215 50216 50217 50218 50219 50220 50221 50222 50223 50224 50225 50226 50227 50228 50229 50230 50231 50232 50233 50234 50235 50236 50237 50238 50239 50240 50241 50242 50243 50244 50245 50246 50247 50248 50249 50250 50251 50252 50253 50254 50255 50256 50257 50258 50259

50260 50261 50262 50263 50264 50265 50266 50267 50268 50269 50270 50271 50272 50273 50274 50275 50276 50277 50278 50279 50280 50281 50282 50283 50284 50285 50286 50287 50288 50289 50290 50291 50292 50293 50294 50295 50296 50297 50298 50299 50300 50301 50302 50303 50304 50305 50306 50307

[PALESTINE NEWS CONTENT WARNING]

You will see: Grainy images on the flickering
screen. Ground shakes with an explosion.
Reporter in a flak jacket gestures to
the chaos behind him, his tone steady,
but the microphone in his hand picks up
screaming and yelling. You see flags
and fists, static and dust, fire clouds
ballooning behind buildings. Barbed wire,
bullet holes and plaster walls crumbled,
children tear-streaked. Caskets carried.
You hear the word *terrorist* describing a single
man, bloody and barefoot, eyes averted, brow creased,
not the cluster armed and helmeted, twisting
his arms behind his back, kicking him, dragging him down
the street. I could tell you not to let your child watch
but your eyes are
trauma-bonded to the images
and you won't
look
away
long enough
to cover
her
eyes.

308 50309 50310 50311 50312 50313 50314 50315 50316 50317 50318 50319 50320 50321 50322 50323 50324 50325
326 50327 50328 50329 50330 50331 50332 50333 50334 50335 50336 50337 50338 50339 50340 50341 50342 50343
344 50345 50346 50347 50348 50349 50350 50351 50352 50353 50354 50355 50356 50357 50358 50359 50360 50361 50362
363 50364 50365 50366 50367 50368 50369 50370 50371 50372 50373 50374 50375 50376 50377 50378 50379 50380 50381
382 50383 50384 50385 50386 50387 50388 50389 50390 50391 50392 50393 50394 50395 50396 50397 50398 50399
400 50401 50402 50403 50404 50405 50406 50407 50408 50409 50410 50411 50412 50413 50414 50415 50416 50417 50418
419 50420 50421 50422 50423 50424 50425 50426 50427 50428 50429 50430 50431 50432 50433 50434 50435 50436
437 50438 50439 50440 50441 50442 50443 50444 50445 50446 50447 50448 50449 50450 50451 50452 50453 50454
455 50456 50457 50458 50459 50460 50461 50462 50463 50464 50465 50466 50467 50468 50469 50470 50471
472 50473 50474 50475 50476 50477 50478 50479 50480 50481 50482 50483 50484 50485 50486 50487 50488 50489
490 50491 50492 50493 50494 50495 50496 50497 50498 50499 50500 50501 50502 50503 50504 50505 50506
507 50508 50509 50510 50511 50512 50513 50514 50515 50516 50517 50518 50519 50520 50521 50522 50523 50524 50525

526 50527 50528
529 50530 50531
532 50533 50534
535 50536 50537
538 50539 50540
541 50542 50543
544 50545 50546
547 50548 50549
550 50551 50552
553 50554 50555
556 50557 50558
559 50560 50561
562 50563 50564
565 50566 50567
568 50569 50570
571 50572 50573
574 50575 50576
577 50578 50579
580 50581 50582
583 50584 50585
586 50587 50588
589 50590 50591
592 50593 50594
595 50596 50597
598 50599 50600
601 50602 50603
604 50605 50606
607 50608 50609
610 50611 50612
613 50614 50615
616 50617 50618
619 50620 50621
622 50623 50624
625 50626 50627
628 50629 50630
631 50632 50633
634 50635 50636
637 50638 50639
640 50641 50642
643 50644 50645
646 50647 50648
649 50650 50651
652 50653 50654
655 50656 50657
658 50659 50660
661 50662 50663
664 50665 50666
667 50668 50669
670 50671 50672

50673 50674 50675
50676 50677 50678
50679 50680 50681
50682 50683 50684
50685 50686 50687
50688 50689 50690
50691 50692 50693 50694
50695 50696 50697 50698
50699 50700 50701 50702
50703 50704 50705 50706
50707 50708 50709 50710
50711 50712 50713 50714
50715 50716 50717
50718 50719 50720 50721
50722 50723 50724
50725 50726 50727 50728
50729 50730 50731
50732 50733 50734 50735
50736 50737 50738 50739
50740 50741 50742 50743
50744 50745 50746 50747
50748 50749 50750 50751
50752 50753 50754 50755
50756 50757 50758 50759
50760 50761 50762 50763
50764 50765 50766 50767
50768 50769 50770 50771
50772 50773 50774 50775
50776 50777 50778 50779
50781 50782 50783 50784
50785 50786 50787 50788
50789 50790 50791 50792
50793 50794 50795 50796
50797 50798 50799 50800
50801 50802 50803 50804
50805 50806 50807 50808
50809 50810 50811 50812
50813 50814 50815 50816
50817 50818 50819 50820
50821 50822 50823 50824
50825 50826 50827 50828
50829 50830 50831 50832
50833 50834 50835 50836
50837 50838 50839 50840
50841 50842 50843 50844
50845 50846 50847 50848
50849 50850 50851 50852
50853 50854 50855 50856
50857 50858 50859 50860
50861 50862 50863 50864
50865 50866 50867 50868

869 50870 50871 50872 50873 50874 50875 50876 50877 50878 50879 50880 50881 50882 50883 50884 50885
886 50887 50888 50889 50890 50891 50892 50893 50894 50895 50896 50897 50898 50899 50900 50901 50902
903 50904 50905 50906 50907 50908 50909 50910 50911 50912 50913 50914 50915 50916 50917 50918 50919
920 50921 50922 50923 50924 50925 50926 50927 50928 50929 50930 50931 50932 50933 50934 50935
936 50937 50938 50939 50940 50941 50942 50943 50944 50945 50946 50947 50948 50949 50950 50951
952 50953 50954 50955 50956 50957 50958 50959 50960 50961 50962 50963 50964 50965 50966
967 50968 50969 50970 50971 50972 50973 50974 50975 50976 50977 50978 50979 50980 50981
982 50983 50984 50985 50986 50987 50988 50989 50990 50991 50992 50993 50994 50995 50996 50997 50998
999 51000 51001 51002 51003 51004 51005 51006 51007 51008 51009 51010 51011 51012 51013 51014 51015 51016 51017
018 51019 51020 51021 51022 51023 51024 51025 51026 51027 51028 51029 51030 51031 51032 51033 51034

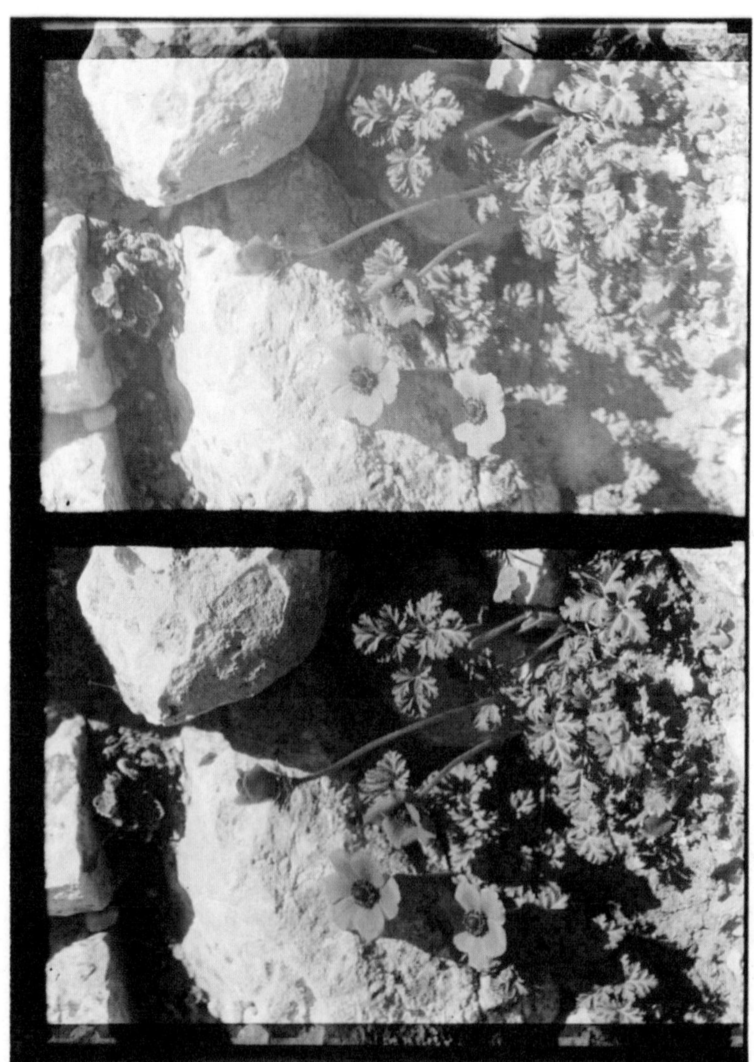

52831
52832
52833
52834
52835
52836
52837
52838
52839
52840
52841
52842
52843
52844
52845
52846
52847
52848
52849
52850
52851
52852
52853
52854
52855
52856

52857
52858
52859
52860
52861
52862
52863
52864
52865
52866
52867
52868
52869
52870
52871
52872
52873
52874
52875
52876
52877
52878
52879
52880
52881
52882

52883
52884
52885
52886
52887
52888
52889
52890
52891
52892
52893
52894
52895
52896
52897
52898
52899
52900
52901
52902
52903
52904
52905
52906
52907
52908
52909
52910

52911
52912
52913
52914
52915
52916
52917
52918
52919
52920
52921
52982
52923
52924
52925
52926
52927
52928
52929
52930
52931
52932
52933
52934
52935
52936
52937
52938
52939
52940
52941
52942
52943
52944
52945
52946
52947

52948
52949
52950
52951
52952
52953
52954
52955
52956
52957
52958
52959
52960
52961
52962
52963
52964
52965
52966
52967
52968
52969
52970
52971
52972
52973
52974
52975
52976
52977
52978
52979
52980
52981
52982

53183 53184 53185 53186 53187 53188 53189 53190 53191 53192 53193 53194 53195 53196 53197 53198 53199 53200 53201 53202
53075 53076 53077 53078 53079 53080 53081 53082 53083 53084 53085 53086 53087 53088 53089 53090 53091 53092 53093
52983 52984 52985 52986 52987 52988 52989 52990 52991 52992 52993 52994 52995 52996
52997 52998 52999 53000 53001 53002 53003 53004 53005 53006 53007 53008 53009 53010 53011 53012 53013 53014 53015 53016 53017 53018 53019 53020 53021 53022 53023 53024 53025
53204 53205 53206 53207 53208 53209 53210 53211

Your screen time is up 41% since last week. You spend hours on social media. You always feel worse afterwards but it feels impossible to pull away. You watch videos in bed even after saying you wouldn't. You wake up and open your phone. You forget your body, but weigh it anyway. You've stopped drinking coffee, because the doctor said it might give you a heart attack. Your body doesn't need more stress. You take an ovulation test, convinced you'll never get pregnant. The desire to repopulate and the fear of bringing another Arab child into the world are fighting over the real estate of your body. You avoid gluten and dairy and processed foods, which feed the attack on your body. You try not to think about those starving in Gaza. You fill your day caring for others and it's reassuring until the end of the day when you wish someone was tending to you. You wish someone would express your rage and grief and disconnection. So you open your phone and get into bed.

100 days
of
genocide.

Every time I see Bisan crying into the camera,
I'm reminded of the girl in our collective attic.
I don't say this to be divisive but because I've always
seen our struggles as interconnected, been told
by my family we can never be free if the powers
that be succeed in turning us against one another,
in convincing us there's not enough to go around.
But where would I be without my Jewish family,
friends, husband? You can't tell me my heart
has no room to hold more, my heart
grows meadows every time I meet someone new
whose voice echoes mine in the crowd.
So take my hand, plant your feet on the land
and let's bloom this world together.

54057 54058 54059 54060 54061 54062 54063 54064 54065 54066 54067 54068 54069 54070 54071 54072 54073
54027 54028 54029 54030 54031 54032 54033 54034 54035 54036 54037 54038 54039 54040 54041
53997 53998 53999 54000 54001 54002 54003 54004 54005 54006 54007 54008 54009 54010
53970 53971 53972 53973 53974 53975 53976 53977 53978 53979 53980 53981 53982
53938 53939 53940 53941 53942 53943 53944 53945 53946 53947 53948 53949 53950 53951 53952
53909 53910 53911 53912 53913 53914 53915 53916 53917 53918 53919 53920 53921 53922 53923 53924
53867 53868 53869 53870 53871 53872 53873 53874 53875 53876 53877 53878 53879 53880 53881
53815 53816 53817 53818 53819 53820 53821 53822 53823 53824 53825 53826
53765 53766 53767 53768 53769 53770 53771 53772 53773 53774 53775 53776
53713 53714 53715 53716 53717 53718 53719 53720 53721 53722 53723 53724
53665 53666 53667 53668 53669 53670 53671 53672 53673 53674 53675 53676

54074 54075 54076 54077 54078 54079 54080 54081 54082 54083 54084 54085 54086 54087 54088 54089 54090 54091 54092 54093 54094 54095 54096 54097 54098 54099 54100 54101 54102 54103 54104 54105 54106 54107 54108 54109 54110 54111 54112 54113 54114 54115 54116 54117 54118 54119 54120 54121 54122 54123 54124 54125 54126 54127 54128 54129 54130 54131 54132 54133 54134 54135 54136 54137 54138 54139 54140 54141 54142 54143 54144 54145 54146 54147 54148 54149 54150 54151 54152 54153 54154 54155 54156

54157 54158 54159 54160 54161 54162 54163 54164 54165 54166 54167 54168 54169 54170 54171 54172 54173 54174 54175 54176 54177 54178 54179 54180 54181 54182 54183 54184 54185 54186 54187 54188 54189 54190 54191 54192 54193 54194 54195 54196 54197 54198 54199 54200 54201 54202 54203 54204 54205 54206 54207 54208 54209 54210 54211 54212 54213 54214 54215 54216 54217 54218 54219 54220 54221 54222 54223 54224 54225 54226 54227 54228 54229 54230 54231

54231 54232 54233 54234 54235 54236 54237 54238 54239 54240 54241 54242 54243 54244 54245 54246 54247 54248 54249 54250 54251 54252 54253 54254 54255 54256 54257 54258 54259 54260 54261 54262 54263 54264 54265 54266 54267 54268 54269 54270 54271 54272 54273 54274 54275 54276 54277 54278 54279 54280 54281 54282 54283 54284 54285 54286 54287 54288 54289 54290 54291 54292 54293 54294 54295 54296 54297 54298 54299 54300 54301 54302 54303 54304 54305 54306 54307 54308 54309 54310 54311

54312 54313 54314 54315 54316 54317 54318 54319 54320 54321 54322 54323 54324 54325 54326 54327 54328 54329 54330 54331 54332 54333 54334 54335 54336 54337 54338 54339 54340 54341 54342 54343 54344 54345 54346 54347 54348 54349 54350 54351 54352 54353 54354 54355 54356 54357 54358 54359 54360 54361 54362 54363 54364 54365 54366 54367 54368 54369 54370 54371 54372 54373 54374 54375 54376 54377 54378 54379 54380 54381 54382 54383 54384 54385 54386 54387 54388 54389

54390 54391 54392 54393 54394 54395 54396 54397 54398 54399 54400 54401 54402 54403 54404 54405 54406 54407 54408 54409 54410 54411 54412 54413 54414 54415 54416 54417 54418 54419 54420 54421 54422 54423 54424 54425 54426 54427 54428 54429 54430 54431 54432 54433 54434 54435 54436 54437 54438 54439 54440 54441 54442 54443 54444 54445 54446 54447 54448 54449 54450 54451 54452 54453 54454 54455 54456 54457 54458 54459 54460 54461 54462 54463 54464 54465 54466 54467 54468 54469 54470 54471 54472 54473 54474 54475 54476 54477 54478

54479 54480 54481 54482 54483 54484 54485 54486 54487 54488 54489 54490 54491 54492 54493 54494 54495 54496 54497 54498 54499 54500 54501 54502 54503 54504 54505 54506 54507 54508 54509 54510 54511 54512 54513 54514 54515 54516 54517 54518 54519 54520 54521 54522 54523 54524 54525 54526 54527 54528 54529 54530 54531 54532 54533 54534 54535 54536 54537 54538 54539 54540 54541 54542 54543 54544 54545 54546 54547 54548 54549 54550 54551 54552 54553 54554 54555 54556 54557 54558 54559 54560 54561 54562 54563 54564 54565 54566 54567 54568 54569 54570 54571 54572 54573 54574 54575 54576 54577 54578 54579 54580 54581 54582 54583 54584 54585

54586 54587 54588 54589 54590 54591 54592 54593 54594 54595 54596 54597 54598 54599 54600 54601 54602 54603 54604 54605 54606 54607 54608 54609 54610 54611 54612 54613 54614 54615 54616 54617 54618 54619 54620 54621 54622 54623 54624 54625 54626 54627 54628 54629 54630 54631 54632 54633 54634 54635 54636 54637 54638 54639 54640 54641 54642 54643 54644 54645 54646 54647 54648 54649 54650 54651 54652 54653 54654 54655 54656 54657 54658 54659 54660 54661 54662 54663 54664 54665 54666 54667 54668 54669 54670 54671 54672 54673 54674 54675 54676 54677 54678 54679 54680 54681 54682 54683 54684 54685 54686 54687 54688 54689 54690 54691 54692 54693 54694

54587 54588 54589 54590 54591 54592 54593 54594 54595 54596 54597 54598 54599 54600 54601 54602 54603 54604 54605 54606 54607 54608 54609 54610 54611 54612 54613 54614 54615 54616 54617 54618 54619 54620 54621 54622 54623 54624 54625 54626 54627 54628 54629 54630 54631 54632 54633 54634 54635 54636 54637 54638 54639 54640 54641 54642 54643 54644 54645 54646 54647 54648 54649 54650 54651 54652 54653 54654 54655 54656 54657 54658 54659 54660 54661 54662 54663 54664 54665 54666 54667 54668 54669 54670 54671 54672 54673 54674 54675 54676 54677 54678 54679 54680 54681 54682 54683

54684 54685 54686 54687 54688 54689 54690 54691 54692 54693 54694 54695 54696 54697 54698 54699 54700 54701 54702 54703 54704 54705 54706 54707 54708 54709 54710 54711 54712 54713 54714 54715 54716 54717 54718 54719 54720 54721 54722 54723 54724 54725 54726 54727 54728 54729 54730 54731 54732 54733 54734 54735 54736 54737 54738 54739 54740 54741 54742 54743 54744 54745 54746 54747 54748 54749 54750 54751 54752 54753 54754 54755 54756 54757 54758 54759 54760 54761 54762 54763 54764 54765 54766 54767 54768 54769 54770 54771 54772 54773 54774 54775 54776 54777 54778 54779 54780 54781 54782 54783 54784 54785 54786 54787

54788 54789 54790 54791 54792 54793 54794 54795 54796 54797 54798 54799 54800 54801 54802 54803 54804 54805 54806 54807 54808 54809 54810 54811 54812 54813 54814 54815 54816 54817 54818 54819 54820 54821 54822 54823 54824 54825 54826 54827 54828 54829 54830 54831 54832 54833 54834 54835 54836 54837 54838 54839 54840 54841 54842 54843 54844 54845 54846 54847 54848 54849 54850 54851 54852 54853 54854 54855 54856 54857 54858 54859 54860 54861 54862 54863 54864 54865 54866 54867 54868 54869 54870 54871 54872 54873 54874 54875 54876 54877 54878 54879 54880 54881 54882 54883 54884 54885 54886 54887 54888 54889

54890 54891 54892 54893 54894 54895 54896 54897 54898 54899 54900 54901 54902 54903 54904 54905 54906 54907 54908 54909 54910 54911 54912 54913 54914 54915 54916 54917 54918 54919 54920 54921 54922 54923 54924 54925 54926 54927 54928 54929 54930 54931 54932 54933 54934 54935 54936 54937 54938 54939 54940 54941 54942 54943 54944 54945 54946 54947 54948 54949 54950 54951 54952 54953 54954 54955 54956 54957 54958 54959 54960 54961 54962 54963 54964 54965 54966 54967 54968 54969 54970 54971 54972 54973 54974 54975 54976 54977 54978 54979 54980 54981 54982 54983 54984 54985 54986 54987 54988

54989 54990 54991 54992 54993 54994 54995 54996 54997 54998 54999 55000 55001 55002 55003 55004 55005 55006 55007 55008 55009 55010 55011 55012 55013 55014 55015 55016 55017 55018 55019 55020 55021 55022 55023 55024 55025 55026 55027 55028 55029 55030 55031 55032 55033 55034 55035 55036 55037 55038 55039 55040 55041 55042 55043 55044 55045 55046 55047 55048 55049 55050 55051 55052 55053 55054 55055 55056 55057 55058 55059 55060 55061 55062 55063 55064 55065 55066 55067 55068 55069 55070 55071 55072 55073 55074 55075 55076 55077 55078 55079 55080 55081 55082 55083 55084 55085 55086 55087 55088 55089 55090 55091 55092 55093 55094 55095 55096

55097 55098 55099 55100 55101 55102 55103 55104 55105 55106 55107 55108 55109 55110 55111 55112 55113 55114 55115 55116 55117 55118 55119 55120 55121 55122 55123 55124 55125 55126 55127 55128 55129 55130 55131 55132 55133 55134 55135 55136 55137 55138 55139 55140 55141 55142 55143 55144 55145 55146 55147 55148 55149 55150 55151 55152 55153 55154 55155 55156 55157 55158 55159 55160 55161 55162 55163 55164 55165 55166 55167 55168 55169 55170 55171 55172 55173 55174 55175 55176 55177 55178 55179 55180 55181 55182 55183 55184 55185 55186 55187 55188 55189 55190 55191 55192 55193 55194

55195 55196 55197 55198 55199 55200 55201 55202 55203 55204 55205 55206 55207 55208 55209 55210 55211 55212 55213 55214 55215 55216 55217 55218 55219 55220 55221 55222 55223 55224 55225 55226 55227 55228 55229 55230 55231 55232 55233 55234 55235 55236 55237 55238 55239 55240 55241 55242 55243 55244 55245 55246 55247 55248 55249 55250 55251 55252 55253 55254 55255 55256 55257 55258 55259 55260 55261 55262 55263 55264 55265 55266 55267 55268 55269 55270 55271 55272 55273 55274 55275 55276 55277 55278 55279 55280 55281 55282 55283 55284 55285 55286 55287 55288 55289 55290 55291 55292 55293 55294 55295 55296 55297 55298 55299 55300 55301 55302 55303 55304

55305 55306 55307 55308 55309 55310 55311 55312 55313 55314 55315 55316 55317 55318 55319 55320 55321 55322 55323 55324 55325 55326 55327 55328 55329 55330 55331 55332 55333 55334 55335 55336 55337 55338 55339 55340 55341 55342 55343 55344 55345 55346 55347 55348 55349 55350 55351 55352 55353 55354 55355 55356 55357 55358 55359 55360 55361 55362 55363 55364 55365 55366 55367 55368 55369 55370 55371 55372 55373 55374 55375 55376 55377 55378 55379 55380 55381 55382 55383 55384 55385 55386 55387 55388 55389 55390 55391 55392 55393 55394 55395 55396 55397 55398 55399 55400 55401 55402 55403 55404 55405 55406 55407 55408 55409 55410

55411 55412 55413 55414 55415 55416 55417 55418 55419 55420 55421 55422 55423 55424 55425 55426 55427 55428 55429 55430 55431 55432 55433 55434 55435 55436 55437 55438 55439 55440 55441 55442 55443 55444 55445 55446 55447 55448 55449 55450 55451 55452 55453 55454 55455 55456 55457 55458 55459 55460 55461 55462 55463 55464 55465 55466 55467 55468 55469 55470 55471 55472 55473 55474 55475 55476 55477 55478 55479 55480 55481 55482 55483 55484 55485 55486 55487 55488 55489 55490 55491 55492 55493 55494 55495 55496 55497 55498 55499 55500 55501 55502 55503 55504 55505 55506 55507 55508 55509 55510 55511 55512 55513 55514 55515 55516 55517 55518 55519 55520 55521 55522 55523

55524 55525 55526 55527 55528 55529 55530 55531 55532 55533 55534 55535 55536 55537 55538 55539 55540 55541 55542 55543 55544 55545 55546 55547 55548 55549 55550 55551 55552 55553 55554 55555 55556 55557 55558 55559 55560 55561 55562 55563 55564 55565 55566 55567 55568 55569 55570 55571 55572 55573 55574 55575 55576 55577 55578 55579 55580 55581 55582 55583 55584 55585 55586 55587 55588 55589 55590 55591 55592 55593 55594 55595 55596 55597 55598 55599 55600 55601 55602 55603 55604 55605 55606 55607 55608 55609 55610 55611 55612 55613 55614 55615 55616 55617 55618 55619 55620 55621 55622 55623 55624 55625 55626 55627

55628 55629 55630 55631 55632 55633 55634 55635 55636 55637 55638 55639 55640 55641 55642 55643 55644 55645 55646 55647 55648 55649 55650 55651 55652 55653 55654 55655 55656 55657 55658 55659 55660 55661 55662 55663 55664 55665 55666 55667 55668 55669 55670 55671 55672 55673 55674 55675 55676 55677 55678 55679 55680 55681 55682 55683 55684 55685 55686 55687 55688 55689 55690 55691 55692 55693 55694 55695 55696 55697 55698 55699 55700 55701 55702 55703 55704 55705 55706 55707 55708 55709 55710 55711 55712 55713 55714 55715 55716 55717 55718 55719 55720 55721 55722

55723 55724 55725 55726 55727 55728 55729 55730 55731 55732 55733 55734 55735 55736 55737 55738 55739 55740 55741 55742 55743 55744 55745 55746 55747 55748 55749 55750 55751 55752 55753 55754 55755 55756 55757 55758 55759 55760 55761 55762 55763 55764 55765 55766 55767 55768 55769 55770 55771 55772 55773 55774 55775 55776 55777 55778 55779 55780 55781 55782 55783 55784 55785 55786 55787 55788 55789 55790 55791 55792 55793 55794 55795 55796 55797 55798 55799 55800 55801 55802 55803 55804 55805 55806 55807 55808 55809 55810 55811 55812 55813 55814 55815 55816 55817 55818 55819 55820 55821 55822 55823 55824 55825 55826 55827 55828 55829 55830 55831 55832 55833

I admit I only read the headline,
Palestinians free birds from pet shops.
At least that's what I think it said.
I could be mistaken.
All of November was a blur.

The article describes the migration patterns of birds.
Gaza's blockade birds soar above
refugees, concentrated, confined.
"Our movement is very restricted," says Lara,
who feels cut off from the rest of the world.
"We wish we were birds so we could move freely."[16]

Birds know no borders, kids learn missile and bird songs.
Birds burrow in bomb-created holes.
"In the past, if people saw a bird, they would shoot it."
Now they buy birds to free them.
Familiar with the plight of being trapped,
they open cages, open minds.
I imagine them, open palms.

flight.

taking

I imagine them,

16 Marta Vidal, "How Trapped Palestinians Fell in Love With Bird-Watching," *International Women's Media Foundation*, Apr. 7, 2023.

I ask my partner to help me write numbers

He wrote less than 20 before tiring

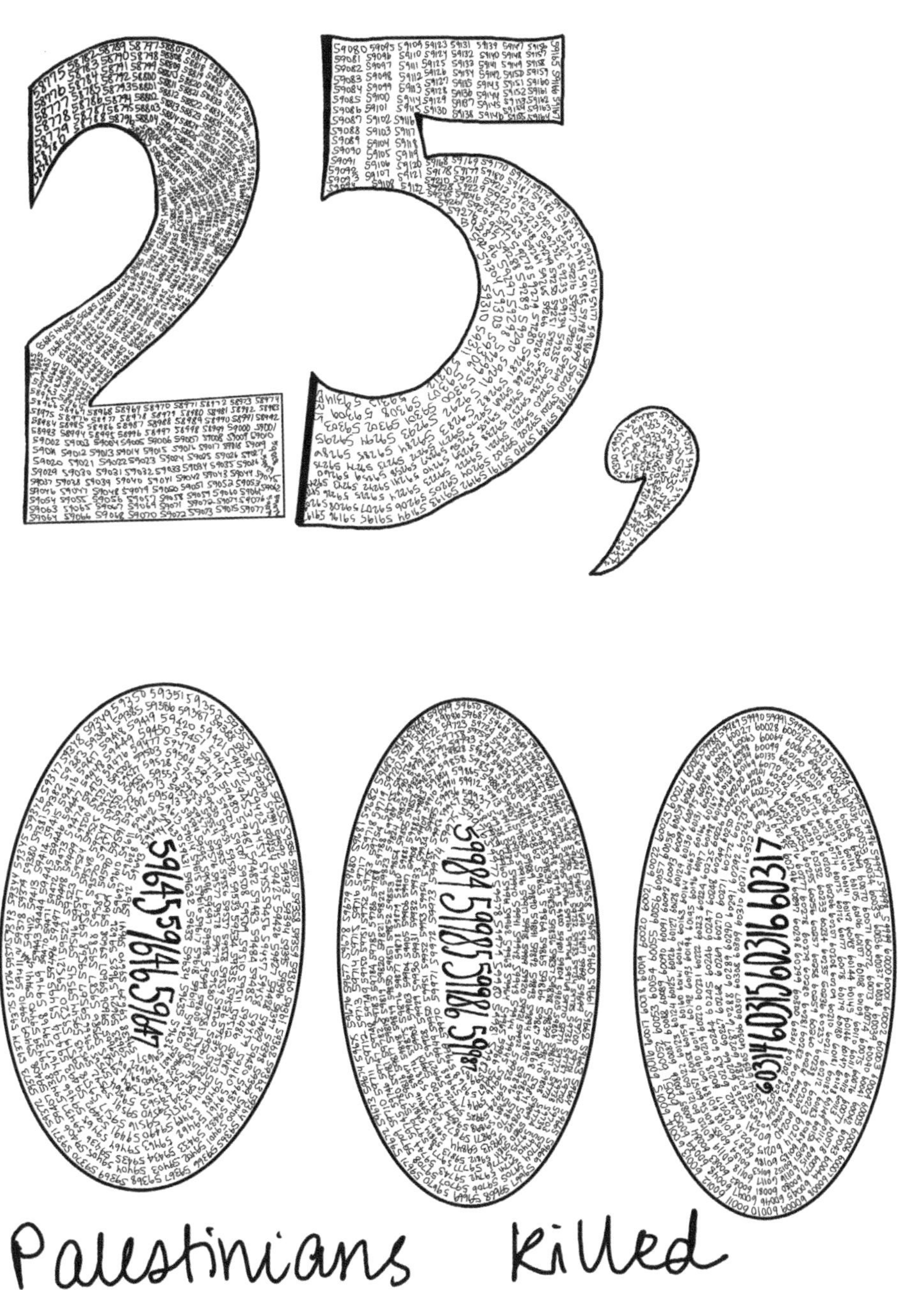
25,000
Palestinians Killed

6 Tips for Anti-Aging in a Time of Genocide

1. Drink plenty of water.
It's recommended to drink at least two liters a day.
~~If you run out, you could always drink sea water.~~

2. Get enough sleep.
Make sure your bedroom is quiet, dark and peaceful.
Don't let the constant bombing stop you
from attaining that youthful glow.

3. Avoid frowning, or furrowing your brow.
These facial expressions can cause wrinkles.
If this is difficult for you, you might try Botox,
or apathy.

4. Protect yourself (from the sun).
When you do leave the house, wear a hat and sunscreen, SPF 30 or higher, and make sure to reapply every hour. If you're outside, seek shade.
If there are no buildings for cover, rubble will do.

5. Don't stress.
The world may be burning, but you are not.
You may ask how we know this.
What about white phosphorus, you ask?
If you were on fire, you would not be reading this.
So, there's no urgency.
Take deep breaths, relax, tune out
the sounds of screaming, crying, bombing.

6. And, the final secret to staying young forever,
if all else fails:
Die young, while the world watches.

318 319 320 321 322 323 324 325 326 327 328 329 330 331 332 333 334 335 336 337 338 339 340 341 342 343 344 345 346 347 348 349 350 351 352 353 354 355 356 357 358 359 360 361 362 363 364 365 366 367 368 369 370 371 372 373 374 375

60376 60377 60378 60379 60380 60381 60382 60383 60384 60385 60386 60387 60388 60389 60390 60391 60392 60393 60394 60395 60396 60397 60398 60399 60400 60401 60402 60403 60404 60405 60406 60407 60408 60409 60410 60411 60412 60413 60414 60415 60416 60417 60418 60419 60420 60421 60422 60423 60424 60425 60426 60427 60428 60429 60430 60431 60432 60433 60434 60435

60436 60437 60438 60439 60440 60441 60442 60443 60444 60445 60446 60447 60448 60449 60450 60451 60452 60453 60454 60455 60456 60457 60458 60459 60460 60461 60462 60463 60464 60465 60466 60467 60468 60469 60470 60471 60472 60473 60474 60475 60476 60477 60478 60479 60480 60481 60482 60483 60484 60485

60486 60487 60488 60489 60490 60491

60492 60493 60494 60495 60496 60497

60498 60499 60500 60501 60502 60503

60504 60505 60506 60507 60508 60509

60510 60511 60512 60513 60514 60515 60516

60517 60518 60519 60520 60521 60522

60523 60524 60525 60526 60527 60528

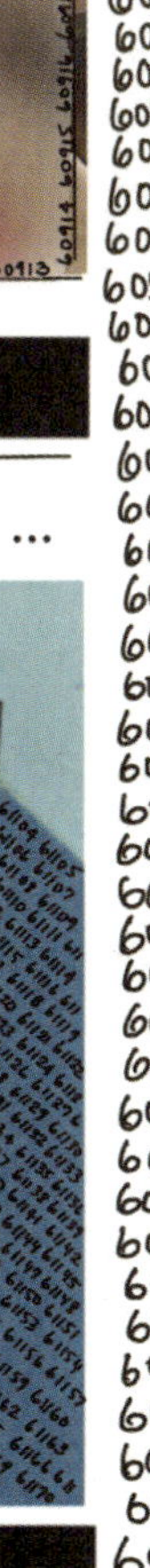

60529 60530 60531 60532 60533 60534 60535 60536 60537 60538 60539 60540 60541 60542 60543 60544 60545 60546 60547 60548 60549 60550 60551 60552 60553 60554 60555 60556 60557 60558 60559 60560 60561 60562 60563 60564 60565 60566 60567 60568 60569 60570 60571 60572 60573 60574 60575 60576 60577 60578 60579 60580 60581 60582 60583 60584 60585 60586 60587 60588 60589 60590 60591

60592 60593 60594 60595 60596 60597 60598 60599 60600 60601 60602 60603 60604 60605 60606 60607 60608 60609 60610 60611 60612 60613 60614 60615 60616 60617 60618 60619 60620 60621 60622 60623 60624 60625 60626 60627 60628 60629 60630 60631 60632 60633 60634 60635 60636 60637 60638 60639 60640 60641 60642 60643 60644 60645 60646 60647 60648 60649 60650 60651 60652 60653 60654 60655 60656 60657 60658 60659 60660 60661 60662 60663 60664 60665 60666

60667 60668 60669 60670 60671 60672 60673 60674 60675 60676 60677 60678 60679 60680 60681 60682 60683 60684 60685 60686 60687 60688 60689 60690 60691 60692 60693 60694 60695 60696 60697 60698 60699 60700 60701 60702 60703 60704 60705 60706 60707 60708 60709 60710 60711 60712 60713 60714 60715 60716 60717 60718 60719 60720 60721 60722 60723 60724 60725 60726 60727 60728 60729 60730 60731 60732 60733 60734 60735 60736 60737 60738 60739 60740 60741 60742 60743

60744 60745 60746 60747 60748 60749 60750 60751 60752 60753 60754 60755 60756 60757 60758 60759 60760 60761 60762 60763 60764 60765 60766 60767 60768 60769 60770 60771 60772 60773 60774 60775 60776 60777 60778 60779 60780 60781 60782 60783 60784 60785 60786 60787 60788 60789 60790 60791 60792 60793 60794 60795 60796 60797 60798 60799 60800 60801 60802 60803 60804 60805 60806 60807 60808 60809 60810 60811 60812 60813 60814 60815 60816 60817 60818 60819 60820 60821 60822 60823 60824 60825 60826 60827 60828 60829 60830 60831

61178 61179 61180 61181 61182 61183 61184 61185 61186 61187 61188 61189 61190 61191 61192 61193 61194 61195 61196 61197 61198 61199 61200 61201 61202 61203 61204 61205 61206 61207 61208 61209 61210 61211 61212 61213 61214 61215 61216 61217 61218 61219 61220 61221 61222 61223 61224 61225 61226 61227 61228 61229 61230 61231 61232

61233 61234 61235 61236 61237 61238 61239 61240 61241 61242 61243 61244 61245 61246 61247 61248 61249 61250 61251 61252 61253 61254 61255 61256 61257 61258 61259 61260 61261 61262 61263 61264 61265 61266 61267 61268 61269 61270 61271 61272 61273 61274 61275 61276 61277 61278 61279 61280 61281 61282 61283 61284 61285 61286 61287 61288 61289 61290 61291 61292 61293

61294 61295 61296 61297 61298 61299 61300 61301 61302 61303 61304 61305 61306 61307 61308 61309 61310 61311 61312 61313 61314 61315 61316 61317 61318 61319 61320 61321 61322 61323 61324 61325 61326 61327 61328 61329 61330 61331 61332 61333 61334 61335 61336 61337 61338 61339 61340 61341 61342 61343 61344 61345 61346 61347 61348 61349 61350 61351 61352 61353 61354 61355

61356 61357 61358 61359 61360 61361 61362 61363 61364 61365 61366 61367 61368 61369 61370 61371 61372 61373 61374 61375 61376 61377 61378 61379 61380 61381 61382 61383 61384 61385 61386 61387 61388 61389 61390 61391 61392 61393 61394 61395 61396 61397 61398 61399 61400 61401 61402 61403 61404 61405 61406 61407 61408 61409 61410 61411 61412 61413 61414 61415 61416 61417 61418 61419 61420 61421

61422 61423 61424 61425 61426 61427 61428 61429 61430 61431 61432 61433 61434 61435 61436 61437 61438 61439 61440 61441 61442 61443 61444 61445 61446 61447 61448 61449 61450 61451 61452 61453 61454 61455 61456 61457 61458 61459 61460 61461 61462 61463 61464 61465 61466 61467 61468 61469 61470 61471 61472 61473 61474 61475 61476 61477 61478 61479 61480 61481 61482 61483 61484 61485 61486 61487 61488 61489 61490 61491 61492 61493

61494 61495 61496 61497 61498 61499 61500 61501 61502 61503 61504 61505 61506 61507 61508 61509 61510 61511 61512 61513 61514 61515 61516 61517 61518 61519 61520 61521 61522 61523 61524 61525 61526 61527 61528 61529 61530 61531 61532 61533 61534 61535 61536 61537 61538 61539 61540 61541 61542 61543 61544 61545 61546 61547 61548 61549 61550 61551 61552 61553 61554 61555 61556 61557 61558 61559 61560 61561 61562 61563 61564 61565 61566 61567

61568 61569 61570 61571 61572 61573 61574 61575 61576 61577 61578 61579 61580 61581 61582 61583 61584 61585 61586 61587 61588 61589 61590 61591 61592 61593 61594 61595 61596 61597 61598 61599 61600 61601 61602 61603 61604 61605 61606 61607 61608 61609 61610 61611 61612 61613 61614 61615 61616 61617 61618 61619 61620 61621 61622 61623 61624 61625 61626 61627 61628 61629 61630 61631 61632 61633 61634 61635 61636 61637 61638 61639 61640 61641 61642

61643 61644 61645 61646 61647 61648 61649 61650 61651 61652 61653 61654 61655 61656 61657 61658 61659 61660 61661 61662 61663 61664 61665 61666 61667 61668 61669 61670 61671 61672 61673 61674 61675 61676 61677 61678 61679 61680 61681 61682 61683 61684 61685 61686 61687 61688 61689 61690 61691 61692 61693 61694 61695 61696 61697 61698 61699 61700 61701 61702 61703 61704 61705 61706 61707 61708 61709 61710 61711 61712 61713 61714 61715 61716 61717 61718 61719 61720 61721 61722 61723 61724 61725 61726 61727 61728

61729 61730 61731 61732 61733 61734 61735 61736 61737 61738 61739 61740 61741 61742 61743 61744 61745 61746 61747 61748 61749 61750 61751 61752 61753 61754 61755 61756 61757 61758 61759 61760 61761 61762 61763 61764 61765 61766 61767 61768 61769 61770 61771 61772 61773 61774 61775 61776 61777 61778 61779 61780 61781 61782 61783 61784 61785 61786 61787 61788 61789 61790 61791 61792 61793 61794 61795 61796 61797 61798 61799 61800 61801 61802 61803 61804 61805 61806 61807 61808 61809 61810 61811 61812

61813 61814 61815 61816 61817 61818 61819 61820 61821 61822 61823 61824 61825 61826 61827 61828 61829 61830 61831 61832 61833 61834 61835 61836 61837 61838 61839 61840 61841 61842 61843 61844 61845 61846 61847 61848 61849 61850 61851 61852 61853 61854 61855 61856 61857 61858 61859 61860 61861 61862 61863 61864 61865 61866 61867 61868 61869 61870 61871 61872 61873 61874 61875 61876 61877 61878 61879 61880 61881 61882 61883 61884 61885 61886 61887 61888

61969 61970 61971 61972 61973

I pull out my phone to check the time and find

Britney twirling naked on the grid / Another dismembered child, orphaned / An ad for Ozempic / Another food truck bombed / NY bans masks / Discount Botox / Israel drops cans of booby-trapped food / How to use your stress to lose weight fast / Cats are feeding on the dead in the streets / Oh and fix those crooked teeth! / In Gaza there's no food, no water / Are you a winter or a summer? / An Israeli soldier poses gleefully with corpses, balloons for a beloved / The word Palestine is banned / 10,000 people believed buried under rubble / Taylor Swift is in love / Students expelled for protesting / This bird looks like a pine cone! / Palestinian child forages for dandelion weeds / Young men in Vermont shot for wearing Keffiyeh / Wear masks so COVID doesn't spread / Wear a mask to prevent getting doxxed / In Gaza, polio exists / Use AI to choose the hairstyle that suits you best / Babies are having heart attacks from the stress of constant bombing / The best nail colors for summer! / Another man burned himself alive in front of an Israeli embassy in protest / Is Taylor's outfit an Easter egg? / Men are being stripped naked and blindfolded and marched into mass graves / Unlikely animal friends :) / A TikTok of an Israeli mocking a Palestinian, grieving, starving, and afraid / A new season of *Bridgerton* is coming / Tim Walz is everyone's cool dad / Sexual assault via electric current / Children's corpses raped / Try this bio-collagen face mask! / If Trump wins it's going to be your fault.

It's been 45 minutes and I forget what I was doing.

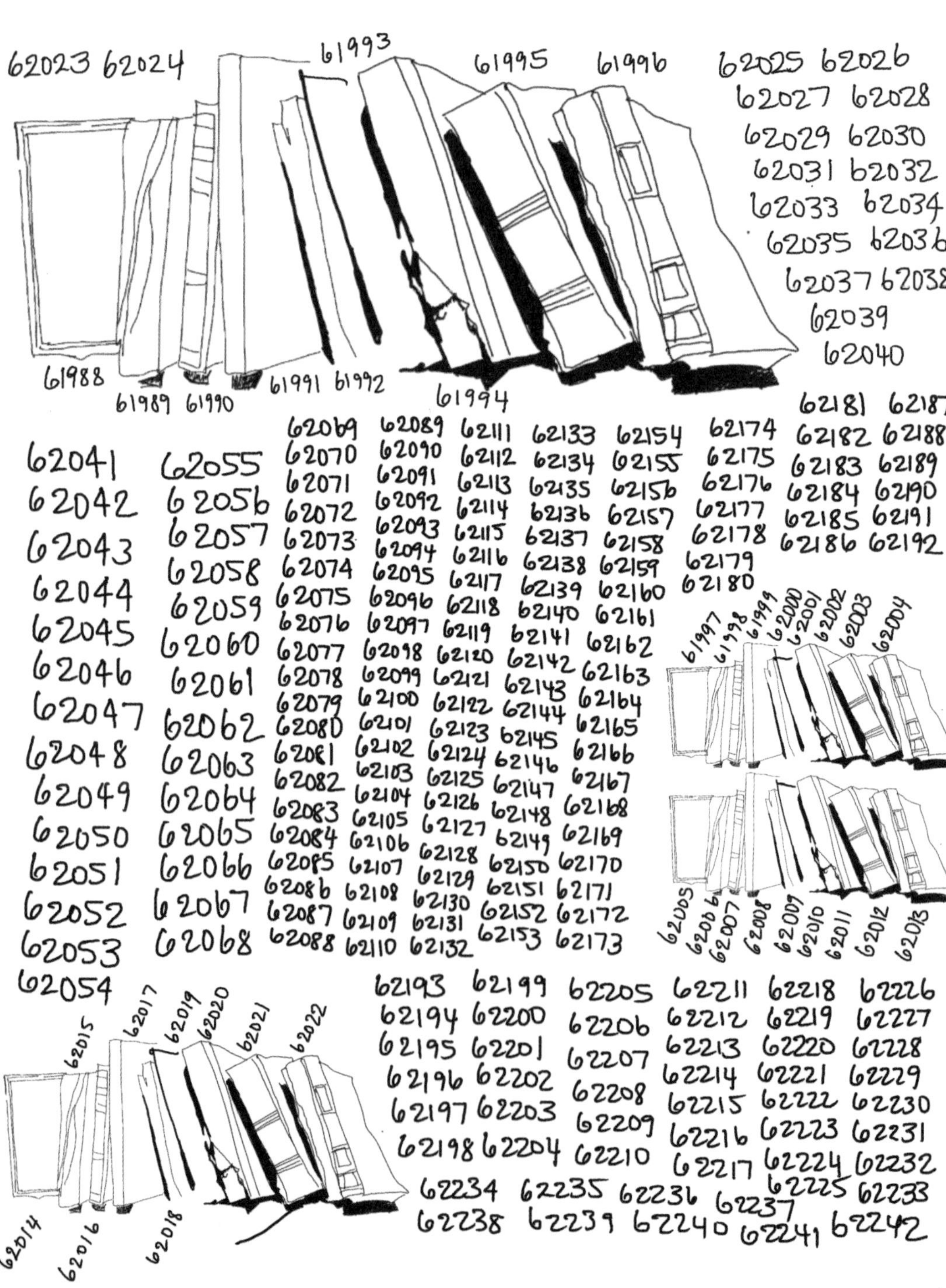
62023 62024
61993
61995
61996
62025 62026
62027 62028
62029 62030
62031 62032
62033 62034
62035 62036
62037 62038
62039
62040
61988
61989 61990
61991 61992
61994
62041
62042
62043
62044
62045
62046
62047
62048
62049
62050
62051
62052
62053
62054
62055
62056
62057
62058
62059
62060
62061
62062
62063
62064
62065
62066
62067
62068
62069
62070
62071
62072
62073
62074
62075
62076
62077
62078
62079
62080
62081
62082
62083
62084
62085
62086
62087
62088
62089
62090
62091
62092
62093
62094
62095
62096
62097
62098
62099
62100
62101
62102
62103
62104
62105
62106
62107
62108
62109
62110
62111
62112
62113
62114
62115
62116
62117
62118
62119
62120
62121
62122
62123
62124
62125
62126
62127
62128
62129
62130
62131
62132
62133
62134
62135
62136
62137
62138
62139
62140
62141
62142
62143
62144
62145
62146
62147
62148
62149
62150
62151
62152
62153
62154
62155
62156
62157
62158
62159
62160
62161
62162
62163
62164
62165
62166
62167
62168
62169
62170
62171
62172
62173
62174
62175
62176
62177
62178
62179
62180
62181 62187
62182 62188
62183 62189
62184 62190
62185 62191
62186 62192
61997
61998
61999
62000
62001
62002
62003
62004
62005
62006
62007
62008
62009
62010
62011
62012
62013
62015
62017
62019
62020
62021
62022
62014
62016
62018
62193
62194
62195
62196
62197
62198
62199
62200
62201
62202
62203
62204
62205
62206
62207
62208
62209
62210
62211
62212
62213
62214
62215
62216
62217
62218
62219
62220
62221
62222
62223
62224
62225
62226
62227
62228
62229
62230
62231
62232
62233
62234 62235 62236 62237
62238 62239 62240 62241 62242

You’ll find me dead in my pile of papers.
Please bury me with my books,
my most valuable belongings.

62243
62244
62245
62246
62247
62248
62249
62250
62251
62252
62253
62254
62255
62256
62257
62258
62259
62260
62261
62262
62263
62264
62265
62266

62267
62268
62269
62270
62271
62272
62273
62274
62275
62276
62277
62278
62279
62280
62281
62282
62283
62284
62285
62286
62287
62288

62289
62290
62291
62292
62293
62294
62295
62296
62297
62298
62299
62300
62301
62302
62303
62304
62305
62306
62307
62308
62309
62310
62311
62312
62313
62314
62315

62316
62317
62318
62319
62320
62321
62322
62323
62324
62325
62326
62327
62328
62329
62330
62331
62332
62333
62334
62335
62336
62337
62338
62339
62340
62341
62342
62343

62344
62345
62346
62347
62348
62349
62350
62351
62352
62353
62354
62355
62356
62357
62358
62359
62360
62361
62362
62363
62364
62365
62366
62367
62368
62369
62370
62371

62372
62373
62374
62375
62376
62377
62378
62379
62380
62381
62382
62383
62384
62385
62386
62387
62388
62389
62390
62391
62392
62393
62394
62395
62396
62397
62398
62399

62400
62401
62402
62403
62404
62405
62406
62407
62408
62409
62410
62411
62412
62413
62414
62415
62416
62417
62418
62419
62420
62421
62422
62423
62424
62425
62426

62427
62428
62429
62430
62431
62432
62433
62434
62435
62436
62437
62438
62439
62440
62441
62442
62443
62444
62445
62446
62447
62448
62449
62450
62451

Reasons to Live When My People Are Dying

Defiance, mostly. But also: The cat purring in my armpit, so soft and trusting. A pot of sweet chai simmering on the stove. The feeling of weightlessness in the ocean's embrace. Getting caught in a warm summer downpour. Turning out the lights to let thunderstorms light up the room. Sharing secrets. Sharing crushes. Sharing silence. The glitter of bioluminescent plankton, dancing across the surface of my skin. A salty slurp of steaming ramen after a cold and tiring day. The way the fullness of the moon can surprise us each month with her radiance. A poem you can read over and over. A book you can't wait to get back to. So many books I've yet to read. Cashmere. Impromptu dance parties in the kitchen. The smell of firewood. Coming home after a long trip. The peace that comes after a swell of tears. Warm hugs. Falling in love. Lighting a candle. Filling my lungs with air and hearing my voice in harmony with others. When I don't know where my skin ends and the air begins. Creating with clay and my own hands. Inspiration. Being lulled to sleep by the voice of a loved one. Dreams. Because I can.

Because I intend to flood the world with my own existence. Because they will never kill us all.

62452 62453 62454 62455 62456 62457 62458 62459 62460 62461 62462 62463 62464 62465 62466 62467 62468 62469 62470 62471 62472 62473 62474 62475 62476 62477 62478 62479 62480 62481 62482 62483 62484 62485 62486 62487 62488

62489 62490 62491 62492 62493 62494 62495 62496 62497 62498 62499 62500 62501 62502 62503 62504 62505 62506 62507 62508 62509 62510 62511 62512 62513 62514 62515 62516 62517 62518 62519 62520 62521 62522 62523 62524 62525 62526 62527

62528 62529 62530 62531 62532 62533 62534 62535 62536 62537 62538 62539 62540 62541 62542 62543 62544 62545 62546 62547 62548 62549 62550 62551 62552 62553 62554 62555 62556 62557 62558 62559 62560 62561 62562 62563 62564 62565 62566

62567 62568 62569 62570 62571 62572 62573 62574 62575 62576 62577 62578 62579 62580 62581 62582 62583 62584 62585 62586 62587 62588 62589 62590 62591 62592 62593 62594 62595 62596 62597 62598 62599 62600 62601 62602 62603 62604 62605 62606

62607 62608 62609 62610 62611 62612 62613 62614 62615 62616 62617 62618 62619 62620 62621 62622 62623 62624 62625 62626 62627 62628 62629 62630 62631 62632 62633 62634 62635 62636 62637 62638 62639 62640 62641 62642 62643 62644 62645 62647 62648 62649 62650 62651

62652 62653 62654 62655 62656 62657 62658 62659 62660 62661 62662 62663 62664 62665 62666 62667 62668 62669 62670 62671 62672 62673 62674 62675 62676 62677 62678 62679 62680 62681 62682 62683 62684 62685 62686 62687 62688 62689 62690 62691 62692 62693 62694 62695 62696 62697 62698 62699 62700

62701 62702 62703 62704 62705 62706 62707 62708 62709 62710 62711 62712 62713 62714 62715 62716 62717 62718 62719 62720 62721 62722 62723 62724 62725 62726 62727 62728 62729 62730 62731 62732 62733 62734 62735 62736 62737 62738 62739 62740 62741 62742 62743 62744 62745 62746 62747 62748 62749 62750 62751 62752 62753 62754 62755 62756 62757 62758 62759 62760 62761

62762 62763 62764 62765 62766 62767 62768 62769 62770 62771 62772 62773 62774 62775 62776 62777 62778 62779 62780 62781 62782 62783 62784 62785 62786 62787 62788 62789 62790 62791 62792 62793 62794 62795 62796 62797 62798 62799 62800 62801 62802 62803 62804 62805 62806 62807 62808 62809 62810 62811 62812 62813 62814 62815 62816 62817 62818 62819 62820 62821 62822 62823

62824 62825 62826 62827 62828 62829 62830 62831

62832 62833 62834 62835 62836 62837 62838 62839 62840 62841 62842 62843 62844 62845 62846 62847 62848 62849 62850 62851 62852 62853 62854 62855 62856 62857 62858 62859 62860 62861 62862 62863 62864 62865 62866 62867 62868 62869 62870 62871 62872 62873 62874 62875 62876 62877 62878 62879 62880 62881 62882 62883 62884 62885 62886 62887 62888 62889 62890 62891 62892 62893 62894 62895 62896 62897 62898 62899 62900 62901 62902 62903 62904 62905 62906 62907 62908 62909 62910 62911 62912 62913 62914 62915 62916 62917

62918 62919 62920

62921 62922 62923 62924 62925 62926 62927 62928 62929 62930 62931 62932 62933 62934 62935 62936 62937 62938 62939 62940 62941 62942 62943 62944 62945 62946 62947 62948 62949 62950 62951 62952 62953 62954 62955 62956 62957 62958 62959 62960 62961 62962 62963 62964 62965 62966 62967 62968 62969 62970 62971 62972 62973 62974 62975 62976 62977 62978 62979 62980 62981 62982 62983 62984 62985 62986 62987 62988 62989 62990 62991 62992 62993 62994 62995 62996 62997

62998 62999 63000 63001 63002 63003 63004 63005 63006 63007 63008 63009 63010 63011 63012 63013 63014 63015 63016 63017 63018 63019 63020 63021 63022 63023 63024 63025 63026 63027 63028 63029 63030 63031 63032 63033 63034 63035 63036 63037 63038 63039 63040 63041 63042 63043 63044 63045 63046 63047 63048 63049 63050 63051 63052 63053 63054 63055 63056 63057 63058 63059 63060

63061 63062 63063 63064 63065 63066 63067 63068 63069 63070 63071 63072 63073 63074 63075 63076 63077 63078 63079 63080 63081 63082

63083 63084 63085 63086 63087 63088 63089 63090 63091 63092 63093 63094 63095 63096 63097 63098 63099 63100 63101 63102 63103 63104 63105 63106 63107 63108 63109 63110 63111 63112 63113 63114 63115 63116 63117 63118 63119 63120 63121 63122 63123 63124 63125 63126 63127 63128 63129 63130 63131 63132 63133 63134 63135 63136 63137 63138 63139 63140 63141 63142 63143 63144 63145

6316 6316 6316 6316 6317 6317 63172 63173

63174 63176 63178 63180 63182 63184 63186 63188 63190 63192 63194 63196 63198 63200 63202 63204 63206 63208 63210 63212 63214 63216 63218 63220 63222 63224 63226 63228 63230 63232 63234 63236 63238 63240 63242 63244 63246 63248 63250 63252 63254 63256 63258 63260 63262 63264 63266 63268

6317 631 6318 631 6318 6318 6318 6319 631 631 63 63 63 63 632 632 632 632 632 632 632 632 632 6326 6326

63270 63271 63273 63274 63275 63276 63277 63278 63279 63280 63281 63282 63283

63327 63328 63329 63330 63331 63332 63333 63334 63335 63336 63337 63338 63339

63383 63384 63385 63386 63387 63388 63389 63390 63391 63392 63393 63394 63395

A moment to grieve / to catch my breath / a mass grave 200 bodies, decomposing People, with lives and loved ones

63284 63285 63286 63287 63288 63289 63290 63291 63292 63293 63294 63295 63296 63297 63298 63299 63300 63301 63302 63303 63304 63305 63306 63307 63308 63309 63310 63311 63312 63313 63314 63315 63316 63317 63318 63319 63320 63321 63322 63323 63324 63325 63326

63340 63341 63342 63343 63344 63345 63346 63347 63348 63349 63350 63351 63352 63353 63354 63355 63356 63357 63358 63359 63360 63361 63362 63363 63364 63365 63366 63367 63368 63369 63370 63371 63372 63373 63374 63375 63376 63377 63378 63379 63380 63381 63382

63396 63397 63398 63399 63400 63401 63402 63403 63404 63405 63406 63407 63408 63409 63410 63411 63412 63413 63414 63415 63416 63417 63418 63419 63420 63421 63422 63423 63424 63425 63426 63427 63428 63429 63430 63431 63432 63433 63434 63435 63436 63437 63438 63439

63440 63441 63442 63443 63444 63445 63446 63447 63448 63449 63450 63451 63452 63453 63454 63455 63456 63457 63458 63459 63460 63461 63462 63463 63464 63465 63466 63467 63468 63469 63470 63471 63472 63473 63474 63475 63476 63477 63478 63479 63480 63481 63482 63483 63484 63485 63486 63487 63488 63489 63490 63491 63492 63493 63494 63495

63496 63497 63498 63499 63500 63501 63502

63503 63504 63505 63506 63507 63508 63509

Rabbi Alana Alpert arrested for trying to bring food into Gaza during Passover She said:

"HOW CAN WE CELEBRATE FREEDOM AS THESE ATROCITIES ARE COMMITTED IN THE NAME OF JEWISH SAFETY?"

63510 63511 63512 63513 63514 63515 63516 63517 63518 63519 63520 63521 63522 63523 63524 63525 63526 63527 63528 63529 63530 63531 63532 63533 63534 63535 63536 63537 63538 63539 63540 63541

63542 63543 63544 63545 63546 63547 63548 63549 63550 63551 63552 63553 63554 63555 63556 63557 63558 63559 63560 63561 63562 63563 63564 63565 63566 63567 63568 63569 63570 63571 63572 63573

63574 63575 63576 63577 63578 63579 63580 63581 63582 63583 63584 63585 63586 63587 63588 63589 63590 63591 63592 63593 63594 63595 63596 63597 63598 63599 63600 63601 63602 63603 63604 63605 63606 63607 63608 63609 63610 63611 63612 63613 63614 63615 63616 63617 63618 63619 63620 63621 63622 63623 63624 63625

63638 63639 63640 63641 63642 63643 63644 63645 63646 63647 63648 63649 63650 63651 63652 63653 63654 63655 63656 63657 63658 63659 63660 63661 63662 63663 63664 63665 63666 63667 63668 63669 63670 63671 63672 63673 63674 63675 63676 63677 63678 63679 63680 63681 63682 63683 63684 63685 63686

63699 63700 63701 63702 63703 63704 63705 63706 63707 63708 63709 63710 63711 63712 63713 63714 63715 63716 63717 63718 63719 63720 63721 63722 63723 63724 63725 63726 63727 63728 63729 63730 63731 63732 63733 63734 63735 63736 63737 63738 63739 63740 63741 63742 63743 63744 63745 63746 63747 63748 63749 63750

63764 63765 63766 63767 63768 63769 63770 63771 63772 63773 63774 63775 63776 63777 63778 63779 63780 63781 63782 63783 63784 63785 63786 63787 63788 63789 63790 63791 63792 63793 63794 63795 63796 63797 63798 63799 63800 63801 63802 63803 63804 63805 63806 63807 63808 63809 63810

Another passover with my in-laws...

63626 63627 63628 63629 63630 63631 63632 63633 63634 63635 63636 63637

63687 63688 63689 63690 63691 63692 63693 63694 63695 63696 63697 63698

63751 63752 63753 63754 63755 63756 63757 63758 63759 63760 63761 63762 63763

63811 63812 63813 63814 63815 63816 63817 63818 63819 63820 63821 63822

63823 63824 63825 63826 63827 63828 63829 63830 63831 63832 63833 63834 63835 63836 63837 63838 63839 63840 63841 63842 63843 63844 63845 63846 63847 63848 63849 63850 63851 63852 63853 63854 63855 63856 63857 63858 63859 63860 63861 63862 63863 63864 63865 63866 63867 63868 63869 63870 63871 63872 63873 63874 63875 63876 63877

63878 63879 63880 63881 63882 63883 63884 63885 63886 63887 63888 63889 63890 63891 63892 63893 63894 63895 63896 63897 63898 63899 63900 63901 63902 63903 63904 63905 63906 63907 63908 63909 63910 63911 63912 63913 63914 63915 63916 63917 63918 63919 63920 63921 63922 63923 63924 63925 63926 63927 63928 63929 63930 63931 63932 63933 63934 63935 63936 63937

63938 63939 63940 63941 63942 63943 63944 63945 63946 63947 63948 63949 63950 63951 63952 63953 63954 63955 63956 63957 63958 63959 63960 63961 63962 63963 63964 63965 63966 63967 63968 63969 63970 63971 63972 63973 63974 63975 63976 63977 63978 63979 63980 63981 63982 63983 63984 63985 63986 63987 63988 63989 63990 63991 63992 63993 63994 63995 63996 63997 63998 63999 64000

[Exercise 2.0. Now it's your turn:

You have been tasked with writing 64,001-70,000: books kept in the Israeli State Archives]

There's no tidy ending,
no ending at all.
No way to properly grieve
when the loss is ongoing.

Calling all poets, I need you to speak out.

Calling all poets, I need you to dream the unthinkable.

I Imagine a World Where Palestine Is Free: A Re-Origin Story

I dream an oasis garden
enchanted by treetop jinn.
I pluck ripe pomegranates off
branches, pry leather open to
collect palmfuls of little ruby
gems, glistening in the ominous
sun, a heavy yolk. I drink cool
clean water from a small pond
and when I bathe in it, time
slips off my softened skin
and I grow wings.

I fly direct to Jaffa, without fear of being detained. I greet the agent with a clumsy mouthful, hand-me-down language like a sweater I haven't grown into yet. I walk through the streets, my intuition a donkey guiding me, until I'm standing in an orange grove, which is flourishing. There are young trees growing amidst the elders, their limbs awkward and joints knobby like newborn gazelle. The smell of citrus transports me, their sunny scent a carpet, to a time when trees never feared being maimed. I spread out on the grass and feast in the shade. Olives, figs and zaatar, tomatoes and cucumbers. A thermos of coffee. I tuck the olive pits in my pockets to plant later. I stroll through poppy fields and olive groves. The old trees tell me stories of the things they have witnessed. I scatter wildflower seeds as I go, over patches eroded. Bulldozers won't bother them here. I bury the olive pits, prick fingertips on rose thorns, water the pits with droplets of my blood. They drink thirstily and awaken from the earth, thousand-year-old trees, unfolding from deep slumber, to tower over me.

NOTES

1 — “The Great Book Robbery.” editorial, *Mondoweiss*, posted January 25, 2012. https://mondoweiss.net/2012/01/the-great-book-robbery/

2 — “Balfour Declaration.” Wikisource. https://en.wikisource.org/wiki/Balfour_Declaration

3 — Sayigh, Yezid. *Armed Struggle and the Search for State: The Palestinian National Movement, 1949–1993*. Oxford University Press, 1997, p. 65.

4 — *Spiritual bypassing. (verb) Using spirituality or belief in a higher power to sidestep or sugarcoat painful emotional issues, psychological wounds, unresolved traumas.

5 — “The 1982 Israeli invasion of Lebanon: the casualties.” (1983). *Race & Class*, 24(4), 340-343. https://doi.org/10.1177/030639688302400404 (Original work published 1983)

6 — “Sabra and Shatila massacre: What happened in Lebanon in 1982?” *Al Jazeera*, September 16, 2022. https://www.aljazeera.com/news/2022/9/16/sabra-and-shatila-massacre-40-years-on-explainer

7 — Quinn, Erin. “This is Artful Resistance: The Power of Tatreez.” (2019). https://blogs.soas.ac.uk/gender-studies/2019/11/05/this-is-artful-resistance-the-power-of-tatreez/

8 — Google ngram viewer, which searches for appearances in a corpus of scanned books. https://books.google.com/ngrams/

9 — Hindi, Noor. “The World’s Loneliest Whale Sings the Loudest Song.” (2023). *Split This Rock*. https://www.splitthisrock.org/poetry-database/poem/the-worlds-loneliest-whale-sings-the-loudest-song

10 — Knell, Yolande. “Oslo Accords: 30 years of lost Palestinian hopes .” (2023). BBC. https://www.bbc.com/news/world-middle-east-66751704

11 — Kubovich, Yaniv. “IDF Ordered Hannibal Directive on October 7 to Prevent Hamas Taking Soldiers Captive.” July 7, 2024. *Haaretz*. https://www.haaretz.com/israel-news/2024-07-07/ty-article-magazine/.premium/idf-ordered-hannibal-directive-on-october-7-to-prevent-hamas-taking-soldiers-captive/00000190-89a2-d776-a3b1-fdbe45520000]. Inlakesh, Robert. “How Israel Killed Its Own Soldiers, Blamed Hamas and Violated the Ceasefire Again.” *The Palestine Chronicle,* October 21, 2025. https://www.palestinechronicle.com/how-israel-killed-its-own-soldiers-blamed-hamas-and-violated-

the-ceasefire-again/

12 — "Israel: UN expert condemns brutal attacks on Palestinians at Al-Aqsa Mosque." *United Nations,* April 6, 2023. https://www.ohchr.org/en/press-releases/2023/04/israel-un-expert-condemns-brutal-attacks-palestinians-al-aqsa-mosque

13 — Bunkall, Alistair. "Hostages taken as Hamas launches biggest attack on Israel in years - with strikes hitting Gaza in response." *Sky News,* Oct. 8, 2023. https://news.sky.com/story/thousands-of-rockets-fired-into-israel-as-video-shows-palestinian-fighters-crossing-border-on-paragliders-12978797

14 — Rascius, Brendan. "US aircraft carrier sent toward Israel is world's largest warship. What can it do?" *Miami Herald,* Oct. 12, 2023. https://www.miamiherald.com/news/nation-world/national/article280300734.html

15 — Reynolds, James Clark, and Kalsi, Gina. "Netanyahu vows to turn Gaza into 'rubble': Israeli PM tells Palestinians to 'leave now' and says Hamas will pay an 'unprecedented price' after they kidnapped grans and launched shocking attack that has left hundreds dead on both sides." *Daily Mail*, Oct. 10, 2023. https://www.dailymail.co.uk/news/article-12605083/hamas-gunmen-kidnap-israeli-grandmothers-gaza-strip-reports-civilians-golf-carts.html

16 — Vidal, Marta. "How Trapped Palestinians Fell in Love With Bird-Watching." *International Women's Media Foundation*, Apr. 7, 2023. https://www.iwmf.org/reporting/how-trapped-palestinians-fell-in-love-with-bird-watching/

IMAGE CREDITS

"Joppa from the sea," photograph by P. Bergheim, between 1860-1880. Library of Congress. (Page 41)

"Jew's Wailing Place", from A Month in Palestine and Syria, 1891. (Page 58)

"Floating in the Dead Sea," photograph by Itamar Grinberg for the Israeli Ministry of Tourism, 2012. (Page 62)

"Peasant women near Joppa Gate, Jerusalem," photograph by C.H. Graves, 1903. Library of Congress. (Page 93)

El-Issa, Issa. "The Zionist Crocodile to Palestine Arabs." Falastin, June 18, 1936. (Page 132)

"Residential tower in Gaza destroyed by Israeli bombardment on the morning of 8 October 2023," photograph by Ashraf Amra, 2023. (Page 142)

"Deir Yassin Massacre," photograph by Thejorge11, 2017. (Page 146)

"Forced Displacement of Palestinians in the Gaza Strip devastated by Israeli bombing, January 29, 2025," photograph by Jaber Jehad Badwan, 2025. (Page 147)

"Al Rimal, Gaza," photograph by Rawanmurad2025, 2024. (Page 149)

"Wild flowers of Palestine." Prints and Photographs Division, Library of Congress, Washington, D.C., 20540-4730. G. Eric and Edith Matson Photograph Collection. (Pages 54, 157-159).

"Displaced Palestinians receive food from charitable Tekiya during Ramadan in Deir el-Balah, Gaza Strip," photograph by Ashraf Amra, 2025; "Images from Gaza war 2023-2025," photograph by Jaber Jehad Badwan, 2024. (Page 172)

ACKNOWLEDGMENTS

Writing is a solitary act, but making a book is a communal one. Thanks to all in my orbit who have worked to bring this all together. None of this would have been possible without my agent, Amanda, and publisher, Michelle, who believed in my work enough to decide it was worth launching into the world. You've made my dreams come true. Thanks to Beau for his careful attention to my words in editing. Thank you to Jenny Xu, who encouraged me to find an agent who would protect and advocate for my work, and then thoughtfully connected me with people she trusted.

The last few years have not been easy, and I have fallen apart and rebuilt myself many times in the process of writing this book. Most of that happened during my time at IAIA, and I want to thank my poetry peers and mentors who spent hours reading, encouraging, and critiquing the words that have come together on these pages. To the classmates who held my heart tenderly during those residency weeks when I felt raw. A special thank you to Layli Long Soldier, who told me I was on the right track, pushed me to keep moving through whatever came up, break the rules that I had for myself in my head, and to trust the words to tell me who they were and where they wanted to live on the page.

Thanks to my therapist, Lynne, whose somatic approach helped me work through traumas I was carrying and to transform them inside my body into art.

To my parents, for being—can I say it?—uncharacteristically enthusiastic about my work. Mom: watching you step back into your art and seeing how it lights you up is such a blessing. I know being visible has not always been safe. I am so proud of the work you are doing. Thanks specifically for letting me share your words, your images, and your art in these pages. Dad: your love of poetry, words, and wordplay started it all. Thanks for sharing that with me. Thanks as well for your ideas for book covers, and for taking my headshots. You are truly multitalented.

Zak: thank you for being there every single day, whether I'm your supportive wife, a heap on the bed, or an absolute wreck. You make me feel easy to love. I appreciate how you hold hope on days when I have no space for it, and your belief that peace is possible and that people can change for the better.

Thanks to my in-laws, who have been cheerleaders along the way. The way you celebrate and champion my work and accomplishments is such a treat.

Thanks to Tin House, Vermont Studio Center, and Sundress Academy for the Arts for making space for me to create and connect. Thanks to Dilja for encouraging me in the visual elements of my book!

Thank you to the writers/artists/activists who inspire me and remind me our liberation is all intertwined. To SJ Ghaus, Jackson Moorman, and Aiya Sakr who co-organized In Water and Light with me, which was such a lantern in the darkness.

Thanks to my friends who have put up with me, distracted me, filled my heart when I was empty, made me laugh, and listened to me complain.

To my readers: Thank you for reading. May my words move you, spark curiosity or grief or outrage. Let your emotions propel you to action.

To the people of Palestine: I'm sorry. I hope my words have an impact, for you more than anyone. I hope you can feel me beside you.

Many thanks to the editors of the following publications, who have published a number of these pieces, sometimes in different forms:

"How to Cure Homesickness," *The Massachusetts Review*

"How to Cure an Olive," *Koukash Review*

"I Imagine a World Where Palestine Is Free: A Re-Origin Story," *The Margins*

"Sowing Seeds and Threads into a Landscape of Grief: Embodied Voices for Palestine," *Chapter House Journal*

Lenna Jawdat is a poet, writer, and psychotherapist of Palestinian and Iraqi descent. Her writing, which explores trauma, identity and resilience, has appeared in journals such as *Poet Lore, The Margins, Passenger's Journal, Rogue Agent,* among others, and in the 2025 Haymarket anthology *Heaven Looks Like Us*. She was a 2021 Best of the Net nominee for her poem "Ode to the Psoas," a 2022 Sundress Academy for the Arts summer resident, and has attended Tin House Workshop for poetry and creative nonfiction. She is also co-organizer of the poetry vigil series *In Water and Light*. Lenna received her MFA in Creative Writing from the Institute of American Indian Arts in May 2024. She lives in DC with her partner and two cats.